The Stuff of Stories

Clues to a Lot of Unwritten Books

by

Donald L. Weismann

DORRANCE PUBLISHING CO., INC.
PITTSBURGH, PENNSYLVANIA 15222

ISBN # 0-8059-4400-1
Printed in the United States of America

First Printing

For information or to order additional books, please write:
Dorrance Publishing Co., Inc.
643 Smithfield Street
Pittsburgh, Pennsylvania 15222
U.S.A.

To:

William Shakespeare
Charles Darwin
and
Buster Keaton

Other Books By the Same Author

The Visual Arts As Human Experience
Language and Visual Form
Why Draw?
Forms (with Hiram D. Williams)
Frank Reaugh—Painter to the Longhorns
Some Folks Went West
Jelly Was the Word
The Twelve Cadavers of Joe Mariner
Follow the Bus with the Greek License Plates
Duncan Phyph and Drum—with Notes for the Bugle Corps
In Four Houses and Out—A Sentimental Return to the Twenties in Milwaukee

Contents

Preface

No matter where a person finds himself or herself at any given time, no matter what they might be doing or saying in that active present, they are also concurrently alive in other times and places—in their worlds of memory, imagination, and invention.

The one hundred and sixteen pieces that have found place between the covers of this book are, for the most part, recordings from the almost subliminal stuff that keeps forming and running in back of the up-front concerns of my everyday responsibilities and actions. Mostly, these undertones, these weakly played melodies of memories, imaginings, and inventions are lost, buried in the cacophony of one's demanding active life.

I think I may be at my most honest when I say that most of these pieces, these "stuffs," have come to life in these pages by way of my listening, then remembering those weakly played melodies that when given a chance, have their own voice and character.

And a wonderful thing about this is that this weak "background music," let's call it, often gives clues to better understandings of the loud "main theme" spotlighted and being played by the orchestra in the pit.

I'll hope for your agreement and pleasure.

Donald L. Weismann
Austin, Texas

We Exhausted Our Neighborhood Junk

When the huge automobile graveyards began to appear all across the country it didn't surprise me. They got bigger than I ever thought possible, but their appearance along highways and streets and open fields was like that of an old, almost secret friend, but a friend turned giant and mad breaking out into the open for everyone to see and know.

At first, back in the early twenties, dead automobiles were junked with other junk. Sometimes they were rolled into garbage pits along with ice boxes and gas stoves, but usually they were pushed into piles of hard junk, and there weren't many of those. They'd be stripped by scavengers until there wasn't much left but the frame and the central part of the body. Sometimes they were left in backyards, dead-end streets, empty lots, and ravines, just like now. But before the massive graveyards appeared, these single stripped cars stood out against the clear-aired scene with a curious and engaging authority like the sculpture of Stankiewicz and Smith. My father's 1918 Model-T Ford came to its end in a weed-covered lot adjoining Weisskopf's garage on Fifth Street in

Milwaukee. My brother Fred and I played on it for over two years while it lost its wheels, radiator, seats, steering wheel, lights, rear end, fenders, spare tire rack, motor, and finally its transmission box with the three pedals on the side. First it died, and then its eyes, kidneys, and heart got used over by someone, someplace. And Fred and I played on the rusting skeleton right up to 1926 when we moved away from near Weisskopf's garage.

It's hard for me to imagine that there ever was a time when most boys, and for that matter girls, didn't go for hunting through, climbing over, sorting out, carrying off, and making things out of junk. We were lucky as kids—we almost always lived right next to junk, fine resources of tough wonderment full of actual possibilities. And just like we exhausted our neighborhood library, we exhausted our neighborhood junk. So we took our junk-made coaster to the other branch libraries—heaps and scatterings of junk along the river, railroad sidings, back of warehouses, foundries, and loading platforms. We even had a name for what we were doing—"alley hunching," and we were "alley hunchers" bringing back lots of good things. And the day finally came when we got to the "Main Library"—the biggest mountain of junk we'd ever seen, with cranes working overhead and hardly any of it we could lift. It was like coming too early upon the Bibliothéque Nationale, the Library of the British Museum, or the Library of Congress. Something about its scale overwhelmed and incapacitated us. From thinking about making things out of its pieces, it seemed we were being asked to shift to an acceptance of an already completed monumental architecture. And then I left all that with those with whom I'd found it—boys like Eddie Nolan and his older brother Joe, and Dietz and Dan and a girl like Lillian Johnston. For, as in lots of other things, what was once an invitation to make had become a cry to destroy, to eradicate.

All I Wanted to Do Was Make Something Perfect

From the beginning, it seems, all I wanted to do was make something perfect. It wouldn't have to be big. Could be small. Very small. Just so it was perfect. That's what I wanted to do.

I even let it out to my friends, that I wanted to make a perfect thing, no matter how small. For a while, maybe from when I was four or five until I was ten or eleven, I told it to everybody who looked like they were listening. Then from about twelve or thirteen to the time I was turning fifty I didn't tell a soul, not even when I'd had a lot to drink and felt awful strong. Then I began to tell people about it again, only in this phase I shifted from saying that I wanted to make a perfect thing to saying that I was already making it. I don't know how this shift from wish to fact happened. It just did. And there was no rational foundation, as some say, for this shift. In fact it was a lie I was telling: I wasn't making any perfect thing, nowhere near it, and I knew it—I was still at the old wishing game as I went manic-depressively at all kinds of things which I characterized to myself as "probings." Probings toward the perfect thing.

Nothing wrong about that. It'd even make a good organizing concept around which a perfectly acceptable deathbed statement could be made. Sort of a deathbed confession of trying and failing, no matter how well intentioned, no matter how well rationalized. Maybe even stand up in court. But who cares about that? What I wanted wasn't an alibi. What I wanted was to make a perfect thing. That simple.

The first attempt I made was trying to use the full moon as a guide to draw a perfect circle. I may have been four years old, certainly not five because at five I wanted to make a perfect straight line, without a ruler, all the way from where I stood on State Street to the water tower my Pa showed me on the only picnic we ever had together down by the lake.

The thing was that the moon had to be full, round, and you had to be looking at it through the glass of the window facing east out of the bedroom window, one floor above the empty flat below. And you had to have your black crayola ready. Then when the moon got free of the window frame and floated there, the thing was to reach up and swing a circle around it real fast, freehand on the glass, like, as you didn't know then, Leonardo da Vinci whipped out perfect circles on his absent friends' doors—leaving his unmistakable calling card. But the moon moves and so do your eyes that see it. And your arms and hands, your head and your whole body standing there on the wide-planked soft wood floor full of splinters two floors up from the traffic of the street below, have to cooperate to one end—drawing that ring around the moon—even late at night when everything seemed so still and ready to help…but I never managed it back then when I was four and gave up never to try again.

In first grade I sat across from Daniel Dadas, a Greek, who drew perfect circles around the inkwells the teacher said we were too young to use, we were limited to our 2-B lead pencils, and I asked Daniel Dadas if he could draw a perfect circle around the moon, and he said, "What?" and I said, "Oh nothing, I just like Greeks."

I Got to Know a Lot of People All by Myself

Besides my conviction that, all in all, I am one of the luckiest men alive, I believe—at least in retrospect—that it was my exceptionally good fortune to get to know an awful lot of inordinately interesting grown-ups even before I was eleven years old. Some of these people I got to know were people who came to the flats where we lived near downtown in Milwaukee. Mostly these people were friends of my father—boxers, wrestlers, six-day bicycle riders, steeple-jacks, circus freaks, and the like. These people I got to know because my father, shall we say, introduced me to them.

But there were lots of other grown-ups I got to know outside our house, wherever we happened to be living at the time. I'll mention only a few of them—firemen, for instance.

I got to know my first fireman when I was about seven years old, back in 1921. That was a bad year for our family. My father—we always called him just Pa—was away again for a long time, maybe out west. I don't think anyone knew where he was. My mother—we always called her just Ma—she hadn't been feeling well and we were past being down on our last penny. The fact is that we had almost nothing to eat and Ma said, "Why don't you go over to the fire station," which was pretty close, "and stand around there. The fireman will be eating their supper, and if you just watch them eat I'll bet they'll give you some."

The fireman took their meals in the basement of the fire house and there were little windows close to the ground that looked right on to the big table with the food on it. We got down on the ground and put our faces right up to the glass and watched them eat. For awhile they acted like they didn't see us.

When they got their ice cream in big bowls, one of the firemen looked straight at us and smiled a big smile. He motioned for us to come around to the open front door. Inside, he asked if we liked ice cream, and we said that we sure did. All the firemen laughed, and the one who'd asked us to come in—his name, I found out later, was Otto, and he was the boss fireman—he brought each of us a bowl of ice cream. It was chocolate, as I very well remember, and we ate it sitting right up at the table with all the firemen.

I don't remember how it came about, but the ice cream feast ended up with me reciting *The Wreck of the Hesperus* for the firemen and them clapping their hands a lot. After that we ate pretty often with the firemen because Otto was the boss and he could do anything—like packing up the leftover meat and potatoes to take home to Ma.

Now Baldy Wasserbach was a bartender, but I didn't get to know him very well. But Baldy Wasserbach used to have shirts done up in a Chinese laundry. And when I was seven or eight, Baldy always had me take his shirts to the "Chinaman's," as he called the laundry. And since I always went back to get the shirts when they were all washed and ironed, I got to know Charlie Lee, the laundry man, better than I got to know Baldy Wasserbach.

Charlie Lee had come over from China long ago to work in the gangs building railroads out west. When he had both of his legs broken, they didn't go back together the way they should so he walked very slow and very bowlegged. That's when he went into the laundry business—all by himself. He never had a wife. He lived in a room back of the laundry and it was there he told me all about China and how it was there when he was a boy my age. Even though he didn't talk like anybody else I knew, I got so I could understand him better than I could understand my Pa when he was drunk. Charlie Lee told me lots of stories, and I believed them for a long time.

One day when he stopped talking for awhile I told him that we had a phonograph record at home, a song about Hong Kong. He asked if I could sing it and I did. As I remember, after these seventy-five years or so, it went something like this:

Hong Kong, Hong Kong
Soon America, so long
In that land of rice and tea,
Soon on my honeymoon, soon I'll be
Where oriental lights are gleaming,
Where little Chinamen are dreaming.
Hong Kong, Hong Kong
. . . and so on.

Charlie Lee let me finish and then he said that the song didn't remind him of China, not at all. I learned a lot more from Charlie Lee than he learned from me.

Years and years later when I was in the Navy we flew along the south coast of China—around Luichow Peninsula—and I remember thinking of my old friend Charlie Lee, almost as if I was back in his laundry, drinking some tea and talking above the noise and rattle of the B–24 Bomber.

Whenever I go across a bridge, the kind that lifts in the middle to let high ships pass, and if I'm not full of other more pressing thoughts, I think of Horace Bligh the bridge tender. I got to know him one day while the leaves of the bridge were up, and he was just standing at his controls in his little bridge tender's house there by the Milwaukee River. After the ship had passed and he let the bridge down, he waved to me, and I went over to look where he worked. He motioned me inside, and that's how I got to know Horace Bligh. He told me all about the controls and machinery that worked the bridge. He used to sail on ore boats, he said, bringing iron down from the Vermillion Iron Range in Minnesota. Mr. Bligh could tell about far away places so that they seemed to be real close—almost right there in his bridge-tender's house.

Not many years after I'd made friends with Mr. Bligh—when I was fifteen—I fell in love with a young matron at the Milwaukee County Home for Dependent Children, and when she told me that she was born in Eveleth, Minnesota, I could talk about the iron ranges as if I'd lived there—thanks to Mr. Bligh. And, come to think of this, I still remember the matron's name, Frances Shudolc, and her address in Eveleth, Minnesota—44 Norman Avenue.

Then there was Miss Drexler—I never got to know her first name. She used to sit near a window on 5th Street and type real fast on her typewriter. Most of the time she faced away from the window, her fingers going so fast they blurred, and I'd stand outside amazed. The day she caught me staring at her she dropped her hands in her lap and laughed so hard I could hear her through the glass. I suppose I looked funny in the kind of clothes I wore in those days, but mostly because I'd been eating an apple which I kept holding in my teeth as I tried to imitate her fast-flying hands with mine.

She came out of her office then, right out onto 5th Street, and talked with me—about all those things that usually come up: my name, her name, how old I was (I was nine as I remember), what grade I was in in school, where I lived, and what I wanted to be when I grew up. I told her I wanted to be an artist when I grew up, and she thought that was wonderful, although what she'd seen of me through her window made her think I could be an actor.

I used to go by Miss Drexler's window pretty often after that—especially when nothing else was happening and I felt lonely. Sometimes, if it was around when school wasn't running, she'd come out, sit on the steps of the Ideal Casket Company, and give me some of her lunch—usually a banana and some cheese. Miss Drexler sure was a fine woman, and I found her all by myself.

Another fine woman I found all by myself was Hattie Wilson. She was what they called a "sport" back then when I was about ten years old in 1924. She was a hooker, a prostitute, but I didn't know that right away, and I don't think that knowing that would have made any difference to me. It certainly doesn't now.

Now and then from a distance I'd see Hattie Wilson walking down Cedar Street or over on Wells. I thought she was always dressed better than the other women in the neighborhood—and she walked better, like she had better muscles in her body, and she sort of glided along with her head held high in a really nice way. I had strong good feelings for her.

One day when I came around the corner at 4th Street, there she was ahead of me, going up Wells Street—not far ahead, and I could smell her perfume. It wasn't all that strong, and not at all like flowers. It was better than that. It made you remember a lot of good feelings you'd had and then forgotten until you walked close enough to Hattie Wilson.

Up near the newsstand at 6th Street, and without warning she stopped, turned around, and looked right at me. "How old are you?" she asked.

"Ten," I said.

"And where do you get these ideas?" she asked.

"What ideas?"

"Oh," she said, "I've seen you around pretending you're on your own business doing this and that—you're following me, aren't you?"

"Well," I said, "not exactly."

"And what's that supposed to mean?" she said with the weakest smile beginning to show around her mouth and eyes.

My God, I can still see Hattie Wilson's face turning into a smile; it was what even then I knew it to be, a real easy, flat out, within-reach beauty.

"I don't know what it's supposed to mean," I said, "I just said it without thinking."

"Not exactly," Hattie Wilson said, "from where I stand I'd say you don't run around *not* knowing pretty exactly what you're about."

And all I could say was, "Yes ma'am."

So then Miss Wilson took me by the hand, like I was three or four years old, saying, "Oh, I know where you live—above Ed Strachota's place on 5th and Cedar, and I'm going to walk you home where you belong." But she was smiling all the time making me feel that we should start skipping together down the street—which we almost did.

I talked with Miss Wilson a lot after that—on the corner outside Ed Strachota's place, under the canopy of the Strand Theater on Grand Avenue, by the cab stand across from the telephone company, up near the courthouse and around. Sometimes we even walked together for a little while.

Just before we moved away from downtown, I saw Hattie Wilson—fine as ever—walking past the main entrance to the Milwaukee Auditorium. I didn't call out to her; I just ran and caught up. "Miss Wilson," I said, "we're moving away, maybe I'll not be seeing you anymore." I swear it was the first time I saw her look the way she did for just a second or two after I said that. Then that slow-sliding smile took over and she said, "Sonny, you'll be all right, no matter where you'd have to go. So take your time, don't try to hurry things, they'll wait—promise me on that." And I did.

The first time I saw Mr. McDermott he was standing outside the Ideal Casket Company smoking a cigar. It was a great long cigar and because it was so big and Mr. McDermott was so small I must have stared at it as I walked past. "No smoking in there," he said, as if I'd asked.

"That's good," I said because I couldn't think of anything else to say, and I wanted to acknowledge his speaking to me.

"You don't smoke, do you?" he asked.

"Once in a while," I said, "one of my big brother's Camels."

"Don't you know that cigarettes will kill you, boy?"

"How about cigars?" I asked.

"I guess everything kills us in the end," Mr. McDermott said. When I asked him what he did inside the Ideal Casket Company, he said, "I'll show you; come inside." Inside, past a lot of fancy coffins, we walked way to the back where he'd been lining a coffin with shiny white satin. He filled his mouth with little tacks, picked up a hammer, and went about pleating and lining the coffin.

"You work fast," I said as he spit out the tacks and drove them home.

"Gotta work fast," McDermott said, "lately they've been dying like flies at the end of summer."

After that I talked with him pretty often, usually when he came outside to smoke his cigar. Another friend I'd found all by myself.

Now, after all the years between, I figure that all these then grown-ups are as dead as doornails, whether they smoked cigarettes or not. As Mr. McDermott said, "There's a coffin waiting for everyone." Maybe that's why, long ago, I promised my beautiful sporting friend Hattie Wilson that I wouldn't hurry things, because they'd wait—just like Mr. McDermott's satin lined coffins were waiting.

Now perhaps that sounds like a moral to this account, but I don't mean it that way. All I meant to do was give you a small sample of the kinds of grown-ups I got to know before my balls came down and the pouch began to grow hair. And so, if we, you and I, should ever meet, you will have some basis for understanding how I talk and why I act the way I do. No matter that since those long dead years I've talked to presidents, generals, admirals, movie stars, writers, opera singers, comedians, philosophers, even a couple of celebrated criminals. What goes in deepest in me—or, more accurately, what *went* in the deepest, are those men and women that I came next to all by myself, and for no *practical* reason when I was very young.

You see, here I am in my ninth decade and still feeling next to Hattie Wilson....

There Is Magic in This World

When I was ten or eleven in Milwaukee, I used to enjoy standing across the street from the Blatz palm garden at night. In summer the doors were left open and the orchestra music came wafting right over to me. And standing on the base of a fountain, now long gone, it was easy to see deep into the huge, darkly wood-paneled room and watch the "acts" put on by dance teams, jugglers, acrobats, concertina players, magicians, and the like. I remember very clearly one night when I was watching from the shadow of the fountain I was grabbed hard in my shoulders and a heavy voice said, "Stealing batteries, eh?" It was a policeman and, with what he said, I was convinced he was going to take me in even though I didn't know what he was talking about. I got a little of that pushing around that looks like one thing from the outside but feels like valet service mixed with judo and sacked BB's inside.

Now my father was a man of average height, average weight, dark hair, and shadowed eyes, just like most of the descriptions given by never-quite-certain eye witnesses of the man who did this or that against the law. Because my father kept very irregular hours and was out late at night and early in the morning on foot far from our house, he was often picked up by the police—even when he was stone sober. Twice he was beaten badly by them in sessions my father called "the third degree." He lost most of his front teeth, uppers and lowers—the one's he'd used to open beer bottles—in one of those sessions, and his ribs were broken in another. Then he found out about a charge he could bring against the police: *false arrest*. I heard a lot about false arrest and settlement damages when I was a little kid.

I was scared, but not quite scared stiff, when the policeman began to handle me there across from the Blatz palm garden. It's mysterious the way policemen and strange dogs can tell if you can't afford a meal or a lawyer, and some of us have had to learn that very early—and we forget it very late, even after we've eaten plenty and have a choice of lawyers on the other end of any phone. But still, that night my voice spoke out and it said, "Officer, I hope you know what FALSE ARREST means." The effect was nothing less than magical. He stopped knocking me around, and after a while in a nice way he asked my name, called me Donald, and said something about the music from the palm garden and didn't I think it was pretty late to be out. I asked him what time it was and offered that I thought I'd better go home—five blocks away. Which I did, feeling that, yes, there is magic, and it works.

My Mother Told Me about the *Titanic*

My older brother, Fred, was born just five months after the RMS *Titanic*, the world's most luxurious floating hotel, sank in the north Atlantic on April 15, 1912. I had to wait over two years after that before it was my turn to be born. Neither my mother nor my father were passengers on the *Titanic* although they had been living and were old enough to have paid full-fare had they been in line to board the ship on April 10, 1912, for its maiden and final voyage.

So far as I know, none of my relatives on either my mother's or father's side were passengers on that fatal voyage, and I never got to know any of the unrelated survivors of which there were 1,517, just one-third of all those on the passenger list. A 1996 report says that only eight survivors are now living. In a roundabout way you could say that my brother Fred was a survivor of the *Titanic* disaster, even though he wasn't aboard the ship. After all, he was born the same year the ship went down, and he continued to live long after that. My claim to be a survivor is a little weaker since I was born two years later. My brother Fred has seniority in this happy situation.

When the *Titanic* slipped under the Atlantic after hitting that iceberg, neither my brother nor I could read the reports. Neither of us, as I've indicated, had as yet been born. We had to wait our turns. In fact, the first I heard of the *Titanic's* sinking was told to me by my mother when I was about two or three years old in 1916 or 1917.

Now, since several of my primary school teachers attested to their belief that I was possessed of a "capacious memory" and was given to "playing vicarious roles" in the events of the day, it was natural that the sinking of the *Titanic* has continued to be part of me in one way or another.

Over the years, from way back, I've amassed a lot of photographs of the *Titanic*, even some taken when the ship was being built, and imaginary drawings of the tragedy like the one printed on the front page of the *New York American* of April 16, 1912. Also, by answering an ad in the *Austin American Statesman* of few years back, I got a copy of the ship's manifest—a long, detailed list of what was in her cargo when she went down. Incidentally that list does not include the coal she was carrying—the tons of coal required for firing the furnaces that boiled the water to create the steam to run her turbines that turned her screws and drove her through the water.

Now today, June 30, 1996, it is announced in *Parade Magazine* that "Rare coal from the *Titanic*" is available in limited quantities for twenty-five dollars each—limit of two to each customer. Well, I've thought about getting my limited share of this historical coal by ordering through the distributor, "Titanic Coal," but so far I haven't done so, and perhaps I never shall. With all my osmotic relations with the *Titanic* and her loss, you'd think I'd want a piece of this coal that never got its chance to fire up under those boilers and complete her voyage. No, it wasn't the sadness of this—the unburned coal waiting patiently in the dark down there in the *Titanic's* hold, and in the end only its *weight*, not its heat-producing powers, was used to hurry the ship's descent two and a half miles below the surface of the ocean. Of course, this is a sad situation, a terrible turnabout of fate, the kind that could provide a rich trove of metaphors for life in general.

But it wasn't any of that kept me from purchasing a piece of coal; it was the *advertising* of the coal's availability: overdone, with guarantees and documents of the true lineage of every piece, every little chip or lump, "certificates of authenticity," and such statements as the one made by "a conservator in Michigan" (a person who collects coal?) is quoted as saying that "this offering of *Titanic* coal is certainly most appreciated by *Titanic* enthusiasts all over the world," and "offered at such an affordable price." And, the ad goes on, "expeditions to recover this coal cost over $100,000.00 a day.... " Sounds like most advertising, doesn't it, with its prose bordering on the fraudulent, the dishonest, and the comical. I expect that if and when some bones of the dead passengers—or just bone chips either from those passengers or from corpses of the poor headed for Potter's Field—are offered for sale, the price will be well above that of the coal "offerings."

Well, as I've said, it was my mother who first told me about the *Titanic*. I seem to remember that my mother's account of the happy people aboard that ship dancing, eating fine food, and enjoying life, with their jewels and money "secure" in the ship's vaults—and then the unheralded appearance through the fog, like one's sins showing up at the Pearly Gates—that huge menacing iceberg; all that, it seems I remember as contributing to my rapidly growing bank of gripping, chilling, and rewarding experiences. Yes, even at the tender age of two or three. I presume that Sigmund Freud, the hysterical Moravian novelist who made so much by exploiting his own psychoses of both the Viennese Waltz and the German Black Forest, would say that my mother had created a deep and lasting *trauma* in me. Not so. In agricultural terms I'd say that this Freudian diagnosis would be similar to spreading manure on solid, infertile rock.

You see, my mother, maiden name Stella Priscilla Custer, had been an actress when still in her teens—played Juliet in Shakespeare's *Romeo and Juliet* on a collapsible portable stage in towns like Fort Madison, Iowa, and Mitchell, South Dakota. So she had the "know hows" about dramatizing and projecting, and I figure that she dramatized and projected the sinking of the *Titanic* straight into my post-infant hungering consciousness. And there it has survived as a positive force, a waxing and waning recollection through the years. Thanks, Ma, you were terrific.

On a rainy Texas day about twenty-five years ago, the recollection came into one of its waxing phases. Without forethought, it seems, I went into my studio, picked out a piece of quarter-inch pre-sized plywood about seven feet long and two feet wide, spread my palette, as some say, and began painting a picture. It quickly became the makings of a wide seascape. The horizon line, running the full seven feet, divided the picture area into thirds—the upper third becoming a clouded sky, the lower two-thirds a dark blue sea. Then, mostly from photographs, I painted an accurate image of the *Titanic* sailing peacefully along the horizon from far left toward center. Then in the sea area at far right, I painted a big menacing shape seen the way we see underwater life through the front glass of an aquarium. This became the iceberg waiting to finish the *Titanic*. Only a very small pointed area of the submerged iceberg showed above the horizon. Later I gilded that little triangle with twenty-four karat gold leaf—point of fatal contact of ship and iceberg. And barely discernible on the ocean floor I painted a lot of Latin crosses—grave markers already in place for the unsuspecting people still having a swell time on that ship sailing so steadily from the far left of the painting.

So you see how it is: From something your mother tells you when you were two or three years old can turn into a painting sixty years later. That's why, in some kind of tribute, I titled the painting, *My Mother Told Me about the* Titanic. And, no, it's not for sale; it's part of the collection belonging to long-standing friends, Rick and Betty Adams, and hangs in their home near Panajachel in Guatemala.

And then you know how it works: One thing leads to another, and they're never unrelated. So it was that I made another painting-collage about the *Titanic* and its tragic end. It's approximately the same size and shape of the one I've just told you about, except that this later one is a vertical, not a horizontal. However before I tell you about it I must let you know that during the 1930s, when I was painting in a mode the critics named "American Regionalism," I got to be called "Social Message Weismann," and I knew why: because I drew and painted pictures of hobos in boxcars, homeless people sleeping in abandoned warehouses, the slums of Milwaukee and Chicago, and because I sympathized with and often talked about the Social Democratic party and its leader, Eugene V. Debs, and Victor Berger. I even worked for a little while doing odd jobs at the socialist newspaper, the *Milwaukee Leader*, where Berger was editor. I went to school with the son of Daniel W. Hoan, the many times re-elected Socialist mayor of Milwaukee. "Social Message Weismann" indeed, and I'm still what's now called a "Populist." I am unavoidably concerned with social issues and social conditions, especially how the power of material riches in the form of corporate collusion has changed the very nature of life in America as well as in the wider "advanced" post-industrial world. And my judgement is that this change, a really harrowing one, is for the worse.

So with the large painting-collage having to do with the sinking of the *Titanic* to which I've alluded, this is how my social consciousness found expression:

At the very top of the seven-foot panel I glued down a Xerox copy of the whole front page of the April 16, 1912, edition of the *New York American*. Over an artist's rendering of the *Titanic* as she rammed the iceberg, the top headline reads, "J.J. Astor Lost on *Titanic*." Below that is another headline that reads, "1500–1800 Dead." A case of what's thought of as the "elite," the *cream of society*, floating to the top: one forty-eight year old, terribly rich, and powerful banker and financier getting top billing over almost sixteen hundred "other" people.

So, just below the *New York American* front page, and in beautiful isolation against a black background, I mounted a photograph of John Jacob Astor framed in a beautiful, baroque gold-leafed frame. Below that, and running clear to the bottom of the panel, I stenciled a falling cascade of anonymous white numbers for all those "others" who went down with John Jacob Astor. I titled this painting-collage "Priority Drowning," my silent negative comment about the early twentieth century journalistic respect for the controlling rich, the corporate, the so-called "elite." And that, boys and girls, was eighty-four years ago! Haven't you recognized the elitist refrain now cleverly counterpointed in our *National Anthem, The Sermon on the Mount, the Pledge of Allegiance*, and the curriculums of programs that lead to a degree called "master of business administration"?

When my mother told me about the *Titanic*, she was twenty-two years old, old enough to vote, but back then women were not allowed to vote—only men, except Indian and "Negro" men. Now, so far as I know, I'm not an Indian or a "Negro," and my mother knew that, and that some day, almost for sure, I'd be voting. I like to think that her memorable dramatizing of the sinking of the *Titanic* for me has had something to do with how I've been voting during these last sixty-one years.

As I recall, my mother never mentioned John Jacob Astor though she used to say depreciatingly of some passing floozy, "Look, she's dressed like Mrs. Astor's pet goat."

Under Mrs. Peterson's Chicken Coop

Mrs. Peterson, who lived next door when we lived at 707 Chambers Street, was generally a quite mysterious person but nice. Her curtains and shades were most often drawn, and there was a story, rumors, that the chicken coop in her back yard was built over a trap door that opened into a downward passage that led to a huge room deep under Mrs. Peterson's yard. The story also had it that down there four men sat around a table. They were all dead but held playing cards, and there was a lot of money on the table—all thick coins covered with white dust.

You hardly ever saw Mr. Peterson because, we were told, he worked at night at the Schlitz Brewery and slept during the day.

Mrs. Peterson, we were told, had a lot of canaries in her house. Sometimes when she came out in her yard to put her curtains on the curtain stretchers, a few canaries came out with her and sat on her head. She had a lot of golden-colored hair made up high on her head and the birds sat in it like in a nest. The birds never flew away, and when Mrs. Peterson finished pinning on her curtains, the canaries rode back with her into her house.

Sometimes I used to sit on our back porch and watch for Mrs. Peterson to come out into her yard. She was always dressed in a long dress like a bath robe, pointed shoes, and pretty often the canaries in her hair. She walked differently from other people—when she walked across the yard it didn't look like she was putting one foot in front of the other. It looked more like she was first leaving one foot behind and then the other. And she sort of floated as she did that.

Sometimes when Mrs. Peterson's chickens laid too many eggs she'd hand a few over the fence to my mother. I always looked real carefully at these eggs because they made me think of those dead men playing cards for that thick dust-covered money under the chicken coop.

"They're perfectly all right," my mother would say, "what's the matter with you?"

"Nothing," I'd say. "It's the eggs." But we always ate the eggs—very hard-boiled.

"Why take a chance?" my mother said. "Why gamble?"

"Like those dead men gambling for that funny money down there?" I said, and my mother would say, "I wish you'd forget that ridiculous story about what's under Mrs. Peterson's yard. I wonder who started that anyway."

Even with all of my learning since we lived next to Mrs. Peterson—with everything that's happened in my life since then, now over seventy-five years ago, I still find it mysterious that only *some* of the people, events, and happenings inside and outside of me attain the status of active memories. Why do I remember even in much more detail than I recount here all this about Mrs. Peterson? Maybe it was that story of the gambler's den far below the chicken coop in her yard that got to me so strongly that it cut deep traces in my gray matter, or made solid electric connections in my brain. But there were thousands of other happenings, much more important, that I lived through, even way back then. Why do experiences of the Mrs. Peterson variety insist on enduring? Maybe we really don't know which are of more fundamental significance to us; we just go with those that the society deems are *the* significant ones. Psychiatrists are supposed to tell us about this, I'm told.

No matter, all that: One day I went with my mother to give Mrs. Peterson a letter addressed to Mrs. Peterson's house number—a letter to a Mr. Tom O'Reilly—that was put, instead, in our mailbox.

With all the shades down, it was pretty dark inside Mrs. Peterson's house. Mrs. Peterson was in her long dress, really a bathrobe with big flowers printed on it. "Oh," she said, "that's strange, there's no Tom O'Reilly here, is there? But I'll take it anyway, thanks for bringing it over."

While Mrs. Peterson talked with my mother in the kitchen, I looked into the dining room. There, laid out neatly on the big round dining room table, were a lot of what looked like that funny money supposed to be lying on the gambler's table way down under Mrs. Peterson's chicken coop. From where I was standing in the kitchen I couldn't see exactly how this funny money was, but it looked thick, at least around the edges, very round, and covered with white dust—just like the gambler's money was supposed to be. I thought that Mrs. Peterson must have gone down under her chicken coop and scraped up these coins for her own, but I didn't say anything.

On the way back to our house I asked my mother about the money on Mrs. Peterson's dining room table and my mother said it wasn't money and that I was nosey and it was none of my business.

It was some years later, by one happenstance and another, that I learned that condoms—which we always called "safties" back then—could be reused. After being removed and washed they could be re-rolled for the next use—and that it was best of when re-rolling they should be dusted with talcum powder. So I figured the mystery of the "funny money" on Mrs. Peterson's dining room table was used condoms, neatly rolled and dusted, ready for the next time Mrs. Peterson was ready to be screwed. But screwed by whom? Mr. Peterson who was hardly ever at home? Or that Mr. Tom O'Reilly we had never even seen but who, perhaps, lived down under Mrs. Peterson's chicken coop.

A Reflection on Foulness

Because of a statement I recently made to a member of the jury selected to judge a state-wide chicken-sexing contest, the local newspaper accused me of using foul language. Knowing myself pretty well, I didn't choose to argue with or sue the newspaper.

Now, because I figured the newspaper had made a fair criticism, I found myself reflecting on the whole subject of foulness—no matter how slight a role it has had in my life. I discovered during that reflection that, yes, even from the time I was a little kid, foulness had a place in my life—as you will see from the following summary I've made of it.

My father, who played a lot of baseball when he was young man, achieved the height of his baseball career in those seasons he played third base for the Slocum Hatworks in Milwaukee. Long after he stopped playing, he attended baseball games, and I suppose it was no accident that back around 1920 or '21 our family rented a house at 707 Chambers Street directly behind home plate of what was then called Borchert Field—home of the Milwaukee Brewers Baseball Team. Even though there was ball-stopping screen up along the top of the grandstand, a lot of foul balls arched over it and landed in the street in front of our house or on our roof and, on more than one occasion, came crashing through our bay window. I suppose that if we had lived on the other end of the field—that is, out on the street behind left or right field, and could have hoped for home run balls to come over the fence and in through the front window of our house over there—if that had been true, I suppose I'd have a special fix on the home run ball. But as it was, our house was back of home plate, and I developed a fix on the foul ball.

In those long ago days before radio and certainly before television, the way you got to witness a sports event was to actually attend the sports event, unless now and then you got to see some weeks-old spectacular plays in the Pathé Newsreel. In those days admission to see a professional baseball game came pretty high for our means. We didn't often attend baseball games though it was a fairly regular custom to let the kids in free of charge after the seventh inning. So when there was a ball game going on Sunday afternoon we very often sat on the front porch and, sitting there, we could visualize the game as it went along. We could hear the umpire calling strikes and balls and safe and out. We could hear the crack of the ball against the bat, and we could hear the crowd stomp and roar. It was simple matter knowing what inning it was by keeping tab of the relatively quiet times between; and no game ever ended while we sat on our front porch with our being surprised at the fact that it was over. So, on Sunday afternoons, very often as I remember, at least a couple of us kids and my father and now and then my mother, would be sitting on the front porch of 707 Chambers Street hearing the baseball game. And every now and then the wonderful thing would happen: A foul ball would go up from the bat, up over the screen, and come bounding toward our front porch. More than that, if we kept the street swept with our eyes, and if we were always ready to run, we could pick up other foul balls that were not aimed specifically at our house. In those days we had a lot of balls, all foul balls, lined up on a special shelf in the living room, a kind reliquary, and there they stayed until I don't know when. My father used to say that when a baseball pitcher took up the ball, he held in his hand a fair ball. All balls were fair, my father said, unless they were hit foul. I can remember that this pronouncement which I'd heard more than once—he used it as a kind of moral that he'd recite in special circumstances—I can remember that as I heard my father say this, I was a little troubled by the whole thing. I'd stare at one of those balls on the shelf in the living room and think about how it had started out fair but then it became foul. And there it was, nothing more and nothing less than a foul ball on the shelf. I wondered whether some balls were really foul from the beginning and that this fact was proved when the batter hit it foul. Years later when I played third base on the Milwaukee County Home for Dependent Children's baseball team, and when I came up to bat, I often heard myself saying like a litany: Don't throw me a foul, oh, please don't throw me a foul. Then, too—back there on Chambers Street—I thought that some balls had been created to be fair forever and that no batter, not even Zip Hauser, could hit them foul no matter how hard he tried. As a kid I knew something about fair balls but an awful lot more about foul balls. So maybe from this you'll be helped to understand, that even though I consider myself a very fair person, a tendency does exist in me that comes in the direction of what could be called foul.

Lester Urkey's Birthday Party

When the time comes for explaining just how a person's life got to be what, in the end, it turned out to be; when the time comes for survivors to account for the life of someone who's "gone west"—thanks to remnants of Sigmund Freud's theories—much is made of that person's very early life: infancy, childhood is where it got going, never to be truly outgrown. At least that's the way most lives are explained these days: in terms of childhood traumas.

The difficulty with this—for the psychologists and psychiatrists going back into the lives of older or deceased people—is how to discover those very early traumas. In just about all efforts made in that regard, the researchers, let's call them, must depend on hearsay and metaphors: what someone said or says about the person under scrutiny—and even what the scrutinized person himself or herself tells the researcher about himself or herself, whether under hypnosis or truth serum, or not.

Through the years, I've had occasion to consider my life as it was running along—partly because I took somewhat seriously that Greek bumper sticker which read "An unconsidered life isn't worth living." I don't believe that I ever searched my past life for excuses for what I was then presently doing. I don't think I would have found any such excuses, anyway. And I never felt that I needed any.

For instance, even though I'm from what has been called "a broken home"—which until these most recent years, was not the ordinary conditions of a home—even though I'm from a broken home, I never felt that that was a negative factor in my life. Quite the opposite, for me it was a positive, a good factor.

Jesus! When I think of what my life would have been if the Weismann home, such as it was, had not broken up, it scares me a little. Not that I would have known, or could know, how life would have been in a unbroken Weismann home. My firm assumption is that one of the best things that ever happened to me was that my home got broken up. And—off the record—I'll bet that some of you who may be reading this wish that *your* home had broken up long, long ago.

So many things, events, situations of the past get misread in their recounting. The clichés and myths of psychiatric scientism are too often forced onto the body of actual human experience. Too often psychiatry operates with the assumption characteristic of the computer, which is, "I have the answer, what's your question," and psychiatry's answer is usually original sin, yes sir!

No matter that, let me tell you of an experience I had as a child of seven, back in 1921. On the few occasions that I've told this little story to friends they got to feel sad. Some even experienced tears. To me, however, it wasn't sad at all; my friends didn't appear to get the point—they misread the data, as some are prone to do, and I do mean *prone*.

Here's the story:

> One of my friends in third grade was named Lester, Lester Urkey, and, as you might expect, he was often called "Turkey," but I didn't call him that—just Lester, or Lester Urkey.
>
> Well, one day at school he told me that on the next Saturday he was having a birthday party at his home which was on the third floor of a wobbly wooden tenement

not far from the as yet unbroken home of the Weismanns. It was just breaking but hadn't as yet really busted.

From what Lester Urkey told me, this was going to be quite a thing: lots of expensive food, big birthday cake, decorations, games—the works. And Lester Urkey wanted me to come to his party, to be there on Saturday at two in the afternoon.

Back at my not quite yet broken home, I told my mother about this grand birthday party, and that I was invited. My mother said that was very nice and that she'd wash and iron my one light-colored shirt, fix and press my pants, put fresh cardboard insoles in my shoes to block the holes in the soles, and so on. Early on Saturday I shined my shoes, took a bath in the copper boiler Ed Wolfe had given us when he came back from the Army of Occupation in Germany, and got ready—way ahead of time in clean underwear. "You don't want to be late," my mother said, and I said she was right.

About a quarter to two I was ready to go; Lester Urkey's home, let's call it, was close—I could even walk slow from our place over to his. With the regular admonitions of my mother which were: "Don't tell them any of our business; don't let them pump you," I was off.

As I remember, the sun was out bright that day in 1921. There were a lot of flies out too, but they stayed in bunches in the gutters. I didn't kick cans on the way; would've spoiled my shoeshine. I had on my older brother's underwear and it kept sliding around under there, but I got it held up okay by tightening my belt which I figured I'd have to let out when I was eating all that expensive food at the party. But, I figured, I'd be sitting down then and my brother's big underwear would stay in place.

Halfway down the alley, there were those tiers of sagging porches and the wooden steps up to Lester Urkey's home. I figured I still had time, so I went up the steps slowly, and counting them. I always, even then, like to count steps. I still do, and I wonder what a psychiatrist would do with that—if I ever let one of those shrinks at me.

No one answered when I knocked on the screen door, so I waited, and after a long time, as I remember,

I knocked again, just a little harder. Finally a woman opened the door. This was Lester Urkey's mother as I found out later.

"Yes," she said. "What do you want?"

"The birthday party?" I said.

"What birthday party?" Lester Urkey's mother asked.

"Lester's party," I said. "He's eight years old today."

"Tell me something I don't know," his mother said.

So I just stood there, up on that porch, three years after the Germans had surrendered and World War I was over.

"Lester ain't having no party," Lester Urkey's mother said.

"No party," I said.

"Lester gets crazy ideas," she said.

"Crazy ideas," I said.

"That's right, crazy ideas," she said, and closed the door.

This is the point in the story—when I've told it to friends—that they get to looking real sad. Some even experience the beginnings of tears. That poor little boy (me) having such a disappointment, traumatic, etc. So, with the mood in the air, I have to tell the rest of the story which is that I was very *glad* that there was no party—and not only because my brother's big underwear was a bother to me, but because I could get back to my regular life—out of this light-colored shirt and all the rest of it. Truly, I was relieved and happy—and I don't think happiness is traumatic...is it? Actually, this Lester Urkey non-party experience was as positive an experience as the breaking up of the Weismann home—for as you may say, but don't necessarily believe—as I do believe: everything works out for the better—and by God, it has.

Look, I'm in my ninth decade and I'm here still alive and telling you this—and I can tell you that if the ancient Greeks were still prancing around they'd have a bumper sticker that said, "Fuck psychiatry and the snake it rode in on." You see, the ancient Greeks missed Christianity and along with it Sigmund

Freud's restatement of the Christian *sine qua non*—the Viper in the Garden and Original Sin.

Well now, there's always someone in the audience who lives on non-sequiturs and asks the foolish question: "Whatever happened to Lester Urkey?"

Well, it so happens we kept in touch, Lester Urkey and I, so I can tell you that he died very young, the product of an unbroken home, in that case.

In Folkloric America

My maternal grandfather was named George Custer, but not after General George Armstrong Custer who, after a brilliant career in the Union Army during the Civil War, died in the ill-fated attack he led against the Sioux Indians encampment on the Little Bighorn in 1876. No, George Custer, my maternal grandfather, was just another Custer. Still, he did distinguish himself—first by being the only driver of Milwaukee's horse-drawn streetcars with a perfect record of always being on time—a perfect keeper of the schedules. Then, in recognition of this he was chosen as the first operator of the first electronically operated streetcar put on the streets of the town. My maternal grandfather was Milwaukee's first streetcar motorman. I never had a chance to get to know him. He died when my mother was a teenager, long before I was born. As a very young kid I heard a few things about my grandfather, but the one thing that got hold of me and which still remains in my craw, is the story of his death—what it was that killed him: Spinal Meningitis.

The story, as I got it, around 1919, was that the speed of the new electric streetcars was controlled by a rheostat, a device we all know about from their use in present day light-dimmers and such. Nothing unusual about that. But the braking system on those early streetcars, I was told back then, worked with magnets—something about bringing powerful fixed magnets in contact with the rims of the turning iron wheels—slowing down and stopping them. It was, I was told, that it was these magnets, magnetism, that did in my grandfather—that what happened was his spinal column got negatively charged up and the back of his skull got charged positive. And since in magnetism, like poles repel and unlike poles—negative and positive—attract, my grandfather's spine, negatively charged, suddenly and violently attracted his positively changed skull pulling his whole head off his neck, literally tearing off his head. That's what I was told. And this was called spinal meningitis.

The picture I had as a five-year-old was pretty awful with my grandfather standing there up front at his post of motorman with his head wrenched free and sticking, face turned up, to the top of his spine.

All this is what's called folklore, but believable as bald truth for me, back then.

There were other examples of fascinating folklore that went into my early formative years as a small child in folkloric America.

There was what went for gospel truth about tapeworms. I'll never forget those stories of long, long—maybe a few hundred feet of terribly strong wide flatworms that got to growing inside people. They wound through and down the esophagus, the stomach, and upper and lower intestines and ate up all the food intended for the person with the tapeworm. If these worms were not gotten rid of, the person in whom these worms lived and ate voraciously, died of starvation, no matter how much the person ate. Tapeworms, I was told, had insatiable appetites—no way to feed them enough. If the tapeworm-infested person wished to go on living, the tapeworm had to be gotten rid of, done-in, in one way or another. Various poisons taken by mouth didn't work. In lots of cases, I was told, people died of the poisons intended to kill their tapeworms. The tapeworms went right to the grave with the corpse. They were tough.

It was Barney Clevenger, the Prudential Life Insurance man who used to come to our house on Island Avenue every Thursday to collect the coins for our family's weekly premium—it was Barney Clevenger who, when I asked him how a person with tapeworms could keep it from killing that person, he told me.

While Ma was looking under the sofa cushions in case some nickels or dimes or pennies might have slipped out of somebody's pockets and got lost down there—enough maybe to pay that week's life insurance premium—it was while Ma was busy at that that Mr. Clevenger took me aside and gave me what seemed like the actual, low-down truth of the matter.

First, he said, you have to have the person with the tapeworm stand up, stretch with his arms raised over his head, then bring them down and continue standing in a relaxed attitude with his mouth wide open. A cooperative friend then hands him a bowl of warm milk which the tapeworm person holds about a foot and a half from his open mouth. After a while, the tapeworm, smelling the milk and wanting to get at it, peeks out of the man's mouth. It is very important, Mr. Clevenger told me, not to take the next step too soon. Tapeworms are more clever than gophers, he said. What you have to do is let the tapeworm come clear out *almost* to the bowl of milk. That's when the friend gets a good hold on the tapeworm, with both hands, and pulls. "They're slippery devils," Mr. Clevenger said, "so you better keep getting firm grips each time you grab another length of the worm." And in this way you keep pulling out more and more of the tapeworm until you come to its end—"could be a hundred feet or more," Mr. Clevenger told me.

Naturally as a believing kid, I was wondering how it looked, dead and piled up like a flat garden hose on the floor, and what was done with it. But that's not so important to this report. The important thing is to have us appreciate the wonder, even magnificence, of some folklore. I know that these folktales of spinal meningitis and tapeworms—and many, many more—lent to my very early entirely trusting and imaginative years real romance and color—and in later years they worked to encourage a special desire to invent my own folklore.

My greatest folkloric *invention* to date—has been the invention of myself. This is an ongoing kind of invention which I hope will continue right to the last when spinal meningitis or some still-unborn tapeworm will finally do me in for all time.

Dick Stamm's Invention

One of my best friends for years, until he died of leukemia, not so long ago, was Dick Stamm. His father was a big shot at the A.O. Smith factory where they made automobile frames. Dick's father, with his inflated salary and bonuses as vice president of the A.O. Smith Corporation, was a rich man. At his big house, when everyone was at home, there were always two new black Packard sedans and a Ford in the garage. And Dick's father always kept a kind of champagne on tap—he'd buy some kind of wine by the barrel and then plug in what looked like a twenty millimeter shell—plugged it in real tight—and then he did something—hit that bullet with a ball peen hammer as I remember, and gas, under great pressure, was fired from the bullet into the barrel, thus charging up the wine. Really tasted like champagne, pretty much. On special occasions, which came pretty often, Dick and I sat around on the big veranda drinking this champagne.

We talked a lot then, just sitting on the veranda, but sometimes Dick would roll out one of those classy Packards—the model that Frank Lloyd Wright liked so much, only Wright's

Packards were always painted red—well, sometimes Dick and I drove out to the flat country west of Milwaukee, taking the breeze, and roaring along at ninety miles an hour which was considered awfully fast then. But no matter if we just sat on the veranda sipping that champagne, or went roaring across the countryside—we always talked a lot. We had genuine conversations in the true meaning of that word. Both of us were still not fifteen years old, so we had a lot to say, and luckily, both of us were good listeners—took turn, as it were, first talking then listening, then talking again—simple and genuine as that.

Indeed, Dick Stamm and I were truly good friends. And as I hope you've discovered in your own life—truly good friends can be trusted.

Maybe because we trusted each other entirely we often talked about things, people, and ideas in open ways we knew would go no farther than us two, Dick and me, sitting there on that veranda. And as I think of it now—after all these years—I don't remember much of our talk (and listening) being about girls—sex—and neither of us was a *fruit* as they were called then—before the word GAY was ruined for all traditional use. But that's neither here nor there—not then, not now. All I wanted to say was that Dick's and my friendship was plainly loaded with trust.

For instance, it seemed quite natural and easy—enjoyable, really—to tell Dick that what I really wanted to be was a movie actor, a kind of updated Douglas Fairbanks or Bob Steele. Now you know that your friend would have to be pretty open and trustworthy for you to let something like that out on the air. I even told Dick how I often practiced alone at home in front of our big Princess mirror—the one I'd have to unbolt from my mother's dresser when she wasn't at home—and carry to the back storeroom where I could feel free to go through with all those facial contortions, and gestures as I said things like: "Well, you'll just have to excuse me, Monty, but I won't take that from anybody."

Of course Dick listened to this, and lots of other private-like things I shared with him. He was as good a listener as he was a talker.

I've found out—in all the years since Dick and I listened so perfectly to each other—that most people just don't listen.

All they want to do, if they talk at all, is talk all the time. And if they do stop talking they're not listening. They're thinking up what they're going to say as soon as whomever is talking draws a breath.

Well, I didn't mean to get into matters concerning those other people who don't listen. I want to stick to how it was with Dick and me.

So, like I told Dick about my private life, he told me about his—while I listened, of course. One of the things he brought out was that he had always wanted to be an inventor like Thomas A. Edison or Lee de Forest—and that, in fact, he'd invented quite a number of things he was still keeping at least semi-secret. One invention he said he was about ready to try out was one that would at least double the time of swimmers—make people who swim go at least twice as fast in the water.

"Boy," I said, "that would be something!" And then I went back to listening.

Dick Stamm then said that he'd like me at the try-out for this invention of his, and I said I'd like to be in on it—just as a watcher, of course.

Well the day came when Dick called and said, "How about this Saturday—we'll drive out to Pewaukee Lake and give it a whirl," and I said that would suit me fine—to give it whirl.

Dick picked me up in one of the Packards and we drove the twenty miles or so to Pewaukee Lake with a bundle about the size of the torso of a man—without the legs, that is. I figured that Dick's invention was in the bundle, which it proved to be.

We parked near the pier that ran quite a distance out into the lake, and we walked out to the end, Dick carrying the bundle. Out there, Dick stripped down to his BVD shorts, no shoes on. Then he opened the bundle.

Inside there were two metal and fabric things that looked pretty much like small umbrellas—and lots of straps and buckles. "You can help me with this," he said. And so I did, strapping the umbrellas—one to one leg, the other to the other leg. He was lying down on the pier to facilitate this strapping on process. "Have you figured it out yet?" he asked, still lying down and well strapped.

"No," I said, "not exactly."

"It's really simple," he said. "You know how a person sometimes swims—brings his leg up to his body then kicks backwards, you know,"

"Sure," I said.

"And you know how a regular umbrella works—when it's closed it's like these *Stambrellas,* as I call them, are right now, slim streamlined and when they're opened"—and he did something on the side of one and the Stambrella opened, "then they're no longer streamlined—you have the full surface to push against.

"When I'm in the water and bring my upper legs forward, the Stambrella closes, gets streamlined, and when I push my upper legs backwards, the Stambrella opens, providing one helluva big surface to push against—first one leg, then the other—closed, open. And I should push myself ahead through the water—simple, eh?"

"Sounds terrific," I said,.

"I hope it is," Dick said, "I've put a lot of time on this one, measuring my leg stroke, matching that with the length of opening-closing of the fabric, and so on."

Then Dick Stamm just lay there on the pier looking straight up in the air. It was real quiet—both of us were listening at the same time right then. No talking.

After a bit, as if the prayer was over, Dick said, "Just roll me in now, Don."

So, I rolled my friend Dick Stamm off the end of the pier into Pewaukee Lake.

After the splash there was some thrashing about, something like I once saw in a movie—alligator tails—and then he sank. I waited a little and then pulled him up and out. He wasn't hurt or anything, but he was glad, it appeared, to just lie down in the sun on the pier looking toward something far off which I couldn't see.

I told my friend that things happen in this less than perfect world, that a real person learns from everything, that practice makes perfect, that sometimes the slightest adjustment often makes the greatest difference, that Rome wasn't built in a day, and look at Charles Lindberg, and on and on I went for what seemed like a whole hour while Dick just lay there, breathing normally and looking way far off. But it didn't bother me—it was one of those times when it was my time to talk and for Dick Stamm to listen. Which he did with real style there on the pier.

From the Balcony of the Gaiety Theater

We were pretty little then, my older brother and I, when we saw those other older kids running for their lives with two cops chasing them. They were all coming our way up Wells Street, and we didn't want to get mixed up with that, so we took to the fire escape up the side of the Gaiety Theater at Fourth Street. At the second floor level we got down flat and the whole bunch, cops and all, ran past right under us.

We waited a while up there and then stood up and looked around. It was a pretty sight looking down at the street car making sparks behind that little wheel that ran along the wire, the lights on the bridge across the river and the lighted red, white, and blue barber shop thing that kept turning and looking like it was screwing itself up the front of the shop where the barber had absolutely no hair on his head because, as he once told us, it all got burned off in the big Third Ward fire and never grew back.

Then we heard music from inside the Gaiety Theater and saw that the door up there was open a crack. So we opened it more and looked in. It was the balcony, lots of seats but no one in them. We should have been home before this, but as long as we were already late with the bag of potatoes the Salvation Army gives to poor people just before they go out in the street to sing "The Old Rugged Cross" and "Onward Christian Soldiers"—as long as we were already late, my brother said that a little later wouldn't make much difference, and I agreed.

It was pretty dark up there in the balcony. The lights were all down there on the stage. We hunched down and made our way right to the front row. There was a little band in the pit making music with a lot of loud drum beats in it, and an almost naked woman was walking back and forth out front on the stage. She was taking off the rest of her clothes, and my brother said we shouldn't tell anybody, not even our best friend, Lefty, about this, and I agreed.

About the time the woman looked like she was getting ready to go completely naked, the stage lights turned to dark blue and the woman disappeared behind the curtain at one side. The music got real loud, the white lights came up, the back curtains opened and there was what looked like the pictures of the deck of an ocean liner with painted water behind. A very old man in just his shorts was lifting a huge dumbbell up and down—over his head and then down and up again, over and over. He was very skinny and had a long white beard. When the music stopped another man, a much younger man, came walking along the deck, watching the old man with his dumbbell until he flipped the dumbbell backwards high over his head. When it landed, the drummer in the orchestra made a very loud bang. The young man said, "My God, man, you're strong."

And the old man said, "You bet, that dumbbell weighs 500 pounds, but you see, I can still get it up."

"Way over your head," the young man said.

"Any time, day or night," the skinny old man said, "you bet."

"Jesus," the young man said, "and you're so skinny—how much do you weigh?"

"A hundred and two pounds," the old man said.

"How old are you?" the young man asked.

"Ninety-eight," the old man said, "born in 1823."

"Jesus," the young man said, "it's a miracle, how do you do it?"

"Monkey glands," the old man said, "got 'em down there in Muscatine, Iowa, from that famous German doctor, yeah, Doctor Steinkried."

"The hell you say."

"Come right over here if you don't believe it," the skinny old man said, stepping behind a waist-high sign that said BRING BACK BEER and making gestures of lowering his shorts, "just take a look." The young man bent over as if looking at the lower part of the skinny old man and gasped a little.

"They're big all right," he said.

"And look at the length of the hair," the old man said.

"Jesus," the younger man said, "has the doctor got more of them?"

"You bet," and he wrote down the doctor's address in Muscatine, Iowa. "Go get 'em kid," the old man said.

Then the curtains closed and the band struck up with a patriotic number *Don't Throw Stones in the Well That Gives You Water*, while a half-naked woman carried a sign across the stage. It said FIVE YEARS LATER, and the curtains opened on the same shipboard scene. The skinny old man, looking even older and skinnier and bent over, is hoisting and even bigger dumbbell while five almost-naked women, saying "Yum, Yum" are tugging at him. "A little later, girls," the very old man is saying— "you draw straws to see who's first, and so on."

Then the young man comes along, walking with a cane. "Well, well," the old man says to him, "haven't seen you in five years. Did you ever get to see Doctor Steinkried?"

"Yeah," the young man said, "sure did, but I want to tell you those monkey glands don't work on everybody—not me, anyway—and me forking over three hundred bucks for them."

"You got 'em cheap," the old man said. "come here, let's just see what you can do with the dumbbell."

"No use," the young man said, "I've tried—I can't get it up."

"Let's take a look," the old man said, and both went behind the sign which now read, AND WHISKY TOO. He bent down as the young man made like he was dropping his pants. After a little while the old man shouted out, "Good God in Heaven, man—no wonder, I'd recognize that tattoo on anyone, he gave you my old ones."

On the way home I asked my brother what happens with monkeys when their glands are taken off, and he said he didn't know for sure, but he guessed that once they're off they can't lift big dumbbells anymore, and I agreed.

The Steam Boiler and Whitey the Rat

When we lived above Ed Strachota's saloon in downtown Milwaukee we didn't pay any rent because Ma worked in the saloon instead.

All of us kids—there were only three of us then back in the early 1920s—all of us helped out around the place even when the barroom and palm garden were full of customers, sometimes way past midnight. I liked it best at night with the electric piano playing and people dancing, sometimes so drunk that now and then they fell right down on the floor—but always laughing and singing along. Ed Strachota had a good reputation for running a decent place, my Ma told us, there was even a "family entrance" as the sign said over the side door. Whole families often came in—mothers and fathers, children, and even grandmothers and grandfathers, always early before the "hard drinkers," as they were called, showed up after nine or ten and stayed until it got light outside.

I enjoyed the life around Ed Strachota's saloon. My Pa was away for most of the time we lived there. I missed him, but the life Ed Strachota's made up for a lot of that. I always thought, as the late "hard-drinkers" skidded and fell down while dancing, that if my Pa was home he'd be on the floor with them laughing and singing along with whatever was playing on the electric piano. He had a good voice, and he sang very loud.

In winter Ed Strachota's saloon, as well as our flat above, and the whole building was steam heated. There was a big boiler in the basement with gas burning under to boil the water that got made into steam and came through the pipes to all the radiators in the building.

Since I could read even before going to school, I'd read newspaper reports of steam boilers blowing up—too much pressure—and exploding. My Uncle Charlie had come back from the Army of Occupation in Germany a couple of years before we moved into our flat above Ed Strachota's. By then he'd gotten to be what was called a "steam fitter." He knew all about steam boilers and he told me about how they work and about some that blew up. He said that the reason most of them blew up was a faulty safety valve. When the steam pressure gets too great, he told me, that very same steam pressure pushes up a piston past an opening in the pipe through which, then, the excess steam escapes, reducing the pressure in the boiler. And, my Uncle Charlie told me, this escaping steam makes a loud whistle that should warn people that it's time to turn down the heat under the boiler. Sometimes, my Uncle Charlie told me, the safety valve gets stuck—doesn't work to release the pressure, and then, BOOM, the boiler explodes.

Well, I used to go down into Strachota's basement pretty often doing chores for the saloon—taking stuff down, bringing stuff up, and such. And when the boiler was making steam in winter I'd look at it, sort of study it, but not close-up. I guess I had a fear of it—fear that the safety valve would get stuck and blow up the whole building, including me and our whole family, except Pa, of course, who'd be safe out in North Dakota being a Federal Dry Agent since those were the early years of the Volstead Act, Prohibition, and Pa, who Ma said had drunk enough to float a battleship, and kept on drinking, was out there enforcing the law. My Uncle Charlie once told me that Pa would make a good politician...or preacher.

Well, the safety valve went off twice while we lived in the flat above the saloon—once in the middle of the night, and one of the bartenders, Baldy Bill Wasserbach ran downstairs and took care of the situation. The other time was on a Saturday afternoon with the place full of people. I was in the palm garden which adjoined the saloon proper, at one of my assigned chores—to get a nickel out of the money slot of the piano, because the stuck-nickel kept the piano from playing and my hands were small enough, with part of a corset stay, to get at it.

Well, I want to tell you, I'd heard a lot of whistles in my then seven or eight years of life, but never a whistle like that safety-valve whistle let loose. It beat all the boat and train whistles I'd ever heard. It was more like the siren on the hook-and-ladder, roaring out of the fire house not far away. This time it was Ad Wolgast, another bartender, who flew out from behind the bar and down into the basement. Ed Strachota, yelling over the whistle, kept assuring the customers that it was nothing at all, to keep calm, it was just the safety valve keeping us all safe...and so on.

Well, there was lots more than that boiler in the basement of Ed Strachota's saloon. There were rats, plenty of them. On my trips to the basement, summer or winter, a few would be moving around on the floor among all the piled-up junk, sort of minding their own business. But, when I clapped my hands loud, they'd scurry away out of sight. All except one rat who most always took a position on one of the old, no-longer-used beer barrels. He'd just sit there, looking very much like a squirrel without the bushy tail. And he'd watch me all the time right until I went back upstairs.

Now I'd heard a lot about rats, the diseases they carried, and how at night they bit babies in their cribs—and grown people getting sick and dying from rat bites. But it seems I was more scared of that boiler blowing up than of this bold rat atop the barrel biting me. In fact from a safe distance I got to expect him there each time I came to the basement. And he never failed me. I sort of go to "know" this rat if not like him. He was a well-built rat, not lean, and on occasion quite athletic, reminding me in a way of my Pa, who was very athletic—running, jumping, swimming, tumbling, everything including being voted the most valuable player on the Slocum Hat Works baseball team.

This bold rat had a fine coat—a dark grayish brown—and looking like he'd just come from a bath and being curried. And there was more about this rat: on the top of his head there was a streak of pure white hair. And remember this was, I believe, before it became popular for human beings to bleach a streak of hair, make it white against all the darker hair—men *and* women. Very stylish for some I guess.

Once I mentioned this white-streaked rat to my Ma, but I don't think she was listening. She was too busy helping Ed Strachota water the whiskey for the evening crowd. And after that I decided to keep it to myself; maybe people wouldn't believe it, anyway: A rat sitting up on a barrel like a squirrel and displaying a perfectly white streak along the top of his head—and evidently not afraid of me, though all the other rats were.

I got to feel disappointed, let down, if when I went down to the basement the rat was not there. Once or twice, after all the other run-of-the-mill rats ran to their hiding places, I called the name I'd given him: "Here, Whitey. Here, Whitey!" but he didn't come those times; he had his own schedule, I guess. But when that schedule called for him to be there on that barrel, he was there. Over a period of months I got to talk to Whitey, this rat, always staying my distance. I needn't tell you that he never answered—didn't even squeak.

I was in school, in the third grade, when the boiler under Ed Strachota's saloon blew up, just like I feared it some day would, and I wondered if Whitey had been killed in the explosion. Nobody was hurt, and Ed Strachota went about making all the repairs, practically rebuilding the area of the former steam boiler. It was done in jig-time; after all winter was coming and the building had to be heated—by a new steam boiler.

So then there it all was, this like new basement and no matter now many times I went down there I never saw a single rat. My "Whitey" was gone—and looking at the handsome new boiler standing there, I was convinced that for Whitey and me this was not an altogether happy exchange.

A Thousand Miles and Eighty Years Ago

I like to think that my very early childhood was not, in generic terms, radically different from that of most American boys my age. I'm thinking of those years from about age four to six, especially if there were other boys around, say from seven to eight, who lorded over us younger ones. This is not to suggest that those older boys forced us into doing things. Rather they were the leaders, and we respected them as such—and besides they had ideas that we felt were better than ours, and they came faster. Or so it seemed to me back in 1919 or 1920. And I must say, no matter how I feel about it now, close to eighty years later, I relished and enjoyed what we young ones were helped into by those older ones. In fact I learned from them some things we could do or avoid doing when our time came.

Now, my experience has it that young boys, maybe more than young girls, get belly-shaking fun out of performances as well as just talk about farting, pissing, and shitting, even belching and puking. So, even though we knew that some of the things we were thinking and doing back then were off limits, taboo, so to speak, and way beyond what we assumed our parents knew about—the latter being, of course, unfounded—we still did them and with a certain frightened zest.

Nowadays, in this bittersweet ending of the 20th century, we may, if we choose, read about little kids murdering each other; older kids firing spreadshot into their parents while Mom and Dad are peacefully eating ice cream; young and old adults drowning and beating their children to death as well as shooting, knifing, and poisoning each other—the latter ignored by church and government only in times of war. It appears that at least some of the day-to-day violence is whelped on the level of grudges—grudges often based in jealousy, in ignorance, in failed efforts to demonstrate personal differences with the conventions of the status quo. More subtly, some of these grudges appear based in feelings of deprivation—feelings that the person involved is being deprived of exercising his or her "free will." It's as if these people hadn't had opportunities for expressing such feelings while they were still kids long before "fulfillment" came to be measured in hurting, torturing, and even killing people. There was a time when I thought that the experience of actually maiming and killing people in officially sanctioned warfare could satisfy for all time the misanthropic tendencies of some human beings. However, I never did propose this as a "cure" for anything; I've found that the successful romanticized combat warrior sometimes serves only to kill himself—as a truly human being, I mean.

In cultures that depend more on taboos than on living examples of "proper behavior," let's call it, laws are developed to punish violators of those taboos, not necessarily to provide examples and encouragement for the law abiding. When breaking of prevailing customs takes on the character of revolt or contrariness, or even "just fun," there's bound to be disruptions in whatever are considered normal procedures. It is my opinion that if children, very early on, have fun going against taboos, no matter how simple, it is likely that later they'll not go for breaking the big taboos about abusing and killing people. By then they should have gotten that out of their systems. I realize that there could be plenty argument about this; that's why I phrase this in the conditional.

So this is where I come back to the earlier references to my own very early childhood and the taboos we enjoyed ignoring or going against. Some might refer to this as "self-expression."

After the days of infancy when we played in our own shit—or excrement as it rests cleaned up as a word in our language—after those finger painting days it became clear to me that talking about it, especially at the supper table, was forbidden. The same went for farting, even though there often was giggling when someone let one fly. To a less degree than farting, pissing, more acceptably referred to as peeing, lay in a territory of only so-so forbidden. If I can trust my memory then I can truthfully report that I never heard the word urinate until I went to kindergarten; that's what the kindergarten teacher called pissing. One just didn't dwell on such bodily functions, or at any length on such events as belching, or worse, puking also known as vomiting or "throwing up."

Well, when my daughter at age three laid a turd on the grill covering the cold air intake of our central heating system, I didn't reprimand her beyond frowning a little, wagging my finger in her direction and saying, "no-no." I don't recall saying anything beyond that—not even "shame, shame" as is sometimes said in stories of less earthy quality. I figured that getting this sort of thing out of her system so early in life might not make it alluring to her when, spying the grill over an air intake in the sorority house, she'd be tempted. My figuring proved to be correct: she'd had this kind of "fun" early, got the idea it was a "no-no" and went on to other matters, never feeling she'd been deprived.

Now to come back to me when I was four or five years of age. To "center" you in time, as some psychologists say, we are now talking about goings-on in the far-off time of 1919 and 1920, way over seventy-five years ago. President Woodrow Wilson was still living; the Great War during which millions were killed, and which is sometimes characterized as Great Britain's "attempted suicide," was over; and the mentally and physically unbalanced man mostly responsible for starting it in efforts to satisfy his grudge against the British and his lust for personal power, Kaiser Wilhelm the Second of Germany, was living in comfortable retirement in the Dutch city of Doorn. I, not ignorant of some of this, was living in Milwaukee, Wisconsin, on a street named Chambers across from the Milwaukee Brewers' baseball park.

Now, under the direction of a boy named Fritz, the bigger boys, aged about seven to eight years, built what Fritz called his "Tent Club" on an abandoned tennis court a couple of blocks from our house. It was made out of scavenged wood supports covered with old rugs. There were no windows and just one doorway accessible by pulling aside a big flap made out of one of the rugs. Inside the older boys smoked cigarette butts that the younger ones, under Fritz's instructions, picked up for them in the baseball park once a game was over. For every twenty good long butts we brought in we were allotted one each for our own personal smoking. It was a clubby atmosphere that I was reminded of a half century later when, as guide, I took a lot of older women in a crowded rented bus to an art exhibition in Nashville.

Now this long ago Tent Club was run in a strict manner by Fritz, the eight-year-old who'd invented it and assumed its presidency. We, as younger members, did his biddings, which we generally enjoyed. President Fritz invented an initiation ceremony as part of becoming a member in good standing in the club, very much like I later learned there is for college fraternities. All recruits—all new, ignorant prospective members, were required to play a game called "Church on Fire." In this game the recruit had to lie face-down just outside the tent and be covered all over with lots of grass and weeds. It was required that the recruit lie deathly still through the entire ceremony. All regular members were to stand around and close to the prostrate recruit. President Fritz, standing at the foot-end of the recruit, then began to mumble, then increased his mumbo-jumbo ending in his yelling, "Church on Fire." That was the signal for us to get out our donikers and piss all over the covered recruit. I noticed as this ceremony was repeated with new recruits that the stupider of the lot laid the longest under the streams. They got really soaked before they rolled aside and got up.

Now, having had this experience as both pissed-upon and pisser when I was four or five years old, I've never had the urge to do this, except metaphorically, to anyone in my later life. You see, it was like my daughter who never wanted to unload on the cold air intake, either in winter or summer, once she'd had the relatively uninterrupted freedom to do it as a very young child. I'm guessing that psychiatrists have some inappropriate name for this.

Another activity invented by President Fritz was called "Special Delivery" and involved the use of a short shovel and scooped-up horse manure. Back in the earliest days of this century, horses provided a significant share of the city transportation system. Horses were always in evidence in the streets, especially those that pulled the big heavily loaded beer wagons. This period of horse-drawn beer wagons is memorialized in present day advertising which shows marvelous wagons piled high with barrels of Budweiser beer being pulled by six or eight pairs of perfectly curried Clydesdale horses all in beautiful harnesses, straps, and doodads sporting highly polished brass ornaments. And even though these horses may be shown at their work for several minutes on television, I've never seen, and I'll bet no one else has ever seen, these animals drop their "horseapples" on the street, not even if the street is an absorbent country road. That's just another evidence of the difference between art and reality, of course; like I've read that some people in love cannot believe that the loved one ever evacuates.

So, back in the days of the Tent Club, the streets of Milwaukee were richly speckled with real horseshit. It was great for the sparrows and, in retrospect, for President Fritz's event he named "Special Delivery." To pull it off, two volunteers were required and had to work in pairs. One would scoop up a shovel full of it—maybe a pound or thereabouts—and carry it to a house selected by the other volunteer. This house should be the house of a stranger, no one we or anyone else in the club knew, and it should have a button outside the front door that when pressed would ring an electric bell inside. Then, standing close to the front door, making sure, from the enframing woodwork, that the door will open *inwards,* not *outwards,* the volunteer gets ready with his shovel—sort of with a cocked arm. Then the other volunteer presses the doorbell button. When the man or woman opens the door both volunteers yell out "Special Delivery" as the first volunteer flings the shit from his shovel into the house and at whomever was in its way. Then both volunteers take off, usually laughing their guts clear up to their tonsils.

After twice being a volunteer for the "Special Delivery" event, I didn't volunteer anymore. It seems I'd had my fill of making those unsuspecting people feel awful, and for no real reason except to accidentally develop my incapacity for unfairness and disgust. There have been times, years and years later, when it occurred to me that the "Special Delivery" treatment would be the perfect order of the day for someone like the dean and a sergeant I once worked under. But no—I'd had that, just like my daughter had had the satisfaction, let's call it, of laying those turds on the cold air intake in the winter she was three years old.

Even though the Tent Club lasted for only a year or so, President Fritz had developed a pretty full program of events. Besides the "Church on Fire" and "Special Delivery" events was another called "Bicycle Race, Standing Room Only." President Fritz, even though he was only eight years old, was already in fifth grade. He was very intelligent, or smart, whichever you prefer. He invented all the names for the club's events and the tactics required for their successful execution. He invented the name "Bicycle Race, Standing Room Only," before any of us had any idea of what it might mean, but President Fritz knew and we soon found out. Getting ready for this event took careful planning and concerted efforts. Even at his early age, President Fritz had the self-conviction and planning ability of a present-day Chief Executive Officer, say, of a corporation like that Columbia health delivery outfit.

First of all, what was required was a pretty big supply of fresh shit of the right consistency. So, all club members, under the president's orders, provided it on a common pile in back of the tent. It took most of one day to provide what he considered to be sufficient to do the job. He said it was better to have too much than too little. When the time came to get on with it, he passed out stiff cardboard pie plates and flat wooden tongue blades, the kind doctors used to hold down your tongue when they were painting your tonsils with iodine because you had a sore throat, and the same kind that, in those long ago days, was given out with the bulk ice cream you bought at the drugstore.

Then, calling all the kids together, he had them sit around him as if this was a corporate board meeting or an Indian pipe of peace ceremony while he outlined the tactics for this bicycle event. First of all, he said, we'll go into action tomorrow. The Milwaukee Brewers will be having a game so we'll move out just before the ninth inning. That will give us the whole inning to do our job. You all know where the bicycles are parked—in that special place on the east side. And the kids said, yes, sure, Mr. President. Now, President Fritz went on, each of you will help yourself to a plateful of shit and two tongue blades each in case you lose one or if one breaks. Then you will move to the bicycles. Since I see that our supply is mostly dark brown, get to bikes that have brown seats. Stay away from the black or white ones; the shit will show up too much against those colors—got it? And they responded as one—yes, Mr. President, we got it. So now you take your supply to a bike with a brown seat, and with your tongue blade you spread it all over the seat. Spread it out nice, shape it so it looks like the seat. Do as many seats as you have time for; I'll be there to tell you when to quit and get the hell away. Got that? Yeah, Mr. President, they said, we got that.

Now, said the Tent Club President pacing in the small space in front of the members, I've watched those bikers as they come out of the baseball park right at the end of the game, or just a little before. They're all trying to beat the other guy, getting on their bikes and tearing out lickety-split down the street. I've watched them; they don't sit down on the seats right away. They wheel out their bikes, get them going by running alongside, and then with one foot on the nearer pedal, they swing their other leg over to the pedal on the other side. They stand up on the pedals to get their weight into the act and in seconds they're going like hell. They don't sit down until, maybe, they're up at 8th Street. But sooner or later they'll sit down—right into your shit.

And that's exactly the way it actually happened.

I was one of the spreaders in this event, the only time it was performed. I can still recall the experience, the fun, the dirtiness of it coupled with a nervous fear of being caught in the act. I can still see my friends of eighty years ago manically spreading shit on those bicycle seats, and President Fritz standing to one side in the shade, raising both arms and yelling out the agreed upon words signaling the end of spreading. They were "Standing Room Only." I can still see him walking calmly, even slowly away after we dispersed—with a big satisfying smile all over his face. A born leader, I guess; maybe one like Richard Milhous Nixon.

In my generally happy long life I've had lots of chances, even impassioned invitations to join up with and run organizations, academic, political, and undetermined, and I've kindly refused them all. At five years of age I sure did admire Fritz, the eight-year-old president of the Tent Club. He had what I thought I took in this life. But thinking of him by the time I was ten years old scared the shit out of me—and still does. I don't think I was overtaken by cowardliness or feelings that I was too good or too precious for President Fritz's creative special events. While I was part of them I enjoyed them. And then, for me, the show was over. I cannot deny the importance in my very early childhood of those events as is certainly documented by the fact that I can still recall and re-experience them here in Texas over a thousand miles away and eighty years ago.

And as for my daughter who has provided me with two grown and beautiful grandchildren, she's never relieved herself again on any hot or cold air intake. And that's not only because she's too busy being a high level manager of a billion dollar corporation. There's a lot more to it than that including that she's a much "quicker study" than her father ever was or claimed to be. In her case only one misplaced turd was sufficient.

Curable and Incurable Insane

In my walks from the west end of the Wells-Downer streetcar line, out that mile to the Milwaukee County Home for Dependent Children, more than seventy years ago, I saw and talked to a lot of women certified as insane. They lived at the Milwaukee County Asylums for both the "Curably" and "Incurably" insane. For a period of several weeks, back then, a woman of about thirty used to appear out of a hedge almost every evening I set out on that walk. She'd come at me, harmlessly enough, with the heel of a loaf of rye bread in her hand and ask me to tell her that she wasn't crazy. From the first time she appeared with that request, I obliged. And each time she'd smile, say "I love you," and rub the heel of rye bread against my shoulder and walk back through the hedge toward the asylum for the curably insane where, I suppose, she stayed.

It was spring, April, I think, of 1931. I got off the streetcar at the end of the line, had my last cigarette in the car shack, and started to the Home. In those days both sides of the Watertown Plank Road stretched out into open rolling fields. The County buildings stood back a good distance nestled among trees. Everything, it seemed, was delicately green; it was about five o'clock, warm, and wonderful. And then I heard singing coming from off to the south, from the direction of the Incurably Insane. It was the voice of a man and it was singing "Asleep in the Deep." It was a good voice and would have to be a strong one to carry so clearly the quarter mile across the fields. I followed it to a four-story brick building with screened porches across one end.

Stripped to his waist and standing barefoot on a stool, George More (whose name I learned later) was singing out from the fourth-floor porch. He was wearing one of those folded newspaper soldier hats all of us have made, and he was grossly exaggerating a vibrato by shaking his belly with both hands. He carried the song to its end again, holding the last bass note surprisingly long. "Hello, I've just walked off the cross," he said, getting down from the stool and showing his hands, "see, they're still bleeding, the bastards." Then, smiling very broadly and looking like a photograph I'd seen of Pete de Palma after winning the Indianapolis 500, he held his paper hat over his heart and asked if I was the Duke of Kackiack. I said no, that I was just coming from school and heard him singing. "Then you must be the Duke of Kackiack," he said,

"All right," I said, "I'm the Duke then; how are you?"

"The question," George More said, "is how are *you*, and from here you look like you could stand some learning. You see that shed over there? Well, you go on over there and get those newspapers on the shelf by the wheelbarrows and bring them back here."

The door of the shed was open, and on a wide shelf there were two stacks of newspapers. I took two or three inches off the first stack and carried them back to my place way below George More. "All *Christian Science Monitors*, right?" he asked.

"All *Christian Science Monitors*," I said.

"Now," said George More, "you open up any of those papers and tell me the date and the page and I'll read you it from up here."

"October 14, 1929, page 12," I called out and he began to "read." He started at the upper left of the sheet and in a sing-song voice rattled off the whole column including the texts of the ads below the last article. Then pacing up and down on that high screened porch, and with the other inmates as heedless of him as only stones could be, he looked out at the sky and kept reciting the exact wordings of the page.

"How about this one?" I asked, pointing to another sheet, "August 25, 1930, page 16."

And after a little pause George More said, "Oh, that's the sad one about the woman," and again he rolled off the words as if he had the page before him.

George More asked if I wanted to be the smartest man in the world, and I said why not. He directed me to the general reference room of the Milwaukee Public Library downtown on Grand Avenue, to a particular stack and shelf where I would find a German lexicon. We talked a little more, about tomatoes, as I remember, and I left him singing "Asleep in the Deep."

The German lexicon was where he said it would be, and a few days later I was back on the grass below George More's porch. "I found the book," I said, "you knew it was there."

"Oh yes," said George More, "and I'd know them all if those telephones would've stopped ringing."

"Telephones?" I asked.

"Yes, the goddamned telephones," he said, "they drove me nuts; I told all about it in my book."

"What book?" I asked.

"My book," George More said, *"The Mind That Found Itself,"* and he told me where to find it in the Milwaukee Public Library.

The book was there all right, but the author was a man by the name of Clifford Beard. And I read the book; a pretty interesting one about a man who'd gone insane and then came back.

It got to be a habit, stopping to talk to George More. I told my friend, John Mimier, about him, and we went together to stand on the grass in the early evening and talk up at that darkening porch. Then, on one of the regular visiting days at the Asylum (George More called it the "Hotel de Rupp" after his doctor) we posed as relatives of his and were allowed to walk with him in a fenced in special grassy flower-planted area of the grounds. We waited in the visiting room for him to come down and when he arrived he was carrying a Panama hat. "See," he said, pointing to his name stamped on the leather sweatband, "I'm your man all right." He was carrying a bundle under one arm and we asked him if he'd brought lunch. "Oh no," he said solemnly, "much more than that."

For a while we just walked around talking mostly about gardening, and then George More said, "Let's go to the bower over there," pointing to two benches arched over by a white trellis laced with little pink and white flowers. "Sit down," he said, "you on that side, and you, brother John, on this side. Now, I know you're wondering what I've got in this bundle...well, I'm not just going to tell you, I'm going to show you what no other person in this world but me has ever seen." George More carefully set down the newspaper-wrapped bundle on the grass between where John and I sat facing each other under the arch of flowers. George More got down on his knees, the bundle in front of him, and stroked it. We waited. Then George More began to peel layer after layer of newspaper from the bundle, then one damp cloth after another including pieces of underwear, until the bundle was no bigger than a baseball. He began to tremble a little; his voice lowered. "No other man in the world," he said, and he slowly took away the last wet rags to reveal a peeled hard-boiled egg and some canary feathers which he carefully positioned on either side of the egg. "See," said George More, "there it is," and he put his finger to his lips, "shhh...and now with the addition of my sperm...it will turn into an angel...and...fly away...shhhhh...but not quite yet." We stared at the egg, the edges of the canary feathers moved the slightest bit in the breeze, and we waited. Then, a little playfully, George More wrapped up the egg and put the bundle under his arm. "Time to preside at my supper upstairs," he said, and the three of us walked back to the visitors' room and returned him to his keepers. "We'll see if old Judas comes by tonight; so long," George More said.

I heard George More sing four times after that; once from his barred window on the same floor. The last time I came to hear him sing there was a rumpus going on in his room, then great cries and figures flashing past the window and George More rushing for the bars and being pulled back, and shrieks and a great gurgling, coughing muffling sound that made his voice sound as if he was drowning.

Thinking About Legs at the Supermarket

I'd done my part of our shopping and parked my well-loaded cart in front of a toilet paper display to one side in the wide front aisle. You're not allowed to smoke in stores anymore, so I was outside on one of the scarce benches—scarce because if too many are provided it encourages people to stop, sit down, and look around, maybe even meet friends and talk instead of keeping at the business of shopping. And then, too, benches might attract what we used to call "vags," vagrants, the homeless. But that wouldn't be a problem in this upscale neighborhood with this upscale supermarket.

So while Virginia finished her larger part of the shopping, and looked around for whatever might be new in ready-to-microwave dinners, I just sat in the shade facing out across the huge parking area packed with BMWs, Mercedes, Lincolns, and the like. Oh, there were some lesser cars, Chevrolets, Fords, Hondas, but without exception, as far as I could see, they'd all recently been washed and polished.

And for the most part the people, kids, babies, and all appeared to have been bathed and gotten into nice clean clothes for their trips to the big shopping center. Most of the grown-ups were young—20s, 30s, early 40s—and, to me, well into my 80s, they appeared extremely agile; the way they took the curbs, the two steps to my right, and the way they seemed to slither out of their cars and bound back in with such ease and surety.

Usually I don't stare at people, or even look directly at their faces. I've found that that makes some people noticeable uneasy. So if I take notice of a person passing, I generally do that for only a short time and if I focus at all it will be at the area below the head. And with the way a lot of people dress these days, men and women, plenty of their legs show.

Maybe because of a spinal operation I had a couple of years back, my legs aren't, as they say, what they used to be. But I do remember how wonderfully they had been to me, dancing, even running in marathons and walking almost endless miles. Except for a relatively few people who use those reserved parking spaces labeled "Handicapped Only" with a wheelchair painted on the pavement—except for those, the people I see have, or seem to have, marvelously strong-looking legs, well shaped, and obviously performing with perfection the lightning commands coming from their brains. Really beautiful and utterly practical.

For the short time my father was around when I was five or six years old, he took me, now and then, to boxing matches. Earlier he'd been a boxer himself. Once he showed me a big pocket watch he'd won boxing. He was proud of it because, as he told me, the winner of a match was awarded a watch, the loser got only a watch fob. In those long ago days my father was at least one of my heroes. He seemed to know everything about boxing, and he told me lots of things about it: how a boxer keeps positions that avoid giving the opponent a broadside view—you meet your opponent at an angle and if you're a "righty" you keep him off with jabs delivered with your left. The opposite is true if you're a "lefty." The movement of the head, he said, was very important—side to side, forward and backwards. And the whole body, my father told me, depends on the speed and rapidly changing movements of the legs. They carry the weight, he said, and function as the moving base of all the actions in the upper body and for the power needed for both defense and offense.

We'd be watching a boxing match at the old Bahn Frei hall in Milwaukee and after a couple of rounds he'd lean over to me and tell me which of the contestants he thought would win. He was often right. One of the things he watched were the fighters' legs. I often heard him say in reference to some fighter, "He's just thirty years old, and already *his legs are going*." In retrospect I'd say that I saw a lot of boxers lose because *their legs were going*. And I've seen a lot of just regular people who have the same thing happening, some because they never gave their legs a fair chance to become strong enough to lose that strength—people who, perhaps, lived with "gone legs" all their lives, cases of never noticing the loss of something they never really had. This, of course, does not apply to bona fide, certified cripples.

With boxers, my father said, when the legs go they might as well forget about boxing, maybe go into playing poker or checkers.

Well, as I sat on that bench outside the supermarket and somewhat nostalgically took stock of all those perfect young legs, a learned truth of life floated up and in clear contour reminded me that only the young who die early—in overdoses, car crashes, or whatever—only those avoid losing their legs. It's the *Riddle of the Sphinx* all over again.

I Knew Early What He Was Saying

From the first time I could hear my father talk, and feel I knew what he was saying—long before I went to school—I got a picture of a man with lots of friends who still wandered alone or almost alone in the world. For longer than it perhaps should have been, the world to me was just America, the United States of America, from "Fifty-four-forty or fight" to the Rio Grande, and "from the rockbound coast of Maine to the sunny shores of California." I read Frederick Jackson Turner's *The Frontier in American History* while I was still in grade school. I read Walter Prescott Webb's *The Great Plains* the year it came out, and thirty years after that I got to know the man, eat over an open fire with him and—with Roy Bedicheck, Harry Ransom, Frank Wardlaw, and J. Frank Dobie—drink Jack Daniels with him. From the first pictures of the world that my father drew in me, the clearest and most powerful ones were of the West. They were big pictures of immense lands, rivers, deserts, gorges, and mountains all against the kind of sky I saw when I lay in a backyard in Milwaukee and stared straight up. And they were pictures that didn't fade, pictures that got made into drawings and paintings long before I'd seen the places from where my father's voice had brought them. And then when I'd gotten there and walked where my father had walked, the places asked to hear my own voice if only in lots and lots of soliloquies never completed over the years:

> In September the sun goes early down the edge of Wyoming;
> Half-past six and the twilight dark is coming, as he came
> To the long abandoned jail open wide to the empty slanting countryside
> Around the forgotten remains of a nameless town.
> No one was there, nor was there any reason to be,
> Unless to escape the night beside the road,
> Shielded some from the wind
> Turning, now, to cold.
>
> With a split erratic lying near the stoop, he propped up the three-legged bed,
> Spread a double sheet from the *Deadwood Times* across the tired springs,
> Ate a biscuit from his bindle in the dark,
> Buttoned up and went down deep
> Into Wyoming sleep.

"And now," my father said, after covering the whole floor of Ed Strachota's saloon with suds from the mop, "before we dry it up for the boss, I'll draw you a picture of the saddest, most godforsaken state in the union." And then with the handle end of the mop he scored through the yellow-white Fels Naptha foam to the dark wet oak below, one single straight line all the way from the State Street plate glass window to the Family Entrance at the other end. "What state is it, Pa?" I asked in the early morning of that day in 1923. "It's South Dakota," he said, "too far one way to be Wyoming, and too far another way to be Texas or Louisiana." And then my father sudsed the floor again and drew the west beyond and south of South Dakota, and I saw him walking in it, young, on the go to the sea; and I heard him playing in the wind, his own shiny *Honer Marine Band* harmonica, and dying away.

Double-breasted Pinstripes

Long before I became familiar with the movie-type developed to stand for high rollers and gangsters—the average height man with dark eyes and dark complexion, dressed in a broad-brimmed fedora and a double-breasted suit with widely spaced pinstripes—long before I became familiar with that type, long before I knew of a man by the name of Humphrey Bogart, double-breasted pinstripe suits stood for something very specific to me.

When my Uncle Charlie, who had been a machine-gunner with the 32nd Division in France during World War I, came home to our house on Clybourne Street—after a year of "mowing 'em down like Kansas wheat," and after something like two years in the army of occupation—he announced that from there on out it was going to be double-breasted pinstripes for him. My Uncle Charlie stayed with us for about two months, and during that time he had his first double-breasted pinstripe suit made by a tailor with a high reputation. When the day came for my Uncle Charlie to go Out West, my father and I went down to the Union Station with him to say good-bye. My Uncle Charlie was wearing his new double-breasted pinstripe suit; and when the engine began to puff and blow and that whistle let go, he swung up the steps and into what seemed to me a car headed straight for the Promised Land.

It was three years later and I was in the fourth grade when my Uncle Charlie returned to Milwaukee for a visit. He'd made a lot of money Out West. My father said that he was a rich man—and he came back wearing a double-breasted pinstripe suit. The stripes were very white and the suit was very dark all around the stripes. My Uncle Charlie stayed at our place for a couple of weeks, time enough for me to notice that after he'd unpacked and hung his things in the closet, there were four double-breasted pinstripe suits hanging there.

Since that day back in the twenties, fashion has had pinstripes and double-breasted suits come and go. But so far as I know, the feeling I have that such a suit is hard evidence of a decision to change life, to be some sort of dapper success in this world, dates back to two years after the first World War with my Uncle Charlie standing in the living room and announcing with absolute finality that for him, it would be double-breasted pinstripe suits from there on out. His reappearance some years later, dressed in such a suit and carrying three more in his orange leather bag, only served to reinforce this conviction to me. And I suppose that series of events with my Uncle Charlie is really what was responsible for my having tailor-made in Guadalajara right after World War II, a very dark double-breasted pin-striped suit, quite out of fashion at the time, but it seems never out of fashion for me even though I haven't had such a suit, nor worn one like it for the last fifty years.

The Snowbird with the Ladder

Maybe it was because of the almost continual television coverage of the drugs-in-America story, the cops-and-robbers docudramas, and the fact that an old former friend of mine, William Bennett, was presidentially appointed to a new office—that of United States Drug Czar. Maybe because of all this I got to thinking about how I knew something about drugs when I was seven or eight years old.

It was, as they say, common knowledge, that our family doctor, Doctor Ingham, was a morphine addict back then in the early 1920s. I can remember that I thought this was sort of special—more special than smoking cigars or men opening up their pants in the shadows around the skating rink. Still I cannot recall there being any aura of deep sin or threats of early death in this matter of drug use, not back then. Maybe that's because not so many people were on morphine, heroin, or cocaine in the 1920s. Quite a bit was made of "reefers," marijuana, but mostly its use by musicians and movie stars, though it seems that everyone "knew" that the romantic movie star, Wallace Ried, was a cocaine addict.

Trusting my memory after all this time may not be sound or reasonable, but my memory has it that we knew that some people used drugs, and that we didn't take much notice of it or them. We called the cocaine people "snowbirds," and we could see them in the evening sitting on the wall around the Milwaukee auditorium and sniffing off the backs of their hands. It's true that many of these men had funny noses—sort of like festering potatoes, but in those days before the norms of health and behavior were so severely drawn, there were lots more "odd" people running about. "Odd" by our present-day standards—not considered odd back then. Psychiatry hadn't really taken hold back then. There were lots more people going about as normal that, I guess, would be considered sick or insane now. Men and women drunks were common in the streets, or was that the case only in the kind of neighborhoods I lived? I don't know. Cripples, the lame, the halt and the blind, and the very old hunched-over people were right out where they could go about whatever was their business. They weren't stuck away—warehoused as they say nowadays—hidden or committed. Those were the days when family ties meant more than they do now—straight out dereliction seemed less common. This was one of the apparent facts that came through to me on my first long stay in Italy: the streets of Florence, Milan, Rome, and Naples were populated not by a *slice* of humanity, but rather by a full lengthwise *cross section*. There the people were, all of them, it seemed, and it reminded me of seventy or eighty years ago in Milwaukee—how it was then.

Now, I don't mean to romanticize, to think of the past as necessarily better than the present—no "myth of the Golden Age" for me. Still I cannot refrain from saying that I believe there was a broader sort of acceptance back then—maybe it was compassion, maybe just an easy feeling of live-and-let-live. A guy could be quite nutty and still be allowed a piece of the fairway, so to speak. Like Louie New, the young ex-boxer, punch drunk and on some kind of dope, who went down the street snorting and throwing uppercuts, lefts and right crosses almost every night. Never hurt anyone, never created a disturbance—and on his way he went—on his way he was allowed to go. And to remind a kid of seven or eight that the world was not all like in those "back to school" ads, or that he himself was *the* model for the rest of the universe.

Sure, there were some real oddities. I think of the man, a snowbird, about 40 years old, who used to come by every so often—mainly, as I remember, on Saturday nights. He carried a very short step ladder—just two steps, and it folded so he could carry it by slipping his arm between the steps and resting it on one shoulder. Seeing him walking along made me think of a story we read in second grade, a story about "Larry the Lamplighter" who carried his ladder each evening to light the gas lights long ago, perhaps in London.

But this man in Milwaukee was no Larry the Lamplighter. He wasn't out to light any lamps, not this tuned-up snowbird. And he might well have gone on for years if he hadn't bothered Jahne the butcher's horse.

In the neighborhood it got to be known that what this man was doing was entering the stable behind the Ideal Casket Company—the casket company delivered its caskets on horse drawn wagons—and once the man was in the stable he set up his stepladder at the rear of the horse—so he could reach—and fucked the horse. One kid, name of Ben Hoefler, said he watched more than once. I was invited to do the same—that is, watch—but I declined, more out of fear, I judge now, than out of a sense of propriety.

It seemed that almost everyone knew what the snowbird with the ladder was doing on Saturday nights, but nothing I heard of was being done about it. Not until the snowbird went across State Street to Jahne the butcher's stable where he kept his delivery horse. Jahne the butcher was waiting for him—appropriately with a butcher's knife.

There were all kinds of stories about what, exactly, Jahne did with the knife, but the snowbird never again appeared in the neighborhood. Some said it was because he was in jail, and some said it was because no horse—the horse of the Ideal Casket Company or Jahne's horse—could ever again serve the snowbird's purpose. And that was that. Neighborhood life kept going on—more concerned with why the U.S. Congress didn't respect President Woodrow Wilson's veto of the Volstead Act in 1919, than with the conduct of one oddball snowbird who was rumored to be an unsuccessful jockey.

My Father Fell off the Roof of the Bakery

It was winter when my father fell off the roof of the Omar Bakery and down between the bakery and the abandoned building right next to it. There was a pile of rubble in the gangway there, and my father must have hit it hard. It was revealed later that he'd fractured his skull, broken his pelvis in three places, broken his left leg in two places and his right arm above the elbow. His bladder was ruptured, and he'd swallowed broken parts of his upper denture—pretty well busted up. But that wasn't all: He lay in that gangway between the buildings until someone passing on Clybourn Street noticed him in there. By that time my old man had contracted pneumonia.

My old man hardly ever carried any identification on him, so it took quite a while before I was notified of his compounded misfortune.

The telephone call came to the principal of the Wauwatosa High School where I was teaching—and he sent his secretary to my classroom where I was trying to explain something about multiple perspectives in drawing. The secretary was a nice lady with no make-up and herself looking pretty broken up by the message she was carrying. She put it simply, "Your father has had an accident and may be dying in the emergency hospital over on Grand Avenue."

Once I was in his room at the hospital, it appeared that after all he'd been through in his life—and that was plenty—this was curtains, the final losing round for him. He'd had a couple of transfusions already, and he was doped up. Looked like he was out cold.

So I stood there looking at my old man and remembering the scrapes he'd been in, mostly from fighting in saloons long after he'd given up being a regular boxer at the old Star Theater. I thought of the times I helped tape his broken ribs with regular black friction tape, stared at his knuckle bones poking out of his hands, and wondering if he'd ever see again through that mess of black and purple where his eyes used to be. I felt sad about everything—how it all ends, for everybody, even, in time, for me. But then I began to think of the good times I'd had with my old man—mostly when I was a very little kid and he was training me to be an acrobat.

I was looking out the window, then, staring at the falling snow and the cars, now with their headlights on, going silently up and down Grand Avenue—when I heard my old man saying, "Hey, is that you, *Donutz*?"—that's what he often called me. I turned to see my old man rising up a little from the pillow and, so help me, grinning. "I heard that they gave me a blood transfusion, is that true?"

"Yes," I said, "they told me—twenty of your buddies came immediately the call went out that you needed blood."

"They're a great bunch," my old man said, "whose blood did they put in me?"

"Well," I said, "the doctor told me that all twenty of your buddies came drunk and they couldn't use their blood—too much alcohol in it. So they sent for Andy" (that was my old man's kid brother) "and they used his blood."

"Good kid, Andy," my old man said. "Did Otzie,"—that was John Otzelburger, my old man's closest friend in those days—"did Otzie show up?"

"Sure," I said, "I'll bet he was the first guy on the scene."

"But they didn't put Otzie's blood in me, did they?"

"No," I said, "they put in Andy's blood."
"Jesus," my old man said, "I'm thankful for that. If they'd put Otzie's blood in me I'd be a drunk for the rest of my life."

That was in October of 1937 when my old man was forty-eight years old. He died when he was seventy-five, having made what was described as a miraculously full recovery.

"There was nothing miraculous about it," my old man said. "Good blood will always tell."

Andy Used to Know About Pa

I presume that a lot of people know a lot more about their parents than I got to know. My mother died when I was just a kid—long before most of us get interested in their parents—how they got to be what they were. My father lived to see seventy-five, but he was a quicksilver guy, away from home a lot, and for extended time, like a year or so. Even in the short time I had with my mother, it seemed I got to know her better, by far, than I ever got to know my father, even though according to second and third hand evidences he had a rich and varied, if often seemingly pointless, life.

As a little kid I'd overheard my mother and father talking personal things—late at night when they thought I was asleep, through bathroom and bedroom walls, and when my pa's friends were in the kitchen, also late at night—drinking whisky and talking about "old times." Stuff about my pa diving off the high North Avenue bridge into the Milwaukee River with lots of spectators willing to express their admiration for the feat by putting money on the bridge wall for Pa, and about my pa, on some kind of wager, swimming alone the twenty miles from Milwaukee to Racine in Lake Michigan. Stories about what a great amateur boxer my pa was; stories about the rescue work done by my pa in the San Francisco earthquake and fire in 1906; stories about how he could figure arithmetic problems in his head faster than anybody; how he could do magic and juggle and tumble; how he was always mistaken for Wallace Reid, the big time movie star, when Pa was out in California doing only God know what; how he made pots of money—in bribes it seems—when he was a Federal Dry Agent during Prohibition in the Dakotas. And my pa was a heavy drinker—what they call an alcoholic now, even back then. And I'd overheard my Uncle Charlie telling, one night, how my pa deserted from the Army during the First World War and was never caught—or never missed.

So I'd heard lots of stories about my pa's younger years—even stories about how he'd romanced my mother, and the suicide of his father, my grandfather, done with a pistol on a park bench on a long ago Thanksgiving Day. Still there was lots more—true or not—that I wanted to know about as I got older.

That's the way it goes, you know: We're so taken up with ourselves when we're young, as if each one of us is the center of the universe, that we have little or no place for lots of others. We go along in ways, that as we get older and we look back, appear at least heedless, if not downright brutal.

Well, I was a long, long way from being young—years after my pa died—that I again got a strong longing to know more about him. I had been writing to Andrew, my pa's kid brother who had been close to my pa all along, so I asked him if he'd like it if I drove up to Milwaukee, brought a tape recorder and plenty of tape—and for as long as he could stand it, I'd ask him questions, anything that would help to have him talk, tell, about his brother, my father.

Andrew's response was 100 percent: "Let's make a week of it; you haven't been back here for a few years; by all means come."

Even though my Uncle Andrew had already had his eightieth birthday, I want to tell you he was still all there. So it was arranged, the date I'd arrive up there and all that, and I set out for the north, full of excitement. At last I was going to fill in one helluva lot of blanks in my pa's life—and in mine. And it was going to be fun—my Uncle Andrew and I had hit it off for a long time—he taught me to ski around the time I was ten—and even though he may not have, in his entire life, read a line of Shakespeare, he gave me the "Complete Works" when I was twelve. Simply put he had often felt like a father to me. Uncle Andy was one of those few I'd always had feelings of love for. Even without our planned mission of talking for days about the man he knew as brother and that I knew as Pa, it was going to be a very special time together.

I stopped over in St. Louis, the end of my first day of driving, and as customary when I was away, I called home to let my wife know I was okay, that all was going hunky-dory—and how were things back there, and so on.

"Hobart called a couple of hours after you'd left," my wife said, "Andy is dead. A stroke...heart, everything." Then that awful descent into the darkness inside ourselves, the shape of our own waiting shroud. "Are you all right?" my wife asked.

"No," I said, "but I will be—I'm going on anyway...yes, and be there for the funeral."

I guess it helped, having all those people there—Andy's old friends from the time he worked with them in the slaughter house back in the depression, friends of his all the way up to his getting to be the Union's principal arbitrator and a real power for what he believed. Old and young people—it helped. And then it was over. Ceremonies end; the reasons for them, never.

It was gray the day I started returning home to Texas.

I drove west across Iowa and the corner of South Dakota where the fields were still muddy from the last of the melting snow and only a little planting going on.

Then south through Nebraska where little green shoots were appearing, the beginnings of a carpet that would be wheat.

Then, slowing down a little, south into Kansas where already, you could see for sure, that it *was wheat*.

Then into Oklahoma—you bet...that's wheat!

And then Texas...and the marvelous stuff—my God; already blowing in the wind....

Who's Keeping Who Out?

The "Holy Rollers," as some called them, used to meet in a place on National Avenue near Ninth in Milwaukee, back in 1929. Before they took it over it had been a grocery store that never appeared to be doing any business. I used to sit on the steps in front of Loretta Gergo's father's saloon talking to Loretta while the place was still a grocery store with two bare electric light bulbs shining out the two windows across the street. I used to look across at those bulbs a lot when I was sitting so close to Loretta, and I could feel her heart beat. I used to talk to her and put my arms around her, and all the time I'd keep staring at those lights across the street. It was easier that way; not seeing, just feeling how Loretta was taking to my lies about where I'd been and what I'd done, and what I was going to do the next day and the next year and for all my life. And then one night when I looked over there the lights were gone and the store had moved out. Two men came one day and painted the bottom halves of the show windows solid black, and soon after that Loretta and I used to sit in front of her father's saloon and listen to the shouting and singing of the Holy Rollers inside.

And pretty soon I was standing at the front door looking in, and then sitting in the empty back row listening to their preacher talk about the strength of Jesus when Jesus possessed a truly repentant sinner. The preacher was a tall, skinny man who usually wore overalls and sounded like he was from some place like Arkansas. Every time I heard him preach he got everybody stirred up, and then, one by one, the people would come up to the front to testify. And even when there were only a few people in the place, he still got them to call out and yell as if they were a hundred. They often brought rolled-up newspapers with them, and after the preacher had got their spirits up, and while the testimonials were being shouted out about how Jesus came into their lives, right into their bodies and intoxicated them with joy, they'd begin swatting each other with those rolled-up newspapers. The longer and louder the testimonial, the harder they swatted each other and the louder they all got.

I took a rolled-up *Milwaukee Journal* with me one Saturday night and sat in the empty back as usual. After they got to swatting each other, a very small woman with a bald spot whacked me on my shoulder and I whacked her back. This must have been taken as a sign of my coming into the Holy Rollers because most of the men and women in the place that night came around and swatted me all over. For a while after that I used to come in the evening with my newspaper (once with the whole Sunday edition, Rotogravure Section and all) and wait for the swatting to begin. It was fun and everybody appeared to enjoy it even though they didn't laugh, and very seldom smiled. I got to the point where I'd prepared a testimonial, based for the most part on Jack London's story, *To Build a Fire*—that one about the man in the frozen north with only one match, his last, trying to light a fire; and when he does just get it going, it melts the snow from a bough of the tree under which he'd foolishly built his fire and the snow slides down and extinguishes it. There was something in it, too, as I remember, about how the man was thinking of cutting open his faithful dog and putting his freezing hands inside to thaw them. But I never gave my testimonial, I just thought about it an awful lot. Instead, it seems, I went to the Holy Rollers' Convention in Waukesha, about twenty-five miles west of Milwaukee. And there in a park-like place on the edge of town a thousand or two gathered to hear a whole slew of men and women shout the intoxication and jump and kick and roll, some wildly together, in the grass.

I never made much of the Holy Rollers. I never connected what they were doing with the vague concept I had of religion. To me, the mood and actions that went with their meetings in Milwaukee and with the day I spent among them in Waukesha at age fourteen, was more like those days I'd known at the circus, or at a friendly fight at the skating rink over on Greenbush Street, or like what often happened after a Boy's Tech-Washington High School football game. And even though the men and women who preached appeared dead serious, I still thought of them in the way I thought of the three-legged man I'd seen with Ringling Brothers and Barnum and Bailey: the freak show guide stopped in front of the three-legged man's place, introduced him and told something about his family life and growing up, and about the tailor who makes his three-legged pants, and such; and then the three-legged man produced a football, put it down on the ground, and with his right and left feet firmly planted, kicked the ball with his middle foot. And then as the group began to move on to the six-hundred-pound "Fattest Woman in the World," in the next enclosure, the three-legged man went into his own pitch to sell photographs of himself in a swimming suit. With both the Holy Rollers and the three-legged man, I felt a mixture of the macabre, the sad, and the funny. With them, I never felt anything like the presence of strange power and people caught up in a terror generated by a leader as I did when I heard the evangelist Bob Williams, Jr. in a tent outside Sheboygan, Wisconsin, in 1935.

It wasn't even a big tent; maybe it had folding chairs and benches for three or four hundred people. But when husky young Bob Williams, Jr. came on to the platform after the guitar music in his tight-fitting black pants and white silk blouse open at the throat and begin to talk slowly in a strong low voice about evil and its agent the devil, and how not even a baby is immune to evil's disease, the vilest, most deadly of all— when he held various statue-like poses as the reed organ backed him up, I could feel what he was doing with those people— as if they were all just one frail shell-shocked kid. And at just the right moment, and perhaps by using confederates, when some people were already crying out loud, he pointed out into the audience and called for this person and that person to come forward in a public sign of repentance and an invitation of Jesus to come into their hearts and be "loved, loved, loved; oh sweet love!" And as the women and girls came up, husky young Bob Williams, Jr. put his arms around them and they moaned and cried all over his silk blouse. And then even men and boys came up, all the while the reed organ, played by a plump older woman who looked very much like Bob Williams, Jr., and hooked up to a public address system, played a kind of waltz-march and young male and female assistants passed out Love Offering envelopes with Bob's picture in jockey shorts on the front and a place to write your own name for Jesus.I never did sign up for Jesus. Not back then and not in the almost seventy intervening years. For me, these conning evangelists with their storefront and tent "churches" constituted a form of entertainment, the excitement of which bordered on the pornographic— a sort of foreplay that never achieved anything natural or unnatural.

So I guess you might say that at this level of demi-religious performance, I was never induced to sign up for Jesus, perhaps because something in me kept him out, and perhaps because something in him kept me out. No matter how that might or might not be, I still find myself, in odd moments— even now in my ninth decade and after having tried out a variety of respected and sophisticated churches— I still find myself vacantly wondering if I'm keeping Jesus out, or if Jesus is keeping me out.

But then, as an Episcopalian seminarian once put it to me: "Weismann, you're not even Agonist to be a good Agnostic"— and without really knowing what this seminarian meant by saying that, I decided I'd leave it at that— which I have, right up to now.

Illegal and Legal

The hidden abortion clinic I once knew of, back in the 1930s, was in a large ex-residence on Oneida Street in Milwaukee, and I never got beyond the high-ceilinged, narrow-windowed reception room. But I'd known about the place for a long time and walked past it and wondered how it was that so many could know about the place, standing there in its upright Victorian trappings, and even the doctor's name, and that nothing was done about it.

There was a scent of carnations mixed with the smell of cigar smoke in the heavily draped reception room. The woman who answered the bell was about sixty, and her vaguely uniform-like dress must have been designed to make strangers think of nurses, or of sympathetic attendants, to go with the very small card that showed through the leaded glass front door: REST HOME. I told her of a problem I said I had, and she began to fill it out for me. We stood near a large oval marble-topped table with black legs, and she kept one hand on it as if she were having her portrait done full-length by someone like Charles Willson Peale. When my eyes left hers to search about the room—over the velvet covered settee, past the stiff Frenchy blue and gold chairs facing a fragile table, around to the large blue and white vases that stood on the floor near the portieres to the next room—her eyes followed mine. She said it could all be taken care of for a hundred and twenty-five dollars, but that would depend of course. I raised my voice in faked surprise and repeated the amount as if I were slowly saying beads. There was something wrong about the woman's jaw, and she sucked at her ill-fitting dentures. I raised my voice still higher. She sucked in the lower part of her cheek and looked toward the door to the next room. I pushed against the marble-topped table with my thigh, a sudden little push, and she jerked her hand up from it as if she was replaying Galvani's electrical experiment with those jerking frog's legs. I straightened up and made an obvious sweep of the room with my eyes. Then very loudly I said, "One-hundred-and-twenty-five-dollars-for-what?" It was then that the man in a white barber's coat appeared between the blue and white vases, just inside the portieres.

"Mrs. Lewis," he called in a low voice, and the woman turned and followed him as he moved back out of sight into the room beyond.

I stood waiting there in the reception room for a while. Except for footsteps on the floor above, the house had fallen silent. I wanted to walk across the room and look beyond the portieres, but I didn't. I had the feeling that if I did, something would die and I didn't know what.

No curtains moved in the second story windows as I walked the short path to the pavement and away north on Oneida Street.

All but the mood has changed. Here in London almost forty years later, the pregnant land at Gatwick or Heathrow bound for prearranged legalized abortions in clean professional clinics, the operation to be performed by bona fide surgeons. But the scalper-pimps lurk by their impressive rented cars and make their authoritative talk and lead the nervous to the neat operating rooms that keep many a Rolls Royce rolling and many a villa swinging on the Portuguese coast. And the thought is that the drains carry it all away to the sea.

A Strong Willful Hope

In the course of my life I've read a lot of newspaper stories about kidnapping. Besides those political and absolutely insane ones that for a while went briskly along with the hijacking of airplanes, besides those, perhaps the most recent one that interested me at all was the strange and never publicly explained kidnapping of the son of Frank Sinatra. And beyond newspaper accounts of kidnapping, there are all those accounts in literature, and, for me as a kid, certainly the most important of all those was Robert Louis Stevenson's. However, when I was still seventeen, on March 1, 1932, the son of Charles Augustus Lindbergh was abducted from the Lindbergh home in Hopewell, New Jersey. Less than five years before that day, Lindbergh had flown across the ocean alone in that airplane which now hangs suspended in the Smithsonian Institution. He crossed the ocean from west to east, as we all know, on May 21, 1927, and after his return to the United States, he went about the country. I saw Charles Augustus Lindbergh riding in an open car and I ran after it trying to get closer to this living image of courage and romance. Charles Lindbergh and his trip across the ocean was, and is, something very real to me. After all he crossed the ocean when I was just thirteen years old. I can remember that after his return from Europe he made a ceremonial flight for the United States Mail Service. He'd been one of the early air-mail pilots before he soloed to Paris and so this later flight was in the character of a sentimental journey. I was a sophomore in high school at the time and my history teacher, Mr. Alvin E. Rutenbeck, encouraged us to invest the twenty-five cents for the special air-mail stamp, and address a postcard, via St. Louis, to ourselves. We addressed our postcards in Mr. Rutenbeck's American History class one afternoon while he wrote on the board a suggested message that we could send to ourselves. The message read: Lindy says use air mail; let's do it, be modern. We all mailed our cards, and I must admit that I waited rather impatiently for mine to return to me, which it did; and as I sit here thinking about this, I wish I had that card now, but I don't. I gave it to my brother's son when he was thirteen years old, and that's some time ago, too.

So Charles Augustus Lindbergh was a very real person to me back in 1932 and, in my own way, I admired him extremely. This was, of course, years before Lindbergh made that trip to Germany and came back to report to all Americans that the German military machine was of such size and might that perhaps the only role for America was one of appeasement. But in 1932 Lindbergh still was to me pretty much what he had been back on May 21, 1927; and 1932 was the year his infant son was kidnapped. I remember following the story in the press all through the offering of the fifty thousand dollars in ransom money; through the finding of some of the ransom money on Bruno Richard Hauptmann; through the long, drawn-out trial; through the finding of the battered body of the baby more than two years after the kidnapping; and, finally, Hauptmann's execution, more than two years after that. Until the body of the Lindbergh baby was found, I had a strong willful hope that it would turn up in the care of some mysterious person. Like I'm sure was true of all kinds of other people, I hoped that the whole occurrence was not actually real—that it was some kind of ceremonial act, primitive and awful but still without the actual and final truth. I would like to be able to say here that what I had hoped for, way back then, was that this kidnapping was only symbolic in some way—that, really, it didn't take place, that the whole event was a kind of art-form or witchcraft, and that the art-form would be seen for what it was—a work of art, a frightful play, and not reality—and that witchcraft, if that's what it was, would be undone either by breaking the spell or by a simple application of reason. I wish I could truthfully say that back then I had wished that the kidnapping of the Lindbergh baby was only as symbolic as the traditional act we describe as "burning in effigy," but I don't know that I had so specific a wish. However, I do know that on an evening in 1961, when the words "kidnapped a child effigy," appeared under my hand on the paper I was writing I was thinking of the Lindbergh kidnapping of twenty-nine years before.

A Freight Out of Hoboken

My last hitched ride ended at 192nd Street, and I walked the long way into Times Square where I bought a glass of orange juice and an ice cream cone. After that I still had about forty cents in my pocket and a Milwaukee streetcar ticket. I recall leaning against the little wooden ice cream stand and trying to make the five-cent cone last as long as possible. I thought of how now I'd be able to tell that I'd been to New York, to Times Square, when I got back; but I was beginning to worry how I'd ever make it over the thirteen or fourteen hundred miles of highway to the edge of Milwaukee, where I could use the streetcar ticket to get me back to where I'd been staying since leaving the Home for Dependent Children. And there was no one at the other end to pull me in. I hurried to the river and crossed to Hoboken. And there everything changed for the worse—just miles and miles of city pavement, strewn with paper blowing in the dust; no way to hitchhike, no one even noticing that I was there. Night came and I was still in Hoboken. So far as I could tell, there was just one way for me to get back to Milwaukee on that forty cents and that was by hopping a freight train.

The freight yards spread out under floodlights mounted on tall poles. I remembered that the phrase "hopping a freight" means exactly that: You shouldn't climb into a boxcar that's not moving and wait for the engine to pull you on out; you should find the train you want and wait until it starts to roll, and then when there's no longer time for the railroad bulls to get you, you run alongside the boxcar, grab hold of one of the ladder-like rungs that lead to the top and hang on before moving up. So I stood there in the Hoboken yard with no way of telling which string of cars would begin to move or where it might go. I stood in the shadow of a locomotive that must have been used during the day and its boiler was cooling down. The engine gave off high-pitched pings and low-pitched clunks as I waited in the dark. Then one of the strings of cars began to move, and as I watched I became so scared that all I did was huddle deeper in the shadow and closer to the warmth of the cooling engine. The string rolled slowly past, and I could see the supporting rods underneath. I wondered how in God's name anyone could get in under the car and onto those rods while the train was moving as many a hobo of the past has done, giving currency to the saying "riding the rods." Nothing that I could remember and nothing that I could imagine gave me any reason to believe that that operation was humanly possible. So for the next few hours I watched short and long lines of cars move one way or another away from me. Then, suddenly, as if possessed, I shot out of the shadow and ran full tilt alongside one of them. I hadn't known until then how difficult it is to keep upright in the loose gravel—and with all that wind and noise. Snatches of stories filled with images of men and boys stumbling and rolling under the wheels of cars, legless, armless, pieces not enough to fill a peach basket, flashed through my mind. Still I ran searching for an open car that I could throw myself up and into. There weren't any, so I grabbed the ladder of one of the last closed cars and climbed halfway up, so as not to be silhouetted against the last of the yard lights. The train picked up speed much faster than I ever thought something of that length and weight could, and before long the train was highballing along.

With the lights of the yard far behind, I climbed onto the top of the car. There was a moon out and I could see the locomotive far up ahead, and for the first time I felt hot cinders coming against me. For a while I just sat panting on those three boards of catwalk. The sky was almost cloudless and a fifty to sixty mile wind was blowing at me. For a while I felt safe, even good, and then I knew I was very cold. The train was pushing into the Appalachians by now, and looking down I could see brilliantly flashing moon reflections in rivers and little lakes and ponds. I had the feeling of traveling through El Greco's *View of Toledo*, and I kept getting colder and colder and then very drowsy. I pulled my socks up over the bottoms of my trouser legs, lay down with my head facing the caboose, wedged my arms under the catwalk to keep from rolling off and tried to fight off sleep.

I woke up in Hornell, New York, where they coupled on some more cars, including some tankers. Once we got rolling again, I worked my way to one of the tankers, got down to it and for a moment enjoyed the windbreak made by the high reefer just ahead. I stood on the low catwalk holding on to that pipe rail that runs around most tankers, and stretched my aching back. And then again I felt sleep coming down around, so I unbuckled my pants belt, passed the end around the pipe rail, and re-buckled it. Now if I fell asleep and went down I'd remain suspended there.

And then I heard voices, loud threatening voices. I opened my eyes. The sun was shining, the train had stopped, and I was dangling from the railing by my pants belt. Two railroad bulls were standing on the reddish roadbed yelling at me, "How far you want to go, boy? Eternity? If that's where you want to go, boy, I can sure as Hell send you there. Now, you get the Hell off that car, and get your ass off the line or I'll take you on a road we got ready for punks like you," one of them said. So while I unhitched my belt, he was telling me about it. "It's a long straight roadbed, and it ain't for sleep," he said, "and ain't gravel either. The ties are laid in busted bottles just for guys like you, and a couple of great beaters get back of you with baseball bats, and they say: boy, take off your shoes 'cause we're gonna chase you up that line, and we're gonna chase you til all your friends are gonna call you Stumpy 'cause your legs are gonna end where they come out of your guts." I got unhitched, grabbed up my pants, and took off in the high weeds.

That was long ago, but one more reason for thinking that I'm one of the luckiest men still alive.

Two Worlds, Two Times

It was 1936; she was standing outside the dime store in Gary, Indiana, and I was coming up from the South. "My name's Jeff," she said, "just call me Jeff." She was in sagging black and tired, but she was beautiful too, and I went with her. The room was cool and as I stood there I realized how worn out I was. Framed over the dresser was a photograph of a young woman standing on a carved wooden porch with her arms around a man who looked like Douglas Fairbanks. "Far from Gary," Jeff said, "and long ago." She pulled down the buff-colored shade and the room turned into a late Rembrandt. "He's gone," Jeff said, "killed at the mills; never shoulda left Valparaiso...you're tired, why don't you lay down?" I was asleep before the question died in the air, and a dream was rolling out—a dream of the night sky of Gary from the first time I'd watched it boiling black and orange-vermilion above the blast furnaces and stacks when I was twelve. And under the sky the Douglas Fairbanks man was calling, "My God! My God!" but it was too late: he was dead in a photograph with a coming-apart oak frame over the dresser and the molten steel swallowed him up and burned him away, long ago.

When I put my hat back on I tried to say something, but nothing came. "It's all right, all okay," Jeff said. "I was bushed too, and I never woulda come back to rest if you didn't come along."

I used to see them in the morning when I got back from the midnight-to-eight at the Coliseum. They'd be waiting for their taxis under striped canopies outside apartment buildings with names like "Terrace" and "Crest" and "Arms" lettered in gold across the fanlights. Beautifully dressed, they were, in fitted suits, silk stockings with seams running perfectly up the calves from un-scuffed high-heels, and their faces and throats were clear and white and held with the consciousness of models who know how delicate and transient their eligibility is. *Executive, Personal,* and *Very Private Secretaries,* they were, who'd moved up to Chicago's 1942 Gold Coast where the hotel-sweet big bands played in "The Pump Room" and the microphone was set just right so you could hear the hushed dreamy laughter in the background, and every now and then the clink of a glass when you turned it up on your Atwater-Kent or Crosley, no matter where you were.

I lived on the Gold Coast—in a back apartment with wooden steps down four floors to an alley where bent men ate Gold Coast garbage out of Gold Coast garbage cans in the snow—all the time I taught those radiomen-gunners for the United States Army Air Force, and it didn't feel all that different from Gary. But I knew it was, with the likes of Jeff and her Douglas Fairbanks man losing out on that land bought by the United States Steel Corporation thirty-seven years before, and the likes of the means and protection that percolated all the way down to those executive, personal, and very private women going to cover-up work at nine. Of course it was all that different, no matter how it seemed between the tarnished gold coast I knew and the flaming skies of Gary that Jeff knew.

My 1937 Beard

Back in 1937 when beards, those ornamental face growths, were not at all popular—rather rare—I grew one. From time to time as a kid I thought of having a beard—then impossible, of course. I wondered how I'd look, and what people would think, if I had a beard like the old men in those 19th century photographs.

My chance came when I was twenty-three and a graduate student at the University of Minnesota. I tried out for a play—was it *Alien Corn*? I can't be sure—no matter, I got the part of an old man who should be bearded. Instead of wearing a false one, I grew one. And after the play was given and forgotten, I kept and cultivated my beard. I looked in a book, a kind of encyclopedia of beards and selected one I liked. Then, for a while, I kept this style well cut and trimmed.

It was sort of fun seeing how differently I was treated by strangers—different from the ways I was treated when I'd gone about with just my own naked face. I was treated differently in restaurants, for instance, where I was given more attention and more rapid service—especially if I spoke with some kind of fake foreign accent. People gave me more space in elevators—out of respect, fear, or disgust, I never figured out.

My 1937 beard—the only one I ever grew, not even when in recent years they became popular with the young—was very black, and my chosen style made me look quite a bit like Jesus Christ—like some Hitlerian caricatures of Jews.

For a while, it was fun running around in what I considered a disguise. Since I had no facial disfigurements to conceal as many men have, I was just having fun playing I was someone other than myself. But, of course, coming from a line of clean-shaven ancestors. I knew who I was under that mass of hair, no matter how neatly trimmed.

In the 1950s and 60s when beards became popular with the young who posed as either *avant guard* intellectuals or happy-time revolutionaries—for instance, a lot of my college students and even some younger faculty members—I used to have devilish fun asking them why they chose to raise and cultivate their beards. Without exception these bearded guys became extremely self-conscious. I figured that they felt this way because they knew that their beards were nothing more than vanity—"Yeah! All is Vanity—Vanity, their vanity, hiding in those hairs." I never went around asking men why they were wearing this and that kind of clothing—but beards and mustaches, yes. Only a few of those I asked got angry and told me off, most of them just squirmed.

Well to come back to my 1937 beard: After having it for a few months, the novelty wore off—and it required much more work than just shaving clean.

The final decision to drop my disguise came one night while walking home after a night seminar in "English Backgrounds and American Colonies." Up ahead of me in the dark street were a few adolescents under a street light—just leaning around with their bicycles in a little group.

As I approached they stopped talking and stood motionless as I passed with my curried black beard. Once past, the yelled out, all together, "Down with the government, Bolshevik!"

All My Life I've Been a Sucker

All my life I've been a sucker for the darkened dive where someone is playing a piano. I've got my special tastes for what I like best to hear, but for me, they're just inclusive enough. And I usually gravitate to where no one in the place appears to be hearing the piano until it stops. I never went much for those places where some good-enough piano player is set up with an oversize grand and the customers, usually in couples, sit on upholstered stools right up against the lid and use it for a bar and ask for "old favorites." And I guess I don't care much for the piano player who talks more than he plays—about the number he's about to play, how it was when he played in "Frisco," "L.A.," or at the such-and-such groovy club in New York, or how everything fits into some usually outrageous fantasy of the history of the blues, barrel house rock, or subcultures. I care for the piano player who, no matter how far gone he is, feels to me that he isn't a whole man—no matter how small or big—until he sits down, looks at the keys as if he'd never seen them before, but guesses that they can open all the doors, and then goes ahead and opens them and goes on through, and keeps on going through. Years ago, maybe

I was eighteen, there was a woman played in an Italian bar on Jefferson Street in Milwaukee's Third Ward. She was that kind of piano player. I used to be able to pretty well describe the hole in my spirit that her playing could fill. I'd be sitting someplace, or working, or listening to somebody saying something to me, or listening to myself saying something at somebody else in the morning, in the afternoon or in the middle of the night, and I'd feel that aching hole. Sometimes I would beat it across town to Jefferson Street, if the time was right and she'd be there, and slow down half a block away and then saunter through that door as if I didn't give a damn for all the time I didn't have, as if I were Mr. Complete just stopping for a beer that I could take or leave, no matter, and as if I wouldn't hear the piano if it was stuffed, playing, right into my ears. I'd come in and stand near the door, up where it said JEFFERSON INN in red, white, and green in an arch across the window, look at the gilded pictures on the open cigar box covers, and read the labels on the bottles and the marks on the bar—while that woman to whom I never said a word, just went on filling that hole in me with such great gifts that they sometimes made the rest of me feel that it would have to find a way to improve.

There was a man in St. Louis, a black man, who played in a bar on Sarah Street when I was getting ready to teach radio-men-gunners for the Army Air Force. Even though he was propped up on a little platform right back of the far end of the bar with all those people and noise, he played as if he was a lone survivor on a raft becalmed in the open sea. I used to walk over to Sarah Street after my night class in communication math, after I'd sat through a couple of hours of being reminded of still one more gap in my education, and stand there listening to that man who seemed to be playing out his whole damnation and redemption. I'd stare straight down into my glass that would open up—the longer that man played—to more of the star-marked infinity that ever eluded the still lifes of Claez or Renoir. And as he played on, the spirit got mended, made whole again and I'd be launched free into the wide open inviting sea. And, by the way, just because I've mentioned these piano-players from long ago doesn't mean that I'm not the same guy today—that I'm still a sucker for the twilight dive where the right piano is playing.

Different now, however, is that the place doesn't have to be the half-light of a bar or a pub, it can be any place—just so the piano is right. I can fill in the rest—thanks to those like that woman in the Jefferson Inn and that black man on Sarah Street.

My Friend John Mimier Said It

In my freshman year at college, a very small college of twelve hundred students, I carried a course of a general sort which came under the heading of Sociology in the college catalogue. It was required as most of the freshman courses were in those days, and, strangely, still are. A Mrs. Giselda Slaughter taught the course. She was a manly woman of about forty-eight or fifty. All the students, it seemed, knew that she had been married and that she was divorced. That in itself was nothing special, not even back then. But more than that, they talked about Mrs. Slaughter as if they were privy to macabre details of her unsuccessful marriage and prolonged divorce proceedings. Having heard this sort of thing even before entering her class served to focus interest in her rather than in the course.

Now my closest friend in those days was a fellow student named John J. Mimier, later a very successful tax expert with lots of men working under him in Dallas and about the state until he and his wife were murdered in their house in East Texas a few years ago. In those days John was interested in drawing and painting and I thought that he was an excellent writer. To me, his drawings were about as fine as those of Raphael. The stories he wrote and read to me, or just told to me, always moved me. Even now I can recall two of them. One was called the "Saga of a Nickel" and over about twenty-five or thirty pages it followed a five-cent piece through the hands of a lot of only disparately related people whose portraits John drew with an uncommonly revealing line. The other story was called "Mother" and it concerned the death of a woman, a mother, who had been insane for a long time. John told me that he had learned, in some kind of medical journal, of a disease associated with a specific form of insanity and that caused the skin to leave the body. John made use of this in the story, and the final episode of the mother's death with her face coming off in the pillow, was as grotesque as it was moving.

John and I sat next to each other in Mrs. Slaughter's sociology class. Both of us, though at first taken by her nervous power, soon found ourselves thoroughly disliking, if not hating her. By all standards I knew of then and know of now, Mrs. Slaughter was unfair. After ingratiating herself to us she would turn and abuse the trust she had engendered, all the while appearing remotely occupied with something beyond and totally unknown to us. She was caustic, mean, spoiling for destructive argument, and she perhaps was very sick. Before the course was half over, it had become a habit for John and me to take her bait and ask relevant but embarrassing questions in class, and though both he and I received A's on all tests she had given, still we received average grades for the course. There was something about Mrs. Slaughter that called up a profound pity in me. Even though she came to class beautifully dressed and perfectly made up, to me she seemed to be dying, that she knew it, and was fighting back by making signs that she still could affect the living for whom she had lost all love. I can remember watching her move like a mystery about the room, as she talked, often it seemed, to herself. And I can remember feeling with something that felt like certainty, that she was being eaten alive from inside. It was one afternoon when I was thinking things like this that John, who was in the seat to my right, leaned over, and in a very low voice said, "My God, I believe she's robed in worms." It sent a chill through me and as I looked at Mrs. Slaughter standing there at the front of the room, I saw her dark green dress as a fabric of worms—and felt them on myself.

Mrs. Slaughter left the faculty the following year and as far as I could imagine, she left to find some place to die. I have often wondered if I would have remembered Mrs. Slaughter as long as I have if John had not said those words, and with them epitomized the quality of presence that this woman had for me then and for all those years between—from the early 1930s in Milwaukee to 1962 in a room in Florence, Italy, where they came to me again, and I wrote them into a long poem.

In the poem they stand for the sick and the doomed, for those who have fallen from grace and know that the face has turned away from them.

Getting out of Cleveland

I recall very clearly where the hyphenated words "brake-shine" came from. Actually I had never heard these words until 1933 when I was ready to leave Cleveland. These words were given to me by a black man and this is how it happened.

I wanted to get out of Cleveland as fast as I could, so in the morning I was back in that low valley in the heart of industrial Cleveland where I'd come in the night before and which was alluded to as "Cleveland's yard." I wandered around in that wasteland threaded with tracks and scarred with abandoned buildings, trying to figure out where the west-bound freights might stop or at least slow down enough to hop. The sun was shining and it was warm, so I was surprised when I came around one of the boxcars to find an old, bald-headed man sewing buttons on an overcoat. He looked up, "You look like you're in a hurry," he said "that's always a dangerous way to be. Where's your home, son?"

"Milwaukee," I said.

"And you're in an awful hurry to get there, ain't you; sit down here and take it easy, son; winter's coming but there's still plenty of time." And with that, the old man reached into one of his jacket pockets and pulled out a round Copenhagen snuff can. He laid the can carefully in the palm of his left hand and with his right deftly removed the cover. Inside the can was a large round pocket watch with its crystal missing. He looked at the watch, then at the sun, and then with his index finger he carefully moved the minute hand backwards so that the watch read ten minutes to nine instead of nine. "Plenty of time," the old man said, putting the box back into his pocket, "I remember that I was once in an awful hurry out in Nevada. The guy came home while I was saying goodbye to her in the kitchen, and I ran out the back door straight into a swarm of bees. I was stung all over and I itched and scratched and I nearly died. Never hurry," the old man said "never hurry, son, there's plenty of time."

"But I've really got to get home," I said.

"Tain't good to be anxious," the old man said "what's the matter with just living here in Cleveland?"

"I don't know anybody in Cleveland," I said, "and this place isn't for me. All I want to find out is where the trains going west slow down enough to get on," I said.

"I'd cool off if I was you," the old man said, and he went back to sewing the button on his overcoat.

I walked down the line of cars and turned across a lot of tracks toward a little path that led up the side of a slag heap. I thought I heard someone singing and I stopped. It sounded like a lullaby, or blues, and it was coming from the top of the pile. I stood and listened for a while and the singing voice reminded me of years before when my father played very slow music on the mouth organ and his eyes fogged over as he said, "Now I'll play you a song about a man who lost his way and never found it again." And then my father, with a jelly glass cupped over the end of the mouth organ, played the saddest slowest music I'd ever heard.

I followed it up the slag heap like one of the kids of Hamlin. There was a crazy white picket fence at the top and it ran around a shack built of tin signs and weathered plywood. Out in the sun on a wooden box a huge black man sat facing away from me and singing to a tiny black girl child. I think he must have heard me coming up the hill but he waited, and then without losing his song, he turned and looked at me. I smiled;

he smiled back and let the lullaby dwindle away. "You comes from up or down?" he asked.

"I just came up," I said, "I was wondering where the trains going west slow down."

"That's easy," the black man said, "don't you know yet how to tell where just any old train slows down? You see, it's a funny thing; the place where trains slows down is where they also speeds up, but that ain't no trouble at all, because you're interested to find yourself a slow train. Ain't that right?"

"Yes," I said, "that's right."

"Well, now," the black man said, "if an engine speeds up, that must mean it was just going slow before it started to speed up; ain't that right?"

"That's right," I said.

"Now it's a funny, natural thing," the black man said, "that when a engine speeds up the wheels skids on the tracks. It's just the same when he puts on the brakes to slow down—the wheels skids on the tracks. Now, when an engine skids on the tracks, the wheels plain polishes them tracks; they makes them shine awful nice. It's my true experience for lots more years than you got, that where the trains goes slow is where the tracks shines. And now you say you wants to find yourself a train going west that's slowed down, or just going slow. Right?"

"That's right," I said.

"Well," said the black man, "I'm not going to worry you about freights pulled by engines that's getting up steam; I'm just going to let you know now where the westbound number is going slow. Yes, I'm going to tell you where them tracks brake-shines." And with that, the big black man walked over to me and pointed down from his little mountain to a concrete bridge about a half mile off. "You can almost see them shines from here," he said. "Now, you just go over there and wait on the other side of that bridge, and before it gets much later than now, you're going to hook yourself a ride out west. The engineer will be putting on the brakes over there, and them big wheels and them little wheels is going to be sliding and polishing them tracks just like you'll see it when you get there."

"Thank you," I said.

The black man squinted and looked off beyond anything to be seen. "And just as soon as this little one of mine," he said, waving to the little girl, "is big enough and smart enough to have herself a right man, then I'll be right back down there by that shine myself—been too long already."

"Yes," I said, "I sure do thank you; I better go now."

"You be careful," the big black man said. And as I went down the heap of slag to where the tracks brake-shine, I heard him singing.

On the Nickel Plate Railroad

Ever since then I've looked at legless people in a different way—especially those with nothing from the knees down. And ever since then it seems that there are more and more of these amputees—and not because I saw lots of them on that hospital ship coming out of the South Pacific, because the war that made those was still eight years in the future.

It was 1933, and I was at last getting out of Cleveland, Ohio, in a gondola of the Nickel Plate Railroad. The freight was still going slow out of the Division when these two guys appeared running alongside. They sure didn't look like bums, or hobos, as they were once called. Both had on black suits—regular black coats and pants like preachers often wear—and white shirts with dark colored neckties. Both wore black fedoras and carried cheap-looking oil-cloth briefcases.

With admirable agility, they caught hold of the box car just ahead of my gondola, climbed up to the top walkway and sat down looking at me below. I was sitting on the cargo of huge sheets of steel, my feet dangling between the steel and the front wall of the gondola—very comfortable.

One of the preacher types up above asked me where I was going and I said Chicago. "You're pretty green, aren't you," he said.

"Well," I said, "I suppose you could say that."

The train was beginning to hit it up when the man said, "Don't you give a shit for your legs?" And then, as the train began to brake, he yelled out, "For Christ's sake pull up your legs, get back!" And as I did just that, the whole load of tons of smooth sheet steel slid forward, closing the space where my legs had been—with a dull thud against the front walls of my gondola.

After I'd come out of the scare, I said, "Thanks," to the preacher type who just smiled.

Then both of them, sitting up there on the walkway and looking back at Cleveland, made what we used to call the "Kaiser's Salute"—thumbs on their noses and the fingers spread wide—and yelled out, "Fuck you, Cleveland!"

I Visit My Uncle in Webster, South Dakota

We were coming back from California where our most interesting experience had been driving through Death Valley from Beatty, Nevada, to Death Valley Junction, California, in mid-August. It was just under 140 degrees at Furnace Creek in the Valley—I thought you'd like to know that, so you'll know what kind of clothes to take with you when you drive that way.

When we got to Rugby, South Dakota, I began thinking of my Uncle Feodore, called Ted, whom I hadn't seen since I was two years old—and I was *told* that I'd seen him, I had no memory, whatsoever, of him. Also, in all the years between, I'd never seen any photographs of him.

Well, Rugby, South Dakota, is only about thirty-five miles from the town of Webster, and that's where I'd heard—at sometime long ago—that that's where my Uncle Ted lived. And so we decided we'd run over there just in case he might still be alive and living there.

It was Sunday when we saw the sign: "WEBSTER, POPULATION 800," as I remember. Out there in South Dakota all roads run either north and south or east and west. All intersections are at right angles. Diagonals are unpopular out there—it's really flat; the lake nearby is named *Dry Lake*, and it really was—and so was Webster, dry and dust blowing enough, almost, to cover the town forever.

The only evidence of life we saw that Sunday morning was a man coming out of the drugstore. We drew alongside and asked if he knew if there was a man in town by the name of Feodore Weismann. "Sure," the man said, "you mean Ted—you wanna go there?" By then he was on the running board. (Do you remember that great "standard feature," the running board? This was back in 1937—lots of running boards then.) Before we knew it, the man said, "Here's Ted's place," and he hopped off saying "It's okay, I'll walk back"—not so generous an offer, we'd gone only three blocks from the drugstore. So off he went, as we sat in the car looking at Uncle Feodore's house standing there like a ramshackle outpost in a desert. "Maybe we should forget it," my then-wife said.

"Maybe," I said, "but, hell, we're here, let's see if he's at home." When I heard myself say "at home" it sounded wrong, inappropriate. It would have been better, I thought, to have said, "Let's see if he's inside." It was the *house* that had me thinking it wasn't really a home—there was just this low pile of clapboards precariously nailed together: a person would be either inside or outside this little heap, but never *at* or *not at* home.

My then-wife waited in the car, and I went up to the door in the front. The torn rubber WELCOME mat was off to one side with the first three letters missing. I think I took a deep breath, then knocked on the plywood door, gently at first, then harder as I was beginning to suspect that there was no one inside which wouldn't have surprised me at all. Then a little harder, and a heavy voice from inside, "Yeah, just a minute."

Then the door was opened and there stood a very tall man—maybe 6'5" or 6"—in long underwear, winter underwear, and for a split second I was reminded of how my father almost always wore winter underwear all summer—he said it kept the sweat in, evaporated more slowly and kept him cool longer. Also, he used to say, "You don't see baseball players running around in summer underwear, do you?" Which you didn't, I guess, way way back then. No matter, that—there stood this tall, barefoot man in long winter underwear in August in Webster, South

Dakota. He didn't look a thing like my father, nor like my other uncles Charlie and Andrew. He had a huge hooked Hittite nose—big enough and hooked enough to pull himself out of a bathtub, should he ever lose the use of his arms and legs. And that had me wondering whether or not our name, Weismann, had Jewish connections—not that that would matter one way or another to me: I knew who I was—I'd been living with myself since I was born. This man with the nose had big matted eyebrows and hair to go with it. And there he stood.

"I'm Fritz's kid," I said, "second oldest, Donald." By explanation I'll tell you that my father's name was Friedrich, and he was most often called Fritz. And because his middle name was Othello, he was sometimes called Tallow, like candle wax. He used lots of other names during his lifetime, but the most used was Fritz—Fritz Kelly. So, I said, "I'm Fritz's kid, Donald. We were just passing and I thought we'd see if you were home."

"Fritz's kid," the man said. "Well, I'll be God damned; and you were looking for you Uncle Ted, eh? Well, here he is. And who's the other part of that we?"

"My wife," I said.

"Well," said Uncle Ted, "I'll get some clothes on—worked awful late last night—and you bring the little lady in." Which, using plenty of time, I did.

Uncle Ted came out of what looked like an empty side room dressed in a unironed white shirt, white bib overalls with different colored paint spots all over the front and shoes likewise. This costume didn't surprise me since I knew from long-ago talk that he was what was called an "interior decorator"—an "artistic painter" of the insides of houses. But it was Sunday, a no-work day.

"So," said Uncle Ted, "take a seat," which we did. Uncle Ted sitting on a wooden box since there were only two chairs and a card table in the otherwise empty living room. In fact, from where I sat, the whole house looked empty.

"And you're the second oldest," Uncle Ted said.

"Yes," I said, "Fred is the oldest."

"Oh, yes," Uncle Ted said.

And that's the way it went—little questions about almost nothing, and answers even smaller—until Uncle Ted said, "It sure is good when you came; I'll be umpiring a kid's baseball game in a half hour or so. You'll enjoy that," and I said we sure would—why I said that I'll never know. Just being nice, I guess.

So a little later we were at the windy, grassless, dusty baseball field. There weren't any bleachers or seats—just a few boxes down the first-base foul line that had been drawn with a broom handle in the dust.

Uncle Ted was all business as the players came around him for instructions. That's when it became clear that the visiting team had only seven players, the Webster team had nine. No problem for Umpire and General Officer Ted. He said that, to make-up for his lack of two players on the visitor's team they would be allowed four outs per inning and the Webster team, the usual three outs. And so the game was begun—for some reason, only a six-inning game that seemed much longer. I forget who won, because Uncle Ted did something about counting the runs scored—something about what he called a "discount" for the under-manned team. So, at least it was over.

Walking back to Uncle Ted's place he talked about the wonderful pheasants in South Dakota—how hunters came from all over the world to hunt, right around Webster, even, but that that last couple of years there weren't so many of the birds around. "We'll have some pheasant for dinner," he said, "all I have to do is warm it up."

"That'll be nice," my wife said.

Back at the house, Ted put out some tin plates on the card table, some cups, knives and forks, and so on.

About then a man in overalls walked right in the front door into the living room where the table was set and Uncle Ted said, "Good you stopped by, Harry; we're just about to eat." And then to us, "This is Harry Schultz, our mail carrier," and then to Harry, "This is my brother's kid, Donald, and wife, Barbara." Then nice to meet you, and so on, and the mail carrier going off into some other part of the house returning with another box that he put at the table: Two chairs, two boxes ready to go, and Uncle Ted bringing in a plate with the partly consumed carcass of a very small, really a tiny, bird, perhaps not even a pheasant, which he set down in the middle of the table saying, "Now don't be bashful, just tie in."

Now there's no moral to this story. A lot of very fine stories do not have morals. Some of the best stories are, as some say, "moral-free." You could say that this story about meeting up, at long last, with my Uncle Ted, way off there in Webster, South Dakota, is an excellent example of the moral-free genre, and should be appreciated as such. Any attempt to find a moral here would lead to all sorts of abstract thoughts, sorties into linguistics, symbolism and, heaven forbid, "meaning."

You see, it wouldn't help even if I told you that the mail carrier who came to eat with us had his small bag pretty full of rusty horseshoes—and that's why he was so bent over until he put all that weight down.

In Old Mississippi

Mississippi is where the county sheriff told me more than sixty years ago that he'd had to let his black friend be hung because, as a sheriff, he had so many more friends who were white, and the majority rules. Mississippi is where they said, "Why, sure, Yankee, you just go ahead and help yourself," and then punched me in the kidneys when I bent over to get a drink from the fountain outside the filling station. And Mississippi is where that man from south of Osceola picked me up when I was hitchhiking to New Orleans, the first leg of a trip to Yucatan.

We were rolling along at about forty-five, the black man driving, the fat, florid-faced white man on the seat next to him, and me behind on a box in the bed of the Chevrolet pickup when a front tire blew. The white man corked up his pint and the black man brought the truck to a careful stop on the gravel shoulder. The white man called the black man "Camel." "Camel," he said, "let's get that goddamned wheel changed, we gotta get on down."

"Yes sir," Camel said. He jacked up the front axle, pried off the hubcap, spun off the five lugs and put them in the open upturned hubcap close to the wheelless axle. He went around to the back of the truck to get the spare and while he was freeing it from the rack, the white man scooped the lugs from the hubcap and threw them, broadcast fashion, across the road and into a cornfield. He winked at me when Camel rolled the spare into place at the front axle. Camel hoisted the wheel on to the studs and reached into the hubcap. He turned it over and looked around on the ground, then up at his boss. "Whatsa matter, Camel, you go and lose them lug bolts again?" the white man said.

"No sir," Camel said, "I put them right here in the hubcap, yes sir, right here in this here hubcap, sir."

"Well, why ain't they there then, you stupid nigger?" the white man said. "You better get your black ass shakin' and find them lug bolts, boy—we jus' ain't got all day you know."

I started, slowly, to walk away down the road, past the front of the truck. "Where you goin', boy?" the white man called out. "You come back here, Camel might need all the help he can get." Afraid to keep going, and afraid to come back, I just stood there.

"It's shadier here," I said. I wanted badly to kill that fat red faced white man. I could see the headline: HITCHHIKER KILLED IN ROBBERY ATTEMPT—Negro Hand Witness to Fight for Knife. I ambled back to the truck. "These niggers jus' ain't not good," he said, "stupid black sons-a-bitches. God dammit, Camel! Get them lug bolts!" Camel kept pretending to look for the lugs. After about ten minutes the white man said, "Camel, how come you're so stupid you don't know enough to look in that cornfield over there?"

And Camel said, "Yes sir. Thank you, sir."

Camel found four of the five lugs, and a while after that I was let free in Jackson. The white man waved. "You be careful now, boy," he called out the window, "you jus' be mighty careful." I couldn't say a thing. My mouth got full of something sticky and sweet-sour, then like bile, and the busy Jackson street was all blurred and spinning.

A Little West of Kahoka

He was hoeing a field of corn across the road a little west of Kahoka, Missouri, and I was absently feeding the last of my Mexican *Entero Vioforma* pills to some stray chickens as I waited for a ride, years and years ago. After the chickens wandered off and I stood there wondering what kind of eggs they'd maybe never lay again, I called out across the road, "Awful hot, eh?"

"Terrible hot," the man called back, straightening up and pressing his hands into the small of his back.

"Keeps on, it'll burn up your corn," I said.

"Maybe," the man said, "you don't farm, do you?"

"No," I said.

"Takes some faith," the man said, "you know what the Lord said: Wherever I am, there also shall my servant be." And, he added, "I serve the Lord."

"Amen," I said, taking a few steps west on old U.S. Highway 136. When, perhaps because I was till in the vicinity where the Lord was watching over one of his servants, the same Lord had a truck come by to pick me up and carry me all the way west, some seventy miles, to Unionville.

Win Big on the Big Wheel

I drove slowly through Billings, Montana, late one July night in 1938, found it blacked-out and shut down, so I drove on out to the edge of town, pulled into an open field, and went to sleep. When I woke up and got out to walk the kinks out of my back and legs, I saw that a carnival was setting up a little further in toward town. After breakfast in a little café where the conversation stopped as I came in, I went out looking for those prehistoric remains I'd read about, remains that had been discovered in some caves the year before. I never found them, but by then the sun was warm and I stretched out in the grass near the river and slept for a couple of hours. By noon the carnival was just about up—a Ferris wheel, a merry-go-round, a crack-the-whip, a fortune teller, a big bingo set-up, a pellet-gun range, and lots of games of chance. I bought an ice cream sandwich from a man stocking the cold box in a little blue and white striped stand with the name, NORTH POLE, painted on a post that stuck out the top. "You looking for work?" the ice cream man asked.

"Not particularly," I said.

"What do you mean by that?" he asked.

"Nothing," I said, "just that I'm not looking very hard, that's all."

"Ever run a numbers wheel?" he asked.

"No, not much," I said, "what kind?"

"The kind that's worth running and that'll guarantee you a quarter of the take," he said.

"Me, or the guy who owns it?" I asked.

"You," he said, "the guy who handles the wheel. The owner gets his, don't worry."

"They always do," I said, "who owns it?"

"I do," the man said, "come on over and have a look."

I went over with him to a stand that had a sign, WIN BIG ON THE BIG WHEEL, painted across the front. The big wheel was mounted on a four-by-four at one end of the stand. It was a handsome object with ten carved spokes, a large center area and a wide outer edge that carried the widely spaced numbers, one to twenty-five. It was painted in red, white, black, blue, and gold and looked like something off a nineteenth century carousel or Sicilian cart. Very closely spaced brass-headed nails, hundreds of them it appeared, stood out from lines that radiated from the center. Of the hundreds of spaces between these lines, only twenty-five carried numbers; the rest were blanks—no wins. A springy piece of metal extended down from above the wheel to a level below the shafts of the nails, so that when the wheel was spun it made a loud clacking sound. When the wheel stopped the metal came to rest between two nails and pointed either to a number or to a blank. "Not such hot odds," I said, "out of all that, there's only twenty-five of those little spaces that got any numbers at all, and then you've got to hit your *special* number to win."

"We go as high as twenty-to-one odds if we got a good player going," the man said, "We'll pay twenty bucks for every single he shows. They put their chips down on the numbers here on the counter; we can't use money so they buy chips—white, ten cents; blue, twenty-five; red, fifty; and gold, a dollar—any amount on any number, and then you spin the wheel. Every time they lose, you win."

"Why the kewpie dolls?" I asked, looking at two shelves of them behind the wheel.

"Sometimes," the man said, "you can make it easier of the guy loses a lot—just give him a doll for being a good sport, you know; you pay for the dolls you give away, fifty cents apiece."

"It's okay," I said, "but it's not for me."

"You run one before, right?" the man said, "if you're wondering if there's a brake, the answer is yes—works against the axle."

"No," I said, "I wasn't wondering about that, I just don't like to stand up all day and keep talking."

"I need a man on the Ferris wheel tonight," the man said, "you can sit down all the time it's going, and hardly say a word."

I ran the Ferris wheel that night outside Billings on the Yellowstone. Around eleven a fight broke out under the sign, WIN BIG ON THE BIG WHEEL, and in a matter of minutes the whole stand was torn down and people were running away with the kewpie dolls. Maybe because they'd been rooked by the man running the BIG WHEEL and figured that a couple dozen kewpie dolls were theirs for "being good sports" just like the owner had himself said.

About Joe Pool, Louisville Cab Driver

I understand that Joe Pool, driver number six for the Louisville, Kentucky Yellow Cab Company, died of a heart attack—and I think I may know why.

After a day at meetings of the Midwestern Art Association in Louisville, I went out and got drunk. Then, feeling lucky, I wanted to shoot craps, roll the dice, so I hailed a cab. It was Joe Pool's number six. He had ideas where games would be in progress, and he drove me around from place to place for a lot of the night until I was cleaned out. When I looked at the meter in the cab it said I owed something over fifty dollars—just mail it to me, Joe Pool number six, Louisville Yellow Cab Company. Can you imagine such trust? Well on the following day I sent him the money.

I figure that Joe Pool's heart went out on him—too much to cope with, when he opened my letter and there it was—a kept promise.

George Raft Rolled His Own

I don't remember the exact date, but for sure it was in the late 30s when, on the invitation of a friend, a New York journalist, I was watching a series of boxing matches in Los Angeles. The arena was packed with a quiet, well-behaved mass of spectators—quiet, perhaps, because of the generally dull performance of the fighters.

As I remember, my journalist friend and I were seated in the fifth or sixth row, above the level of the ring and over the heads of reporters right up at ringside—clear view, perfect seats.

It was during the second bout—flyweights who flitted about the ring without throwing any punches, when my journalist friend asked me if I recognized the man seated directly ahead of me in the row below. And, yes, it was true, it was George Raft, the ex-hoofer turned movie star, the guy whose fame developed in roles of gangsters as in the 1932 movie "Scarface," and as a big casino/whore house operator in Havana. Yes, George Raft, right there in front of me.

I spent some time wondering how he kept his black hair pasted down and so shiny—maybe with what was then called *Stacomb* mixed with a little *Brilliantine,* I thought. He was wearing a short-sleeved, tight-fitting jersey, perhaps to display his muscles and his hairy arms. Short men often do these things including stuffing their jockstraps with wads of cloth or sponge, I'd been told.

Well, there's not much of a story to tell about George Raft even though after this close-up of him it affected my response to every one of his appearances in subsequent movies.

You see, George Raft continually picked his nose, continually, as if he couldn't quite free a booger, or a nest of them from high up in one nostril or the other. But he did free quite a few without apparent damage to his optic nerve. Nothing strange about this, especially when it's assumed no one is watching. But what was exceptional about George Raft's performance was what he did with the boogers he managed to get hold of and bring out. First he rolled them between the index finger and thumb of his right hand—slowly and reflectively, never looking at them, rolling them to near dryness. Then he switched hands, and continued rolling in an absent-minded way as he stared in the direction of the boxing matches. Then came what was a bit surprising, even to me: With a booger between index finger and thumb, he transferred it to his arm and rolled it over and among the long black hairs. Doing this, I thought I noticed him wince a little as one of the now drying and sticky boogers rolled up a hair or two and pulled it, or them, out. What George Raft now had was a booger reinforced with hair, as he kept rolling this strengthened ball of mucous up and down and around his arm.

This put me in mind of what I already knew about the art of plastering—how interior plaster is applied over a base which will furnish a proper grip—like wood or metal lath. And to secure best results three successive coats of plaster are requisite. What George Raft was doing put me in mind (mainly) of the *first* coat—called the "scratch coat." This plaster coat is composed of sand and lime mixed with *abundant hair*, often cow's hair, to assure against its cracking, while adding greatly to its overall strength. In a way, this incorporation of hair is comparable to the use of iron reinforcement in concrete—what's called "ferro-concrete."

Well, over time George Raft produced a number of these "scratch coat" booger balls. As he quite mechanically and quite non-consciously produced another of these balls he placed it in the center of his open hand, and by using the index finger and thumb of his *other* hand as a kind of catapult—the machine used to throw missiles in ancient medieval warfare, and nowadays used to powerfully assist the take-off of jet fighters from aircraft carrier decks, he flicked the hairy booger ball in the direction of the boxing ring. I found it difficult to sight and follow these; they were small and they left George Raft's palm in great speed and usually in low trajectories.

However, in a couple of instances I saw spectators in the rows below George Raft slap at the backs of their necks as if they'd been bothered by a fly or mosquito instead of being visited by one of George Raft's very own manufactured souvenirs—part and parcel of the man himself.

Waiting for the *Cincinnati Hit Parade*

He pulled the truck over on the gravel, and I ran through the taillight tinted cloud of dust as he swung open the door. It was 1937 on a road that cuts Kansas in half, east to west. "Where you going?" the driver asked.

"To the coast," I said.

"You live out there?" he asked.

"No, back in Wisconsin," I said. He had the radio on low, a Cincinnati station, and he hardly talked at all. "You've got a big one here," I said, referring to the truck.

"Almost empty now; just five left," he said.

"Five what?" I asked.

"Upright pianos," he said, "old ones, reconditioned." He'd started out from Grand Rapids with a full load, and he was selling them in little towns and at farmhouses along the way. "You'd be surprised how many people want a good upright piano," he said, "especially if you can wheel it right up to the front door for them." And a little later, "Music is a wonderful thing."

"It sure is," I said.

We rode along, maybe fifty miles, without saying anything. He kept looking at his wrist watch. Then he asked, "What time you got?"

"A quarter to ten," I said.

"That's about right," he said, turning up the radio a little. "I don't suppose you'd think it was funny if all of a sudden I started to sing, would you?"

"Oh no, not at all," I said, "I like to sing myself."

"Well this is different," he said, "I have to sing alone."

"That's okay," I said, "I don't have much of a voice, anyway."

"Well," he said, "you see it's this way: My girl is back in Cincinnati, and when I'm on the road we both listen to the *Cincinnati Hit Parade*. It'll be coming on pretty soon."

"That's nice," I said.

"When the program comes on we both know we're listening to the same thing," he said, "she's listening up in Cincinnati, and I'm listening wherever I am."

"That's a damn good radio," I said.

"So when the program comes on," he continued, "we both sing and we know we're singing together."

"It's a good idea," I said, "both of you singing along with the music like that together."

"We don't sing along with the radio music," he said, "we just start singing out own song right when the program begins."

"It's a fine thing, having your own song, I mean, and singing it like that," I said.

"Yeah," he said, "it sure is. Our song is *The Rosary*."

"I know that song," I said, "I can even play it—not so good, but I can play it on the piano."

When the *Cincinnati Hit Parade* came on, he started to sing and I began to play *The Rosary* on one of the tied-down uprights in the dark back of the van as we sailed across Kansas, away from nothing, it seemed, and toward something still waiting for a name.

In Lemmon, South Dakota

I was returning from California in a 1934 V–8 Ford convertible, the clearest evidence I had of having taught two years at Sheboygan High School in Wisconsin. I hardly slowed down for the town of Lemmon, South Dakota, but I did on the eastern edge of that scattered group of buildings when I noticed a makeshift carnival operating about two hundred yards off the road. There were some poles against the sky and bare electric light bulbs, not many, strung between. There were a couple of small faded striped tents and some little wooden concessions slapped up on a flat grassless piece of ground and whipped with the dust-laden wind. There were a few automobiles parked around, and I parked mine and got out. Five or six kids were riding in tin racing cars attached to a disc, like the floor of a very small merry-go-round that was kept turning by a belt and a power take-off from a very old truck. The engine was loud, and it missed now and then. The disc wobbled its way around, and the kids rode it with blank expressions. This was the only ride the carnival offered; the price was five cents. There were a few games of chance; as I remember, three of them. I stood for a while at one of the games. Physically, it consisted of a flat surface about eight-by-eight feet, covered with red oilcloth. Setting close together on this surface was a bunch of prizes. There were little plaster-of-Paris dogs and cats, a bundle of cigarettes, some boxes with lithographed pictures of mirrors, brushes and combs and the words, "Vanity Set," on the outside, and a lot of squat bottles labeled "Perfume." The object of the game was to stand back of a rope, and by tossing the three wooden rings—the kind used to stretch cloth when doing needlework—hope to have at least one of them fall around a prize.

The men and women running the concessions looked like the saddest sharecroppers ever photographed by the Farm Security Administration. Most of them were blondish, around forty years of age but looking more like sixty. They said almost nothing, and they appeared not to see anything they looked at. They collected the rings from the board or from the ground where they'd rolled, and then exchanged them for nickels again. While I was there, there may have been as many as twenty people come and go, and, in what was a very real way to me, they didn't seem to move as they came and went. No matter what they were doing, they seemed to be standing and waiting for something. They were like people in a stopped move. They were tattered, earth-colored, and quiet in the blowing dust.

These were the people, that a couple of years later, I'd become more familiar with in John Steinbeck's book, *The Grapes of Wrath*.

And thirty-one years after that, in 1966, while serving on the National Council of the Arts with Steinbeck, I told him how much I appreciated—valued—that book, that it came at just the right time of my life.

He thanked me, saying that sometimes we miss something because we're not quite ready for it, and sometimes we miss it because we're way past having it be of any importance to us—we just hang on—season after season like migrant workers.

John M. Steinbeck, at sixty years of age, and twenty-three years after the appearance of his *Grapes of Wrath*, was awarded the Nobel Prize in Literature—mostly for writing about people I saw in Lemmon, South Dakota—way back then.

In Cleveland, Ohio, in 1933

I had arrived in Cleveland on a fast freight and was looking for a place to stay. With all I'd heard about places for overnight transients being maintained by the Federal Government in those years, I figured there must be one not far, right there in Cleveland. I asked several men on the street and got a variety of contradictory directions, so that around two in the morning I was still looking when I came around a corner and ran smack into a hold-up. The man with the pistol appeared only mildly surprised by my practically walking into him, and casually turned to me and said, "Now if you'll just stand back there, young man, nobody's gonna hurt you." So I stood back of him while he talked to his prospective victim. The man who was being held up turned out to be quite drunk and seemed not to understand what the other man was after. Then I realized that the man with the pistol was also drunk, very drunk. The two drunks kept talking to each other, the man with the gun saying, "Now I'm telling you, this is a stick-up; I want what you got on you." And the other man saying "Well, now, that's not the thing to do, and I don't have much on me, and what I have on me I need, but I'll split it with you if you'll just give me a chance and stop arguing with me." It was actually an unusually pleasant situation with darkened Cleveland lying all around, and these two men talking and going on in a really gentle way about their different roles in life, their different means and purposes, and every now and then turning to me and asking wasn't it right what they were saying. I tried to take both sides and still take no side at all, not even my own, whatever that was. After about fifteen minutes they got sentimental and put their arms around each other and the next thing I knew I had my arms around them and they had their arms around me and everybody had their arms around everybody and we were singing *Bye Bye Blackbird* and *Sweet Adeline*. We staggered down the street for a couple of blocks and then at the corner under a swinging sign, I excused myself as if from old friends and went on my way.

It was right after this that I walked into the principal square of the town, the one with the squarish tower. There was a bunch of about twenty or thirty old and young men off to one side of the square. They were being harangued by a man who stood about three feet off the ground in the hollow of what appeared to be an old horse-watering trough. He was saying those things about class struggle, labor bosses, the common man and redistributing the wealth that I'd heard many times before, especially in that now-vanished place called Bughouse Square in Chicago. He must have been about thirty-five or forty and doing a very good job. Even though the horse trough was no more than six feet long, he actually managed to pace back and forth in it. At the conclusions of many of his sentences he'd stand in the middle of the trough and hold his arms straight out from his sides in a way that made him look very much like Cimabue's crucified Christ. When he implored his audience to do something about the bad conditions he painted, he would throw his head back and moan straight up into the black sky over Cleveland. He went on and on, and from all evidences he could have gone on forever. A policeman appeared from out of the shadows, walked to the outer edge of the assembled group, listened for a little while, and then sauntered across the square and away into the darkness.

Just before I finally faced the fact that I had better find a place to stay or give up the idea of sleeping at all that night, the man in the horse trough began to accuse his audience of lack of interest in what he was saying and a lack of responsibility for the world in general. He began to accuse his audience of betraying the working man by not organizing and mounting a revolution against the corporate capitalist system. The old man on my right turned and looked at me as if he expected me to say something. I looked at him blankly for a few seconds and then said, "Sounds easy, doesn't it?"

The old man took hold of my arm and said, "Why don't you get up there and tell him off? You can do it, I bet you can; go on get up there," and he pushed me a little toward the horse trough.

"No," I said, "I think he's doing just fine and besides if we don't like what he's doing, I guess we can just go away."

The old man let go of my arm and said, "Maybe we all ought to go away—very, very far away."

And I said, "who knows?"

As I remember, I must have hung around for close to half an hour listening to the man in the horse trough and looking at the men around him. Only the man speaking seemed to have any energy. There was a kind of blankness in the faces and a heavy sag in the bodies of both the young and the old standing around. I remember that to me they looked helpless and lost, but, at the same time, as if they were engaged in heavy combat down inside. And in the gaps when the speaker paused for a few seconds, a quality of impending destructiveness emanated from the group. It was in those gaps that I half expected them to be joined and transformed into some horrible but understandable act of revenge. Not that this mood was entirely strange to me. This was 1933, and there had never been anything at home or in school that kept me from knowing what was going on in the streets. I'd been at streetcar strikes in Milwaukee when the scab operators brought the cars out of the barn, and bricks and bullets were fired through the windows. I could remember huge groups of men and women, often with the women in front, running with clubs and yelling and calling for something that sounded like both a threat and a plea. I'd watched fires outside of factories and the police running from their overturned Black Marias. Back on the other side of 1933, us kids who thought we were men used to say good-bye by saying, "I'll see you on the barricades," and as I recall that now I think we at least half believed what our words were saying. So there in Cleveland, that night in 1933, the threat or the promise or the nightmare felt close.

So far as I know, the intense frustration and the will to avenge that I sensed in that bunch of men came to nothing, because as I walked away, they were still standing blank and tense, and the man in the horse trough was making words that sounded like a benediction. Neither he nor anyone else was ready that night in 1933, in Cleveland, U.S.A.—not ready to go against the forces he was describing. But their inaction—as all of us learned later, could never be construed as surrender.

No, the surrender of people like those around the horse trough was taking place in what then seemed a far-off place on the other side of the Atlantic Ocean—in Germany, then the most literate nation of the world.

Misadventure in Rossville, Illinois

I remember racing my brand new, white, 1940 Plymouth convertible with a special twelve-inch speaker under the dash all the way from Bloomington to Rossville, Illinois, just to see Margaret Foster for an hour and then turn around and race back. For miles I had to pee but couldn't afford the time. But when I got to the stop sign at the edge of town that said ROSSVILLE, the slanted stroke of the "R" had been painted out, and the "O" changed to a "U" and I laughed so hard at eighty miles an hour that I began to wet my pants. At the first bar in "Pussville," I stopped, hopped out, went in, ordered a beer and asked, "Where's the washroom?"

"Right here," he said, knocking his knuckles against a copper sink right in plain open sight behind the bar.

"Right *there*?" I asked.

"What's the matter, ain't it good enough for you," he snarled, looking out the window at that brand new convertible with the radio still playing.

"Okay," I said. "Okay, I guess I've come farther than I thought."

So I walked around the end of the bar, stood at the sink, and reached for my zipper. That's as far as I got. The bartender swung at me yelling, "Why, you goddamn filthy son-of-a-bitch pervert, you...!" I went up and over the bar, through the screen door and into that Plymouth and didn't stop until I was out the other side of town. It may seem strange to some, but I never thought that my experience was odd or dirty. It was unexpected, to be sure; but odd, no. All that bartender and I had between us was a language difficulty. He knew well enough, and perhaps for his whole long life, that a "washroom" is where you wash, not pee. I should have asked for the men's room, the john, the gents', the can, the toilet. I just had the wrong word, but, for the gods, I almost paid dearly for it.

And if your wondering if I got to see that girl, Margaret Foster, the answer is yes, I did—after taking the shade under a tree and reflecting on language, semantics, custom, habit—everything that should work to keep us together, but often does not.

E.R. Johnston Used to Teach Journalism

When I was teaching at Illinois State, one of my friends was E.R. Johnston, Associate Professor of Journalism. At the time he must have been pushing fifty, a slightly overweight, gentle soul, always in a dark gray suit, always somewhat retiring but always ingratiating. He was one of that lot who did everything but the dissertation for the Ph.D. at a good school—the University of Chicago. Because of this and because Illinois State was an insecure college hoping to convince the academic world that it was close to first class by having a high percentage of Ph.D.'s on its faculty, it was pretty obvious that E.R. Johnston—even though he wrote incisive but short articles for some of the best journals—pretty obvious that he'd never make full professor. For me he lent some evidence for the arguable belief that "nice guys don't win ball games."

E.R. Johnston lived in a small house with his matronly wife. They were childless. The house—painted pink because Mrs. Johnston wanted it that way, Johnston told me—was directly across the street from the college, no more than a hundred steps from the room where Johnston taught his Journalism classes five days a week.

There was a swing on the porch—one of those varnished wooden porch swings that hung from chains.

I don't know how long Johnston had been at the college, but a good while before I'd arrived, I'm sure. Each day after breakfast he came out and sat in the porch swing. From there he could easily hear the first warning bell ring—the one before his eight o'clock class. When it rang Mrs. Johnston would call out from inside the house, "First bell, E.R., time to go," and E.R. Johnston would say "Okay, I'm going," leaving the swing, crossing the street, and being in his classroom by the time the second and last bell rang. I don't know for how long this had been routine—but long, I figured. And I figured that E.R. Johnston had never failed that routine.

Then, on a spring morning now over fifty years ago, E.R. Johnston was swinging just a little in the porch swing when the eight o'clock class warning bell rang out. "First bell, E.R., time to go," Mrs. Johnston called from inside the house. On this particular Spring day, E.R. Johnston didn't say, "Okay, I'm going," he didn't say anything. Then the second, the last bell, rang and Mrs. Johnston called out, "Goodness, that's the last bell, E.R.," but still there was no answer from E.R. Johnston.

And when Mrs. Johnston, red-faced and wiping her hands on her apron, came out on the porch, the swing hung empty and still.

I had never gotten to know Mrs. Johnston, so what I learned of E.R. Johnston's broken routine I got from the town newspaper over a period of a couple of weeks. As the stories went, it was a case of a sudden and complete disappearance. No reasons were given, no guesses were made. Mrs. Johnston, it was reported, was completely mystified—and broken. E.R. Johnston had packed no bags, had taken nothing from the house, not even the money or the checkbook kept in the big covered dish in the pantry. The car was where it almost always was, month after month, in the garage.

If E.R. Johnston were still living, he'd be over a hundred—and proof, I'd like to believe that good guys *do* win ball games—sometimes by the grace of their ace in the hole, the pinch hitter.

A Very Rare Super Refined Air

In my experience, there's something very special that hangs in the air around games of chance played for real stakes. People I've known for a long time seem to turn into other characters and show faces I'd never seen before the wheel is spun or the dice are rolled out with a good chunk of their money riding with them. The most reasonable, down to earth, two-times-two-equals-four people suddenly expect the answer to be five or three or even eleven. They believe the dice can hear, that they have feelings, and can be offended by bad talk and coddled into cooperation by good. They feel hot or cold, ready to come out on track seven or lie dead in the shed, right or wrong by what amounts to commands from the way the dice fall, from a spirit that enters the room or gets spontaneously generated in the air around the wheel or the crap table. I'm not talking about the guy who stops by for a couple or rolls, to try a pass or two on his way home with the change or a few bucks in his side pants pocket. I'm talking about the guy who troubles to find out when and where a game is coming up, who waits for it to open, who keeps his money in three or four places in his clothing as an easy mechanical check of how deep in he's going—and he's usually got most of the green folded in his last stash, the bundle that'll bring him back up if he really goes under. I'm talking about guys like Hawk Hydal, my roommate in Sheboygan in 1935—the kind of man who believes he can *see* that the last digit on the next-to-appear-Chevrolet license plate will be a six, nothing else, just a six, and who believes that *he,* not fate or destiny or God, screwed him up when the Chevrolet turns into the drag with the number five where the six should be.

There's a very rare, super-refined air around where chance rules and people believe they know how it will unfold. In such air it feels like anything you want to have happen can happen; and if you do your part just right, then, by God, it *will* rain, smack out of a cloudless sky. So, maybe if *The Word,* the question of questions, the answer of answers, the most of all the best, the Alpha and the Omega was to be voiced in the hope that for the very first time it would be heard, then one place it should be called out is over the spinning wheel or the rolling dice.

I Meet the Superintendent of Schools

The graduating class had elected me to be the Ivy Orator for the convocation so I had to remain to personally receive my diploma, my printed-out degree. But I'd been ready to leave for days before that. I'd packed my 1928 Model A Ford roaster ready to go to Canada. So once the benediction was said, I gave my robe and mortar board to my girl—now we say girlfriend, back then we just said my girl—gave her that to return to the rental agency and I got in my car and left.

The year was 1935, the depth of the Great Depression. There were no jobs, not even for teachers for which a separate document said I was qualified—certified. So why not go someplace else? Another country, why not Canada?

I got a job in a lumber camp above Cochrane, Ontario, in a place near Island Falls Junction off the Ontario Northland Railway. As soon as I got my bearings, I called back to my girl in Milwaukee and gave her the telephone number where I could be reached in case anything like a teaching job turned up down there. That was in late June.

In late July she called saying that a Mr. Henry E. Smith, superintendent of the Sheboygan, Wisconsin schools, was coming to interview people for jobs, and that there was an opening for an instructor in art in the high school. When he'd be in Milwaukee she didn't know, so I left Canada on the fly.

Once back in Milwaukee I learned that Superintendent Smith would be arriving at the college on Monday of the following week, so I was nicely dressed and waiting at the main entrance by eight that day. Around ten o'clock a taxi drove up and a business-type man got out. I gambled this guy was Smith so I followed him into the building. He went to the men's john to a urinal. I took the slot next to him, saying, "You're Superintendent Smith aren't you?" Not to my complete surprise he said that yes, he was, and I introduced myself offering my free hand which he met with his—as if he was a lefty.

Superintendent Smith must have been holding his water for quite a time. We must have stood there for close to five minutes and making none of the performances usually attributed to "queers" as we called them at the time. He appeared to be a straight, no funniness guy.

Well, by the time I joined the other candidates up in the college appointment office I was in solid with Smith. When it came my time for interview, Superintendent Smith greeted me as if we were old friends. And yes, I got the job—instructor in art, Sheboygan, Wisconsin High School.

There may be no moral to this account unless it be that *aqua vita,* the water of life, is not always distilled spirits, and that the water-bearer, the *Aquarius,* is sometimes a superintendent of schools.

My Nephew Tells Me about the Fire Department

I was talking with my nephew, Hobart, who was a captain in the Milwaukee Fire Department at the time. He'd been with the department for a long time, been through some of the worst fires, and knew the business, let's call it, from A through Z. He was driving me around town, showing me how it had changed in the years I'd been away—and so the conversation got around to the big advances made in fire prevention and fire-fighting since I watched the Phoenix Hosiery and the grain elevators burn years before.

I asked Hobart if a four-alarm fire was the highest classification—the worst fire.

"No," Hobart said, "there's the worst—the five-alarm fire. It goes by stages. First there's the simple one-alarm fire, usually taken care of by the fire station right in the area. Then there's the two-alarm fire, and maybe a couple of companies get called in.

"With the three-alarm fire you've got still more companies and lot more equipment involved.

"And when you get to a four-alarm you know you're in real trouble—captains in charge of brigades, lots of the best equipment goes to work—it's really pretty much like Hell."

"And the five-alarm fire?" I asked.

"There's not many of those, thank God," Hobart said. "It's then you've thrown all the equipment at it and every last one of your fire fighters."

"So," I asked, "and what's to be done then—if the fire keeps going—and spreading all over?"

"That's when the *chief* comes on.... "

"Yes," I said, "and.... "

"And he arrives in a spotless *gray*, not *red* Oldsmobile sedan," Hobart said. "He drives right up to the hot edge, the car door opens, and he gets out.... "

"Yes," I said.

"Now," said Hobart, "he's in a long *white* rain coat, a white helmet with the word CHIEF lettered across the front in big letters—very clear, you can read that name, CHIEF, a mile off."

"So," I asked, "what does he do, just stand there?"

"Only for a little while," Hobart said.

"Yes...and.... "

"And then," Hobart said, "he raises his arms high over his head...and the fire goes out."

The Transformations of Kenneth Shuck

They put us graduate students in a surplus World War II Quonset hut, there to pursue the art of painting as a corrective, so to speak, to our studies in the history of art. Of the six or seven who shared this work space, I remember only two: John Koos, a genuine genius who never completed requirements for a degree and went off to Burma on a Fulbright Fellowship; and Kenneth Shuck, a married man with two children.

If you have ever spent time with a group of people—all in one space—who are making paintings as part of the requirements for a graduate degree, then maybe you have some idea of how artificial this sort of situation is—and maybe how trying it gets to be, as the weeks and months drag by. The fact is, it gets to be boring as you stand at your easel with another blank canvas staring back at you—daring you to either neglect it or rape it. Long periods of silence in the hut while it rained outside, or snowed, with no music, and the graduate professor in charge stopping by once a week, smoking a few cigarettes and leaving.

Well, into this dull and strangely insulated place, Kenneth shuck usually appeared late and looking tired—sometimes quite worn out. This was because he had to stay up late at night, once the day in the hut was over. He had those two kids and a wife to support—and he did all the engraving for the University fraternities—mostly engraving on metal beer steins that the fraternities used and which they passed out in great numbers to friends—supporters. Kenneth Shuck was paid five cents per letter for his work. So the more letters he engraved, the more money he made, and the later he was up at night. And the more exhausted he was, once he made it to his easel and paint cupboard in the hut.

Still, Kenneth Shuck rose above his exhaustion, once he was seated at his easel and beginning to paint. It was something to behold—to see Ken, as we called him, begin painting and change before your eyes. The night's weariness bled away, a smile played across his face, and it even seemed that color rose in his cheeks.

Now I knew that Ken had fallen in love with a graduate student from Chile, from Santiago, and that she had returned to that far off place. More than that, I knew that Ken was buying silk scarves from a guy in town who may have been stealing them from some outfit he worked for. Ken got them for "a song," as some say. What he'd do with these scarves was this: he'd roll them into copies, especially of the Sunday edition, of the *New York Times* and mail them, duty free of course, to his girl—named Antoñetta Terrazas—in Santiago. Down there Antoñetta would sell them at a good price—putting the money aside until there was enough for airplane fare for Ken to come to Santiago. Knowing these things about Ken, I figured that what made him become happier and happier as he sat at his painting easel, was his thoughts of money piling up in Santiago, and of reunion with his sweetheart down there.

Still to have this transformation from gray exhaustion to bright smiling energy happen every time Ken took his position at his easel remained a little mysterious to me. Not that I spent any time or concern with that mystery. Life begs our interest in more earth shaking mysteries. But even so—one morning I was in my corner of the hut when again I witnessed the transformation of Ken Shuck. So I walked over to his regular place and told him how reassuring it was to observe the power of art—how painting appeared to transport him into a world where the boredom and fatigue of this world was left far behind, where maybe everything was better and happier.

Ken looked up from his chair, smiling and rosy-cheeked and said, "Yes, it seems wonderful, doesn't it?"

"It is," I said, "I envy you."

"There's no cause to envy me," Ken said, "that happy world, as you call it, is just an arm's reach away." And at that he swung open the lower door of his paint cupboard where, with its bright orange label glowing, stood a fifth of Old Grandad bourbon—already knocked off to the halfway mark.

Out a Window to a Past

I went to the window and leaned out. It was the early 1950s. Along Third Avenue as far as I could see there was lumbering out of the darkness toward me an unbroken column of heavy rubber-treaded tanks. The olive drab top hatches were open, and from each a man, visible to the waist, leaned forward. One of them looked up as he went under my window. He must have been about twenty. The old building trembled and I heard the two maiden ladies moving about in the apartment below. They came rushing up the stairs and knocked at the door. I let them in and they asked if America was being invaded. They blurted out about Belgrade in 1941 when the Nazis came and how they didn't know what to do, and how they pulled down the shades as the tanks went by. Trembling, they asked where they could go, and I said that everything would be all right; the tanks were ours, coming, maybe, from the Cadillac plant where they're made, and being delivered, perhaps, to someplace in Korea. We stood at the window, shade up, until the last one and a trailing jeep were out of sight in the direction of the docks along the Detroit River.

But the deadened rumble of their passage lay in the street like a mushy black pavement until dawn and the first light began playing over the terrain of memory: The returned veterans of World War II had melted chameleon-like into the silent younger generation of the 1950s, and I, as one of them, taught an only slightly skewed brand of the history and criticism of art in three state universities. We couldn't play the old games any more than we could play with power based and engendered in fear, with the falsification and forgery of documents, with lies, electronic snooping, the interception of mail, blackmail, and character assassination—the new legacies of "Tail-Gunner Joe" McCarthy, the fake hero-veteran who showed a short TV generation how to suicide by killing others.

For years the university campus played dead at bingo-jargon games full of instant clichés and intellectual chic, at crises concerned with where upperclassman should park their sport cars, and at tables full of charts showing how much a baccalaureate in engineering was worth in the sellers' market compared to one in classics, philosophy, or physics. The "Greeks" played on their aphrodisiac lawns after dinner, the stadium was full every Saturday, and prizes were given for fitting snugly in square holes no matter the shape of the plug, while the vines quietly clawed their way up the wall, and—not quite unknown—some few students were plotting toward truthfulness, no matter how blindly, how romantically ideal.

The Shortest Religious Movie

This movie opens with a standard nineteenth century sentimental image of Jesus Christ—neatly trimmed beard; rosy cheeks; and that vacuous expression in the face so characteristic of the Pre-Raphaelite painter, William Holman Hunt. A model for this image could be Hunt's celebrated painting *The Light of the World*. Full length in a spotless white robe, he is looking straight out of the frame at us. We notice that He is holding a pair of powerful Japanese binoculars.

As we move into a close-up, Jesus slowly begins to raise the binoculars toward his eyes while at the same time turning away from us to begin scanning the background landscape. From this point on we see that landscape as seen through the binoculars—as Jesus sees it.

Plaintive music—harmonica and guitar—barely audible up to this point, increases in volume as, so to speak, Jesus slowly scans the distant landscape. It's seen as if from a rise, as if we're looking along a great flat valley toward distant mountain peaks. Slow pan, left to right and fade in super-imposed credits: *John Wayne*, dissolve to *and Iago Diablo*, dissolve to the word, *in*, and then the title of the movie; *The First Shall Be the Very Last* and fading out, revealing one of the most beautiful Wyoming landscapes imaginable.

Then in the great distance we can barely make out a horseman, slowly, deliberately riding toward us across a meadow. Music up as he keeps coming on—a genuine, first class movie-type hero, maybe twenty-five or thirty years old, tall in the saddle, broad-brimmed white Stetson, plaid shirt, buckskin jacket, neckerchief, chaps, boots, and a sparkle now and then from spurs and saddle. The horse looks like one from that sculptured group above the entrance to *St. Mark's* in Venice crossed with a strain from those on the west Frieze of the *Parthenon* in Athens, but with some Arabia in it and the wild mustang of the Great Plains.

Fade-in and superimpose lines of lettering that roll up over the landscape as the rider gets closer:

> "Spring in the valley and he came riding in from the Great Golden West. At first there appeared nothing remarkable about him, except that he seemed to bring the clear air of Wyoming with him. The closer he came, the more it was evident that this was anything but another drifter. Tall in the saddle, he rode easily with the dust of distance on his white Stetson, his boots, chamois vest, and chaps—easy, deliberate. Broad across the shoulders, narrow through the hips, he moved as one with the grace of his mount. Qualities of endurance, effortless strength, compassion and the reserve power of a coiled spring seemed to emanate from him and bring a special kind of life to the whole wide valley. On he came, lean, tan—slowly, steadily, easily on, with every mark of strength, competence, intelligence, and honesty upon him."

Then the last line disappearing at the top of the frame and our hero, a little right of center, now the only movement against the great western expanse. Then a slow intrusion into the frame from the left—an extreme close-up of another man, from the waist up facing away: Black hat, shaggy hair, side of dark beard showing, black vest, black shirt, and his gloved left hand raising the barrel of a Winchester. Then snuggling the stock against his shoulder, bringing our hero in his sights, slowly squeezing the trigger, the shot gotten off with a report that echoes and re-echoes across the valley, and our hero blown out of the saddle and falling lifeless to the ground. Freeze frame, and fade to black.

After about two seconds of the blackened screen the figure of Jesus, as shown in the first shot of him, is faded-in. He's holding a sign that reads, THE END, and right below that it reads, DAD SAYS IT'S TIME TO HIRE ANOTHER NOAH. Then fade to black, music up and out.

Mrs. Mullen Tells Me My Fortune

A Mrs. Mullen lived upstairs when we lived downstairs in the old Knights of Columbus building in Bloomington, Illinois.

When the delivery boy from the grocery store found no one at home upstairs, he left the groceries in our place. About an hour later I went out into the hall and buzzed her mailbox. She came to the upstairs railing, and I told her we had her groceries down here. "Thank you," she said, and she reached behind her for a large basket which she lowered on a nylon rope. "It's my bad heart," she said, "I have to take it easy and the steps are just too much for me."

I put the groceries in the basket, and she hauled it up, saying, "You teach art at the college, don't you?" and I said, "Yes, that's what I did." Setting the basket down beside her, she said that she always liked art, especially sculpture, and I said that was nice. "I like sculpture better than painting," she said, "you can walk around it—and you can actually touch it, if you want to."

"Yes," I said, "it's a tactile art."

"Whatever that is," she said, smiling and taking the basket of groceries away from the railing and inside her place.

Mrs. Mullen looked about forty-five, maybe five feet four or five, not fat, and red-headed. She looked Irish, which I guess by the name she must have been—and still is, if she's still living. Some things don't change no matter how old you get.

Maybe it was week or so later when I was putting my car away in the garage off the open space in back of the building. When I came out of the garage, Mrs. Mullen sort of hissed down at me from her second floor back porch, then motioned for me to come up the steps to where she was leaning on the railing.

"I didn't want to attract any attention," she said, "come in, I've got something to tell you—something you ought to know."

We sat down on either side of a little table, and there were a few awkward moments before she said, "Maybe you don't know that I read the cards."

"Like some say, a fortune teller," I said.

"Yes," Mrs. Mullen said, "sort of a gypsy..." That's when I noticed the stars and moons and some strange lettering woven into the loose robe she was wearing.

"Yes," Mrs. Mullen said, "I read the cards, and just the other day a young girl came for a reading. Now I want you to keep this secret—her name is Margaret Fischer, and she's a student in one of your art classes, she told me."

"Yes," I said, "I know who she is."

"But do you know," Mrs. Mullen asked, smiling and looking straight at me, "that she's madly in love with you? That's what she told me, and she was wondering what the future held for her."

"So," I said, "what did you tell her, Mrs. Mullen?"

"Call me Rosie, please," she said.

"Well," I said, "what did you tell her, Rosie?"

"She wants you real bad, Donald," Mrs. Mullen said, pausing before using my first name, leaning over the table just a little and smiling.

I guess it was then that I noticed that Mrs. Mullen was a pretty good looking woman, that she had nothing on under her robe, and from what I could see at the opening, her breasts must be large and firm—though you can never tell what sort of supports are under there and pushing them up.

"Yes," Mrs. Mullen said, "She wants you real bad, and she's really a sweet young thing, Donald."

"I guess she has a problem," I said, and Mrs. Mullen said, "Doesn't it mean anything to you, Donald, that someone wants you as bad as that pretty young thing wants you—even if they're not so pretty and certainly not so young—and wants you just as bad?"

"Rosie," I said, "maybe you ought to tell me my fortune."

"My pleasure," Mrs. Mullen said, "no charge, free for you, everything, Donald."

She didn't lay out any cards on the table, instead she said, "In your future I see that you're going to see me stand up, right here, drop this gypsy robe, and walk into the bedroom there and wait for you. Beyond that I cannot see, that will depend on what you see right now." At that, she stood up, dropped the robe revealing an astoundingly young body—no artificial supports under the generous, big-nippled breasts, narrow waist, and swelling hips—turned, revealing buttocks as firm as her breasts and walked slowly into the bedroom.

I sat there for a moment and then called to her, "What about your heart, Rosie?"

"Forget the heart," she called back. "Now you get in here and fuck the rest of me."

Epiphany in the Supermarket

While Virginia went about the block-square supermarket doing the heavy shopping, I wandered with my cart picking up only the obvious items—V-8 juice, orange juice, tasty snacks for the beagle, Rid-X for the septic system, etc. It being Friday afternoon, when little stands crowd the aisles with made-up women offering free samples of miniature bologna sandwiches, cheese spread, and mysterious chip-type things to dip in hot sauce—it being that day, I nibbled my way from one stand to another until I came to one where wine samples in shot-glasses were being handed out.

The man in charge of the wine sampling stand caught my eye right off. Well, it wasn't the whole man that arrested my attention—it was his face, and not his whole face—just the part from below his nose to his chin. You see, this man was heavily bearded, a thick black beard and mustache that between them almost completely covered his mouth. Hidden as if maybe he had no mouth at all. I guess I must have stared at this part of the man's face, because, looking right at me he asked, "Would you like to sample this new

Johannesburg Riesling from west Texas?" As he spoke those words the beard and mustache parted and a red-ringed hole in his face appeared—yup, his mouth, surrounded in a nest of curly black hair. At the end of his question the red-ringed hole disappeared, again almost completely covered, lost.

I said, "I guess not, we're going away for Christmas." This statement had no meaning for me; I just said *something, anything* in hope, perhaps, that he'd say something in response—so I could see that hole appear again. Fascinating.

"Going away for Christmas," he said. And there it was—reminding me of several women I'd known long ago. Ever since I went with Sarah in San Francisco during the war, I usually take a good look at where I am about to plunge. It was Mamie who had that tattoo just below her belly button which said, "PAY AS YOU ENTER." And though that was the first and last time I'd spied any tattooed messages in places like that, I continued to look just in case.

"Yes," I said to the wine sampler man, "we're going to Santiago for Christmas." I just made this up, waiting to see that hole open again between the surrounding bush.

"Santiago, Chile?" the man said.

"Yes, in South American," I said, watching.

"We have some fine Chilean white wine," the man said—and there it was again, for sure it was Hilda Burns: same hair color, same density, same curlicues.

"No need," I said, "to take Chilean wine back to Chile—coals to Newcastle."

"How about some Spanish Sherry—Jerez," the man said, mispronouncing "Jerez."

"No," I said, "we're going via Paraguay Airlines," myself intending this non-sequitur to see if it would confuse the man and produce some odd movements of that hole, but he just stood there looking at me—all hair, no opening among it. So I went on, "Have you ever noticed that big-busted women almost always have inordinately thin ankles?"

"In Paraguay?" he asked, tipping his head to one side a little.

It was then I thought of the wartime myth that Japanese women open in a horizontal direction—westerners in a vertical. So I tipped my head to the side so I could see the wine sampler man's mouth as a vertical rather that the usual horizontal. As I tipped way over to do this the man said rather excitedly, "Is anything wrong? Do you feel all right?"

"Nothing wrong," I said, "I just wanted to see you as a Westerner—straight up and down, you know."

"Maybe a cowboy hat would help," the man said.

"No," I said, "but a clean shave would help—make you into one of those Ingres models—you know, 19th Century Neo-Classical French paintings, looking like a nice pre-puberty girl-child."

This was when the man surprised me by saying, "And, yes, then I'd look like every other man—like you, you depraved anti-Christ."

That's when I realized that every painted image of Jesus Christ I'd seen in all my life had his face pretty much covered with hair—often times right around his mouth—and I left the wine sampler man stand wondering what that might mean to me. Who knows, maybe the next time I stared down to see if the lady-in-waiting was wearing a tattoo I'd see, right below, a *Veronica*, a true icon of the Savior of Mankind.

We Visit Merritt Waldemire in Texas

I was still pretty fresh at that College in Illinois where I was teaching art history and a course called "Art Processes," which I may tell you about sometime. And being new on the faculty and "in art," as they say, I had a lot of odd, extracurricular jobs pushed on to me—like chaperoning dances, designing Christmas Cards for the Trustees, and so on.

One job I got was overseeing a batch of students who were to decorate the gymnasium for the annual Christmas party, just before the holiday vacation. They had the idea of changing the basketball court into a "Florida Scene," as they put it—palm trees, coconuts, and such. Also they wanted to lower the ceiling by crisscrossing wires that would run across the place at a ten foot level, then lay crepe paper on top of the wires.

This took one helluva lot of wire, crisscrossing the gym—thousand of feet of wire. But it got done, and so did the palm trees, bales of straw for seats around the walls, coconuts lying around, colored lights strung, and so on.

The dance, they said, was a huge success. My then-wife and I were chaperones and remained until it was all over.

By prior arrangement, it was understood that the gymnasium would be cleaned out—all decorations down right after the dance was over. And this, de-construction, let's call it, was also my job to oversee. Which I did—rolling up all that wire and getting it into the big trunk of my car—right on top of what was already in there—a pair of my boots, an old radio I'd been planning on fixing, some batteries, my .22 caliber rifle, and some other junk.

So then it was all over, the goodbyes and Merry Christmases were yelled back and forth, and my then-wife and I walked out to our car, where we sat down, lit cigarettes, turned on the car radio, and just sat there for a few minutes listening to Bing Crosby singing off an old record in Gary, Indiana. It was "Let's Turn Out the Lights and Go to Bed"—those were the words, anyway, and I said to my then-wife, "I'm really not tired; I should be, but I'm not," and my then-wife agreed—that she wasn't tired, either.

That was in late December, 1941. It was a pleasant enough night even though the U.S. had declared war a couple of weeks back. I said, out of the blue, as some say, "Let's go see Merritt"—that was our friend Merritt Waldemire who was already in the Army at a place called Camp Wolters, down in Texas. My then-wife was game, so after stopping at the house for some cash, we set out—just like that! That's the kind of thing you can do when you're still in your mid-twenties—so you better do it while you can, believe me.

We blew along those highways—through St. Louis, Tulsa, and Fort Worth, wide open as often as we dared, and just about non-stop, except for gas and something to eat as we kept going. And then there was Mineral Wells, Texas, about a thousand miles from that Christmas party with the false ceiling—and only a few miles from Camp Wolters.

After a rest in a motel, we called the camp and finally got Merritt Waldemire on the phone, who wasn't surprised to hear from us, but not from that close. I asked him if he'd ever gotten a response from Loretta Young, the movie actress—and he groaned over the phone saying, "I'll bet she never opened the crate."

You see, Merritt Waldemire, right up until he'd been pulled into the Army, had planned on being a fashion designer, a designer of women's clothes—even though there was nothing queer about him. What he had done was get Loretta Young's measurements and designed and *made*—mind you, actually cut and sewed—a full wardrobe for Loretta Young. And when he'd finished, he built a fine strong crate with Loretta's new wardrobe inside. He was really going to surprise her, knock her silly when she opened that crate with this great bunch of dresses, gowns, he'd made to fit her perfectly—and which, Merritt believed, would launch him on a spectacular career as a "Designer to the Stars," as he once said. Loretta Young hadn't responded to the letter he wrote her—timed to precede the arrival of the crate by a few days at most. Nor to the crate full of clothes. And then, like overnight, he was in the Army at Camp Wolters, Texas.

I'm telling you this so you'll know why, on the phone, I'd asked him if he'd heard from Loretta Young. And that's why Merritt Waldemire—who'd been calling himself Jon Merritt toward the end—just groaned over the phone: He'd never heard from his Hollywood idol.

Well my then-wife and Merritt Waldemire and I had a great reunion that night in a bar in Mineral Wells where there were a lot of other soldiers celebrating, mainly by getting pretty well stewed, when one of them yelled out, "Bed check in twenty-five minutes." At that Merritt Waldemire, got up, bolted out of the place, waving goodbye as he got in one of the soldier's cars and sped off for bed check back at camp.

All of a sudden, my then-wife and I were sitting alone and wondering if our friend would make it back in time for curfew—the bed check. So we decided to race to the camp to see. Just before we got to the guard house I thought I saw the car that Merritt had sped off in—up ahead of us in the line. So I pulled around the cars in front to get a look.

That's when I heard a voice coming over a bull horn: "Stop! You there in the white one. Stop." And you can bet I did.

The sergeant, gun and all, was alongside like right away. "Turn off the engine, get out!" he said. Which I did without even asking why, I didn't have to: in passing up the line of cars, my front wheels had crossed the boundary of U.S.A. military property—and, remember, Pearl Harbor had already happened.

The sergeant directed another enlisted man to get in my car and drive it off to the side, *inside* the camp. My then-wife and I were hustled into the guard house where we were, as they say, interrogated and searched.

This went on for quite a long time, considering the time spent with the Provost Marshall after the sergeant and other non-coms finished with us. I won't go into the kind of general and very personal question we were asked, their stories of how the "Fifth Column" would be more and more of a threat to America's war effort, sabotage, and whether or not our friend Merritt Waldemire was a homosexual—I'll just say that in the end it ended with the Provost Marshall warning us, taking us back to our car, and letting us go.

The next evening Merritt Waldemire joined us at the same bar. He was surprised at what we'd been through, but now it was pretty much a laughing matter. It was in the middle of one of those laughing periods when I remembered what I had in the trunk of my car: a few thousand feet of wire, a rifle with a telescopic sight and lethal at a mile, radio parts, and old batteries. My God! What they could have made of that—accused my wife and me of planning to set up a land line communication system over that rise to the north and picking off the commanding officer—or setting off their ammunition dump, if they had one. "If they had opened that trunk," I said, "maybe my whole life would have been changed."

"Yes," said our friend Merritt Waldemire, "and if Loretta Young had opened that crate I sent her, just imagine how mine would have been changed, *really* changed."

It Happened on the Greyhound Bus

The story was that the Greyhound bus was on its route between Memphis, Tennessee, and Little Rock, Arkansas, with the usual mix of passengers—about fifty of them. Everything was going as usual, some people sleeping, some reading, some just sitting bolt upright and staring into nothing, a few looking out windows as the bus ran between all those little places, Shell Lake, Goodwin, Brasfield, Hazen, and on toward Little Rock. It was just west of Carlisle when an older man—maybe sixty years old and in a blue work shirt and gimme cap—doubled forward in his seat and began to yell at what must have been the top of his voice. The woman seated next to him, a matronly sort of about the same age and dressed in a kind of house coat that buttoned down the front, leaned toward the yelling man, looked toward his lap, and began letting out her own yells.

The bus driver looked up into his rearview mirror, then brought the bus to a stop on the gravel shoulder and hurried to the seat where the man and woman kept yelling in a strange contrapuntal way. What he saw he couldn't believe. But it was a fact: The man's belly-button had come untied and the loose end was now wiggling around in the man's lap.

"My God in Heaven!" the bus driver called out, staring transfixed. It was then that the woman next to the man who was now trying to get a grip on his untied cord, gave out a whining wolf cry as she opened the buttons of her dress to see that, lo and behold, her belly-button had also become untied. "Oh, my God help us!" the bus driver called out, raising his eyes to the ceiling of the bus. "Now there's two of them!"

By this time most of the passengers were in the aisle or standing on their seats to get a look. That's when the bus driver fell backwards into the arms of people standing behind him. They must have grabbed him pretty hard—he was a big man, maybe weighed close to three hundred pounds—and in grabbing him had torn open his neatly pressed Greyhound uniform shirt. And since he was not wearing any underwear, it was there for all to see; yes, his belly button had, like the others, unknotted itself and the loose end appeared trying to get itself back into a knot. No way.

Then, one by one, each person who got a good look at the three untied belly buttons had *their* belly-buttons wiggle out of their knots, the loose ends looking like thick inchworms at the end of a tree branch, reaching out onto the air in search of firm footings. It appeared a case of panic—like a run on a collapsing bank, like a contagious rumor that the end of the world was at hand, right now.

In an exceedingly short time everyone on that Greyhound bus was hysterically staring at his or her own bare abdomen, yelling or moaning at the place where their knot used to be. Yes, every one on that bus, except a boy who'd been riding way in the back seat. He was about thirteen years old and had a slingshot in one of the pockets of his khaki-colored shirt. When he finally took notice of that writhing mass of people yelling and moaning and calling on one god or another for help, he stood up. He was taller than you'd expect, and very calm when he asked above the din, "What's the problem?"

"Look," an old woman shouted out while holding her belly toward him, "the knot came loose, Lord knows what will happen next."

"Next?" the boy rhetorically asked. "Just you all line up here in the aisle, and I'll take you one at a time." Which he did, after slinging his belt of merit badges over his shoulder. "You'll take note," he said, pointing to one of the embroidered badges, "that I am a certified tie-er of knots."

And as the passengers came to him, one by one, he re-tied their umbilical cords in neat knots. "It's a miracle," an old man called out as he watched the boy deftly fix his cord into a knot more functional and more aesthetically pleasing than the one the doctor had tied at his birth in 1903.

"No miracle, no miracle at all," the boy said, "I'm always prepared." And the bus driver, standing erect, gave the boy the official three-finger salute known all over the world as the Boy Scout Salute—which the boy returned...very smartly and without losing a single loop in the knot he was at the moment tying.

And, as you'd rightly suspect, this Greyhound bus was late when the driver pulled into Little Rock. The bus dispatcher, raised hell with the driver. "You had great weather," he said, "next to no traffic, what the hell kept you?"

And the driver said, "You'd never understand, Mike, but we had real trouble—and then we just got all tied up."

I Was Saved from Going to School in Nazi Germany

I arrived in Madison, Wisconsin, a week ahead of time for that first full year of graduate school and was having a cup of coffee on the lawn back of the Union building when a former classmate from undergraduate days walked up. I'd never been much for Jack Van Koert; he'd chased a girl—in his family's Studebaker—who I was interested in during our freshman and sophomore years while I was still commuting between college and the Milwaukee County Home for Dependent Children. I made consistently better time with the girl, perhaps for the simple reason that she just naturally cared less for Van, but he wondered how I did it. Maybe the clothes I wore were the attraction.... He'd ask me about the shirt I was wearing, or about the one suit I owned—a suit cut down by a matron at the Home from one of the cheap uniform-like suits issued to all the old men in the Milwaukee County Infirmary, up the road from the Home. It didn't fit, and I knew it. It bulged in the middle, bagged in the seat, and skimped in the shoulders; the cuff size was out of fashion, it had too many buttons, and all the seams were rolled so it looked like a clearly outlined patchwork of armor plate. When Van asked about it, I told him I had it made that way. So Jack Van Koert took his mother's money and had a suit made like mine. Maybe I should have liked him for doing that, but instead it made me despise him a little more.

"Are you going to be on campus?" he asked; and I said that I was. "In what?" he asked; and I said, "In art history."

"You're not going to be enrolling in Professor Hagen's seminar, are you?" he asked, blowing out his cheeks.

"Uh-huh," I said, "why?"

Had Van smoked cigarettes, he would have reached for one then, but instead he put his left hand, all except the thumb, in the pocket of his jacket and went into a series of shifting contrapostos while staring out over the lake and stroking his chin with his gold-ringed right hand. "It's tough, Don," he said, "it's the real thing, real scholarship. If I were you I'd wait a year before trying it. How's your German?"

"Only Middle High," I said, "and I can speak and write it fluently—but I can't read it." But he didn't hear what I said; he never had.

Professor Doctor Oskar Frank Leonard Hagen's seminar met in an old room in Batts Hall with seats that rose in curved banks around a point dead-center in a table on a slightly raised dais. Standing down on the dais that first day, he announced that the subject of the semester's seminar would be "Modern European Sculpture," and that at the next session we should be prepared to let him know on what phase of the subject each of us would prepare a paper. The paper would be delivered with slides, a fully documented presentation of two hours—actually one hour and fifty minutes. There would be two copies of the paper, one to be handed to him to follow and annotate as we read from the other. After asking if there were questions, which there were not, the room went dark and Professor Hagen gave a two-hour summary of Modern European Sculpture. The slides went through the twin projectors like shells through pom-pom guns in perfect timing with whatever he was saying. The last two slides, one by Ivan Mestrovic, the other by his main source, Michelangelo, slid into place as Professor Hagen said his last words and the bell rang. The lights came up, and he said he'd see us next week. I was impressed with the timing, so exact, like two second-hands, one on top of the other on the same clock.

The following week I let Jack Van Koert say first what he'd chose for his subject, and then I settled on one, "Esoteric Sculpture from Rodin to Boccioni"; that would give me plenty of room to richly overlap and demean whatever he might say in his formal presentation. Van gave his paper three weeks before I gave mine. In those three weeks I worked like a possessed German professor murdering another in the pages of the hottest professional journal.

Once I had the first draft and the slides it was based upon, my roommate at the University Y.M.C.A.—W. Dean Lowry, who was taking an M.A. in Philosophy and who later became a successful insurance adjuster in Illinois—he and I ran full-dress night rehearsals for the presentation of the paper. Lowry ran the slide projectors and timed his copy of the lecture. Then, making considerations for an increased rate of delivery due to the excitement the final presentation would engender, the paper was brought to its final form with marginal entries indicating what my watch should be reading as I read down each page. These time calibrations were in units of thirty seconds. The final night rehearsal was made, Lowry and I horsed around, joked in the empty hall, and two days later the paper was given with, by special permission, W. Dean Lowry manning the projectors. I lost about ten seconds in handing Professor Hagen his copy as I went to the dais and switched on the lectern light. These I knew I could pick up on a long passage on page twelve. The hall lights went off, the projectors shot on, and Jack Van Koert got murdered for exactly one hour and forty-nine minutes and fifty seconds when, precisely, the bell rang and Lowry flooded the hall with light. The echo of the bell died in the corridor like Shakespeare's "knocking at the south gate" as I came back to reality, gathered up the paper, and stepped off the dais. "Just a minute," Professor Hagen said, rising from his seat in the front row and turning to face the group. "I just want to let you know before you're dismissed that this is the finest seminar report I have heard since 1922." The year on the current calendar was 1938: *Sixteen years*! I said to myself.

That seminar paper, my club for Jack Van Koert, became the basis for my master's thesis and put me in line for a Ph.D.

fellowship and stipend at the University of Bonn in Germany for the following year. But after the rape of Poland, England declared war on Germany, and I heard it come over my car radio outside Waycross, Georgia, that September, and shortly afterwards my fellowship was canceled. Someone "up there" must have been watching over me: I never went to school in Nazi Germany.

The Long Lost Philosopher's Stone

I was never much interested in what's been called "The Philosopher's Stone," an imaginary substance capable of transmuting base metals into gold, until one evening when I was reading about an early eighteenth century blacksmith named Jean Delisle who claimed he had discovered it—discovered the philosopher's stone and went about France turning lead into gold. By 1706 the word was out that Delisle was in possession of the philosopher's stone, and people from all over came flocking to his residence to witness how he could turn horseshoes, axes, and shovels into gold and silver. All by elaborate trickery, of course; which ended with his incarceration in the Bastille and death at the age of forty-six.

I can recall with clarity the first stirrings in me of what some ancient alchemist might have diagnosed as an extraordinary evidence of the occurrence of the philosopher's stone—whole and ready for use.

It was on an early Sunday morning when I awoke in great pain and letting out blood-curdling yells. I was all doubled-up, in the fetal position recently associated with momentous events in the lives of former President Richard Nixon and tele-evangelist Jim Bakker. With my wife's help, I was rolled out of bed and onto the floor. The pain only increased no matter which way I rolled, no matter how hard I tried to straighten out. The center of the pain seemed to be located in the lower area of my abdomen, but it moved around, "Like the worst labor pains," my wife said, doing all she could to help.

"Maybe," I said between gasps, "even feels like there's a baby porcupine in there."

"We've got to get you to the hospital," she said.

Still bent double and with my hands almost dragging on the ground, I made it to the back door of the car, up, and in.

At the hospital they wanted all the entrance data they usually demand, proof of insurance, biography, and so on. I couldn't see the woman who was asking for all this since the counter was way above my eye-level, so it was like talking to an echo on the floor. I never saw her; she never saw me. Then into a wheelchair and up to a semi-private room where the other occupant was sitting by the window and reading a book. The dust jacket had fallen on the floor where I could read the title: *Extraordinary Popular Delusions and the Madness of Crowds.* He appeared interested as the nurse and my wife worked me up and on to the bed. "In pretty bad shape, eh?" he said.

"We'll see," my wife said.

Once flat on the bed, the pain increased, almost to the point I couldn't stand it, and I yelled out. By then the doctor was there, and he administered a pain killer that put me under and out, but not before I heard him say something about a kidney stone.

While I was under I had a lot of dreams, hallucinations, or just plain nightmares. They were all played out against a sort of gigantic billboard that carried the wording of that dust jacket I'd read on the floor: *Extraordinary Popular Delusions and the Madness of Crowds.* There were movie-like scenes that had to do with haunted houses, people being poisoned, witch hunts, fortune tellers, horrors of the children's crusades, and university faculty meetings, but mostly about alchemists, those people who purported to change base metals into precious ones, especially gold. It was clear, in these drug-induced nightmares that what these alchemists claimed to have discovered, and retained for their own use, was what they called *The Philosopher's Stone*. And that name, *The Philosopher's Stone*, kept being repeated, over and over like a leitmotif in my nightmares: *Philosopher's Stone, Philosopher's Stone, Philosopher's Stone*—the magic stone that could turn base metals like iron and lead into pure gold. Also in my nightmare I could hear the doctor saying "kidney stone" which he alternated with pronouncing in a clear voice, *"Philosopher's Stone."* And after a while the doctor stopped saying kidney stone and said only *"Philosopher's Stone."* In retrospect it could be said that by a process of incantation the doctor had assumed the role of alchemist and converted a kidney stone into a philosopher's stone.

When I came to it was determined that, yes, I had a kidney stone, which if I could not pass with my urine would have to be removed by opening up the channel of my penis and going up there and getting it. This was before it was discovered how to dissolve or explode kidney stones inside the patient. When I heard this I resolved to do all I could to pass the stone in my urine. I drank gallons and gallons of liquid, and sure enough the next day out it came: a rock-like object almost a half-inch long and almost a sixteenth of an inch wide—in the shape of an elongated football or zeppelin. I caught it in the basin provided for this purpose. Plunk! it went, and I called the nurse. I was, as some say, "proud as punch." "I guess that's it, eh?" I said.

"I don't know what else it could be," she said.

"Oh," I said, "it could very well be something quite different."

"Like what?" the nurse asked.

And I said what you who are reading this have presumed all along, "Nurse, that could very easily be the long lost philosopher's stone."

Dr. B.F. Skinner and "Operant Behavior"

It has just come to my notice that Doctor B.F. Skinner died at the age of eighty-six.

In case you've forgotten, Skinner was considered one of America's most eminent psychologists. He studied human and animal behavior in ingenious experiments and hopes that his findings would foster creativity and curtail repression. That's what he hoped for, he said.

In his research and writings Skinner advanced the belief—*his* belief—that individuals could understand themselves and build a better world only through systematic modification of their behavior according to principles he promulgated.

Over his long career he worked on projects such as machines that teach, warheads guided by pigeons locked in those warheads, and controlled environments for infants. Some people believed Skinner was a profound thinker. I never did. I saw him as a manipulator whose ideas could have—and to some extent have had—disastrous consequences in the modification of behavior in individuals.

He admired the success of Nazism and Fascism under Hitler and Mussolini—their success in changing human behavior in the direction of support of the State. He said that "Fascism and other authoritarian political systems are capable of applying the technology of behavior modification, and the challenge to democratic society is to develop it first." Maybe like the race with Germany for the Atom Bomb.

Well, Dr. B.F. Skinner is dead, and if the ground, this earth, lies in peace, then he lies in peace. But his books and his behaviorist teachings, sad to say, go on.

In all my life I've been in the same room with Skinner only once—and that wasn't really a room but a large lecture hall in the Roosevelt Hotel, New York, in 1966. And that's what I want to tell you about.

I was in New York to give a "paper," as it's called, at the invitation of a friend, Dr. Sigmund Koch, at the time chairman of a section of the American Psychological Association. This was at the annual meeting of that Association which boasted one helluva large membership.

After I gave my paper, having to do with how psychologists might help understanding works of art—my point was that they haven't done much—my friend, Koch, said, "Why don't we look into some of the other conference rooms, and see what's going on there. Especially," he said, "let's see what they're doing in B.F. Skinner's session."

We got ourselves up like reporters—clipboard pads, a tape recorder, and so on, and entered the back of the hall where the huge crowd was attending the session arranged by Chairman Skinner and given over to papers having to do with "behavior reinforcement"—that is, how you get people to behave in certain ways—the ways *you* want *them* to behave.

Koch took one side of the hall, I took the other. With our reporter's equipment poised like in old movies, we first pretended to be interested in the presentation then going on—a young professor-type talking and showing slides full of statistics. B.F. Skinner, the Chairman and Master, sat in the front row and seemed to be operating the speaker by invisible strings, like a puppeteer.

Observing the church-like quiet of the hall, I knelt down close to a man in the audience.

"I'm from the Associated Press," I said, "we are very much interested in this particular session of the American Psychological Association; could you tell me what's going on?"

"That's Dr. B.F. Skinner, right there in the front row," the man said, pointing.

"Yes," I said. "What's this session about?" I asked.

"It says right here," the man said, showing me his program.

I looked at the program with which I was entirely familiar. "I see," I said, "it's about *operant behavior*; what's that?"

"It takes too long to explain," the man said.

"How about just a quick summary for our readers?"

"You can't summarize it," the man said, "and I'm not sure I could anyway."

"That fellow up there," I said nodding to the professor-type droning on about his rapidly changing slides and often right in front of all those projected charts and numbers so that they made a sort of camouflage outfit of his snappy gray suit—"That fellow who's speaking," I said, "what's his message?"

"I think it's about operant behavior," the man said.

"Like in the program," I said.

"Uh-huh," the man said, "like in the printed program."

This didn't promise much, so I moved on to another man sitting on the aisle in the audience.

"Pardon me," I said, "I'm from the Associated Press, and we're especially interested in this particular session of the American Psychological Association; there's evidently a lot of interest—this place is packed."

"Yes," the man said, "lots of interest."

"In what?" I asked.

"It's Dr. B.F. Skinner," the man said, "right down there in the front row."

"The real Skinner?" I said.

"None other," the man said, "living and breathing right there in the front row."

"What is this particular presentation about?" I asked, referring to the man with the slides.

"It's about reinforcement, I think," the man said.

"Reinforcement of what?" I asked.

"Operant behavior," the man said.

"Could you give me a clue as to what that is?" I asked, "I'm pretty new to this."

"No," the man said. "Doctor Skinner knows all about it though."

In the course of Koch's and my charade, I spoke to six people in that audience. It was the sixth person, a man of about thirty who said he had a Ph.D. in psychology, who, I thought, explained a lot.

"I understand," I said, "that this session is about operant behavior; am I right?"

"As right as the next guy, I guess," the young Ph.D. said.

"You'd rather I just moved away? Left you alone?" I asked.

"Not necessarily," the man said, "stick around if you want to—that's what I'm doing."

"Just sticking around?" I asked.

"Yeah," the man said, "once these guys finish their things, there'll be a chance to talk to Skinner."

"That's why you're sticking around, then," I said.

"Why else?" the man said.

"You want to shake Skinner's hand," I asked. "Shake the hand of the big guy, huh?"

"More than that," the man said, "he's the key."

"To open what?" I asked.

"Look," the man said, "B.F. Skinner's just like this"—and he held up crossed fingers—"just as close as that to the Pentagon, the U.S. Government. You get in with Skinner and your projects got a good chance to get government funding—cash."

"You've got a project, I take it," I said.

"You bet I have," the man said.

"Would you mind telling me about it—just a hint, I mean. Nothing that would compromise your research?"

"It's for soldiers—well for sailors and marines, too," the man said, "to keep them from getting brainwashed—reinforce the democratic ideals—keep them straight, you know."

"Like those pigeons Skinner trained to keep them on the ball, on the trigger of those air borne bombs, those warheads," I said.

"So," said the young Ph.D., "what, in the last analysis is so different, anyway—pigeons, people...."

"And rats," I said.

"Yup," the young Ph.D. said, "operant behavior—and Dr. Skinner really knows, he really does—and he's got the connections—why else do you think all these people are here?"

Along the Way in Academia

Maybe it was foolish for me, a painter from the time I was sixteen, to think that study of the history of art, under professionals, would answer a lot of the questions my painting was posing for me. Maybe it was just my simple ignorance of the fact that art history as taught by the predominantly German professors I ran into between 1937 and 1949 was concerned with something that may have been history, but certainly had next to nothing to do with art. But I went through with the academic program; all the way to the end that came at a sunny five o'clock—after the dissertation defense and congratulations at the coffee and doughnut ritual—when I walked out of that secluded room and rejoined myself in the open air. Not that it was all that bad, for I'd managed to a remarkable degree—by short but flashy exhibitions of "brilliance" in a few seminars and by merely seeing what was right in front of all of us to see—to distort the academic program enough to bring it closer to my own shape.

Common among the men under whom I worked in art history was an occupational incapacity to do their teaching outside of a rather rigid and easily identifiable system. The core of the system was the one first published in Germany about 1915 by Heinrich Wölfflin, and later, under the title *Principles of Art History*. Wölfflin had recognized, in a great number of works from the early Renaissance to the late Baroque, certain recurring characteristics of "form" or "style," each peculiar to the time and place in which it was produced. To these different characteristics he assigned descriptive terms such as "linear," "painterly," "clear," and "picturesque." For Wölfflin these terms had specific meanings in a developmental theory of the history of art. In a word, his *Principles of Art History* holds that Medieval and early Renaissance art is "linear," not "painterly," that it is "clear" and, comparatively speaking, rigid and flat. From that, the *Principles* go on in many words and few pictures, to outline a phase-like development through the Renaissance and Baroque in which the linear becomes more and more painterly, the clear becomes more obscure, the rigid and flat become more and more relaxed, flowing and three-dimensional. With Wölfflin's words, and with his selection of illustrations, the theory works very well. It is convincing enough within the historical "epochs" he chose to work with.

Wölfflin's *Principles* represents one of those terribly simple but beguiling ideas that gets to be much more generative than it deserves—especially in the hands of persons much less perceptive and much less intelligent than its founding father. In this respect Wölfflin's *Principles* is not so different from the theories of Freud, Marx, Lévi-Strauss, and many others. So, back in the late thirties and forties, at least, my major professors taught art history in a Wölfflinian box. No matter if the subject was "Greek Sculptures to the Fourth Century," "American Painting to the Armory Show," "Northern Painting of the Renaissance," "The Etchings of Rembrandt," or "The Sculpture of Gothic France," it was all Heinrich Wölfflin. All the student was given was thousands of slides with names, dates, sizes, locations, and some mixed biographical and bibliographical material—all to be memorized. With the exception of some iconographic nuances to bring to bear, all the student had to do was hang this specialized data on a Wölfflinian scale that ran from clear to obscure, rigid to flamboyant, etcetera, and then he had all that he was intended to get—of both art and history. We wrote papers, of course, but they were meant to exhibit how well we could use the library, cite and footnote sources, and avoid being "subjective."

I suppose I could say many the same sorts of things about courses I'd taken in English literature, history, and economics—all with the never-to-be-forgotten exceptions made wonderfully real and valuable by the few great teachers, regardless of the subjects they taught. And, I suppose, this is little more or less than lots of other people besides myself could say about whole passages of their education in academia. But even as I sat in those classes at Wisconsin, Minnesota, Harvard, and Ohio State, I was aware of the emptiness that all but the very least sensitive of the professors felt in dealing this way with what they must have know as a great part of the human heritage. Often the semi-darkened lecture halls seemed to fill with moans of their own agonized wrenchings as they read out from their labored notes of denial—denial of the import of the work of art projected on the screen behind them; denial of the life breathing in a least many of us in front of them in the hall; and denial of themselves, their own life experience. I can remember sitting in those twilight halls, my hand working from my eye as a telegrapher's "fist" works from his ear, my mind somehow free to range back to Magnasco's making the original of the counterfeit on the screen, back to the professor's young life in pre-Nazi Germany, or even England, back to my own painting and my own life, and to life all over the world—and I knew that I sat where a lingering death dwelt. I wondered how these professors, these men, could go on semester after semester, year after year if not by some mystic and horribly mistaken belief in the rites of their "discipline." I found myself hoping for their own good that in their private lives they were something else, if only alcoholics, snow birds, or flat-out criminals like Jay Gould or even John Dillinger.

In my first year in graduate school I did get some sense of how these men might be surviving as they strangled in the narrow-gauge spasms of their constricted discipline: by turning the minutiae of art history against itself in games and battles with each other. The playing fields and battlegrounds for these encounters were the professional journals for which they wrote "reviews" of each other's sallies in *ex post facto* architectural (or other) theory and old-time unsymbolic logic. With these magnificently honed lethal instruments they went at each other for blood with hopes of killing or at least mutilating. There, in the pages of oversized journals, these dead German professors seemed to come alive as they thrust and parried—their arms and defenses consisting of true or false attributions, correctly or incorrectly quoted documents; postulated monuments, spellings in five or six languages, listings of dates, museums, galleries, stylistic characteristics, and *catalogues raisonnés*. There, out of rigor mortis, they snapped up, twisted, and jerked in the heat of the crematoria they prepared for their opponents, "my distinguished colleagues." And this they did under smiles, ingratiations, and bowings—the civilized manners of the Old World. Linguistic arabesques of timeless wisdom, patience with all the ignorance of the world decorated their camouflaged frustration, never so honestly put forth as on that sign that hung outside the headquarters of C Troop, Second Squadron, Seventeenth Cavalry (Vietnam) showing an angry vulture crouching on a limb and saying, "Patience, my ass! I want to kill something."

The Second Grade Teacher and Outer Space

I was in the slide room getting my slides for my course in 19th century art when this very presentable young woman came and asked me where the "outer space" slides are kept.

Well, the art department slide collection of some half-million 2 x 2 inch color slides is limited to images of painting sculptures, the so-called minor arts, photography, etc. There is *no* classification, no slides about outer space as such.

I told her this. And then I said that maybe I could help if she'd let me know why she wanted those slides—for what purpose, and so on.

She told me that she was a second grade teacher in one of the city schools, and she wanted to help get her children, generally aged seven or eight, ready for life "up there," as she put it. I asked her if she, herself, had ever been in outer space and she said that she hadn't. "How far up *have* you been?" I asked.

"Just in an airplane," she said.

"How far?" I insisted.

"I don't know," she said, "it was between Austin and Dallas."

"That's on the land," I said, "about two hundred miles, but that isn't up or out."

"I don't know how high I was up."

"But," I said, "you want to get your pupils ready for outer space—out in the stratosphere."

"If that's what it's called," she said.

In the next few minutes I got to like this second grade teacher, even though it became clear she had no perception, no awareness of any of the theories concerning outer space, yet she still wanted to do something about it...which may be okay, maybe. Then she said, "You've been in outer space, haven't you?"

"What makes you think so?" I asked.

"I can tell by how you talk," she said.

"Oh," I said, "that's just a little cold in my head—affects the voice."

"It's cold out there, isn't it?" she said.

"Where?"

"In outer space," she said, and "Yes," I said, "it evidently is cold out there."

"Did you take any pictures that I could show my class?" she asked.

My God, this second grade teacher was persistent—now she thought she was talking with an astronaut—and I was beginning to feel like one. "No," I said, "I didn't take any pictures."

"Why not?"

"Because," I said, "my outer space is in my head—in my mind—and that's where it is for everybody except for a few, very few, people who have actually experienced it out there."

"Well, you've experienced it, haven't you?" she asked.

"Yes, indeed," I said, "I've experienced the outer space *of my mind*—where stranger, more wonderful things happen than anything that will ever happen out there way beyond this earth. Where do you think the idea of outer space came from—from outer space? No, not at all—it came from the outer ranges of the human mind working right here on this old earth."

"If that's the way it is, how can I tell my kids that?" she said. "And besides, I don't think I know what you're talking about."

"Don't worry about it," I said. "You're not alone—most people don't even know what Albert Einstein was talking about—out loud—way back almost eighty years ago."

"Who was this Albert Einstein?" this second grade teacher asked me.

"Oh," I said, "he was just a fella who traveled in the outer spaces of his mind and came back to tell us about what he saw in there."

"This sounds funny," she said, "I don't get it."

"Don't worry," I said, "maybe one of your second graders will clear it up for you. . . sometime, if you're still around, and remain in touch."

Potato Printing in Illinois

One of the courses handed me to teach in the first college job I had was a course titled "Art Processes," and it was to be taught to students from the college of education who were majors in education, aiming at teaching in grade schools. They wouldn't be teaching art, no, they'd be teaching the regular subjects taught in the third, fourth, fifth, and so on grades. This "art" course, I was told by the chairman of the art department, was what's called a "service course," and it was planned to acquaint the prospective teachers with some techniques, some "art processes," that they could later pass on to those grade school kids.

Not a very good thing, this—but I'm talking about how it was—and where I was—about sixty years ago.

The first time I did this course—which proved to be the last but one, I was strongly encouraged—told—to follow the outline that had been developed by my predecessor in this, a Miss Gladys Bartle who died on the job at an advanced age, I was told. Died right in front of the class.

Well, one of the "art processes" to be taught was titled "Graphics: Potato Printing." The outline for this process called for one potato, one paring knife, and some different colored poster paints. The process was as follows: With the paring knife, cut the potato in half, thus providing two flat surfaces, one on either side of the cut. Into, first one, and then the other of these surfaces, the student was to make cuts and remove some of the stuff of the potato. This would result in some parts remaining level not cut away—and some parts, *below* the level of the originally smooth level of the cut potato. Then the students should press these half potatoes, "design side down," on to the poster paint they'd spread out on a piece of oil cloth—provided by the State of Illinois. Picking up the color, on both potato halves, the student should then press them, alternating, into some kind of repeat-type of design on a clean piece of paper—*not* provided the State of Illinois.

Well, that was all there was to it—tell and demonstrate to the prospective grade school teachers what I've just outlined.

So the potato-printing process came up on the course outline in about the fourth week of classes, and I had already been chilled to the bone by the generally low level of intelligence of the group in my care. Not that I thought of myself as Einstein or Leonardo da Vinci. It was just that I *never* in all my life up to that time encountered so many underslung IQ's, so many semi-literate, bungling uninteresting people, young or old, all in one group. So the day we were to adventure in potato printing, I took great care, very slowly and with lots of repetition, first outlining in words the process then drawing a couple of potatoes on the blackboard, a drawing of the paring knife they were to bring to the next class session, and so on. Then I performed the whole process with real potatoes and a real knife—right before their eyes. With a question period that followed my presentation, this took one whole class period of fifty minutes—right on schedule in the outline provided me.

There's lots more to it than this—but I'm preferring to leave it out, believing that even if only your dog is listening to this, he or she can already make excellent prints with potatoes.

Well, at the next class period, I *reviewed* my earlier presentation—sound pedagogy! I had them hold up their potatoes for my inspection, then the knives. Being a young college assistant professor, and wanting to be successful and resourceful, I had brought a few potatoes and knives for those who forgot to bring their own—or had their baby sisters run off with their potatoes, or lost their knives on the bus, or between the car seats where they couldn't reach to retrieve them—or whatever.

Then, so to speak, on your mark, get ready, get set, and go—into this process of art known as "Graphics—Potato Printing." And most of these future teachers of America's future went to work. Only one girl—normal enough looking there in the middle of that group of thirty—appeared at a loss. She was sitting there, holding one of her potatoes and staring at it. I looked away, but when my eyes came back to her she was still staring in a very concentrated manner, smack dab at that Idaho potato. When she looked up I was caught staring at her. I walked back to where she was sitting and asked her if she'd been absent when I made my big presentation, and she said no. "I see you have your potato," I said, and she nodded, holding it up to me. "And your knife," I said, and she said yes, holding it out before her. "That's good," I said, "now you go ahead, cut it in half, and get going—if you aren't sure of anything look at what your neighbors are doing—okay with you neighbors?"

"Okay," they said. Things generally appeared to be going pretty well when my problem girl approached me at my desk. She had her potato cut through—not into halves, but what the hell, I thought. "What do I do now?" she asked. I couldn't believe this, I really could not. For a moment I thought that this girl was pulling my leg; then I thought she was just after my attention—but, no way.

In a mood that had been mine throughout all this about "art processes," potato printing and cookie cutting, etc. I said to her, "Look, Mildred, you take your potato halves back to your seat and see how thinly you can slice them—both halves."

"Thank you," she said, and went back to her seat and began slicing. As soon as she had done the lot, she brought them up to me in her hand.

Well, there she was with her very thinly sliced potato halves and holding the stack out to me. I said, "Mildred, please get me a paper towel from the dispenser over there."

"Yes sir," she said. She got a paper towel and came back to me!

"Now, Mildred," I said, "you put your potato slices on the towel, wrap them up, and put them in the wastebasket here." She did—so help me—exactly that. Then looking down at the little package in the wastebasket she said, "Now look what you done."

Spring Does Return

At the end of World War II, and while still on terminal leave in the uniform of a junior grade Navy Lieutenant, I went back to look at the college from which I'd been on military leave for the past three years. I'd already been to Milwaukee to see my father with whose life I'd come to graceful terms during my time in the South Pacific. I must have wanted to make this clear to him in some better way than just telling him that now I really did understand and that everything was okay with me. I took him to a baseball game, the Milwaukee Brewers vs. the Toledo Mudhens, and I carried a case of cold Schlitz to the best seats in the grandstand. For a while it felt like going back to 707 Chambers Street, back to the early twenties and Sundays on the porch listening to the Brewers play, and watching and hoping for another foul ball to fly up and over the retaining fence and land near our porch—for us. It felt like an unwinding back to a place and time before we'd lost each other. Soon the old road, lost at the fork twenty-five years before, would appear and we could travel it as if the time between then and this summer afternoon of 1946 had never happened. We'd come early to the ballpark, but what I didn't know was that an exhibition by the "Hell Drivers" was scheduled before the game. The cars were revving up before we'd finished our first bottle of beer. The helmeted, white-uniformed drivers waved to the stands, and for the next thirty minutes the far outfield was a montage of leaping, rolling, crashing, and burning automobiles. When one of the drivers ran limping from the flames of his capsized car, my father said, "By God, Donny, that's the way to live!" The Brewers lost in a long drawn-out game, and a lot more than half the case of Schlitz was left for the scavengers.

I bought a 1931 Model-A Ford coupe in Milwaukee and drove down to Normal, to the Illinois State Normal University where I'd been teaching before the war. I wasn't sure that I'd ever go back to teaching, but I had to look at the place again, walk the halls, hear the voices coming out of the classrooms, stand where I used to stand before I'd learned for sure that death was the one guarantee in life, and talk to whomever I used to know before the war. Foolishly perhaps I'd expected a lot of change, that besides VJ Day and VE Day there'd be some deeper signs of victory, some hard evidence of trying to do better with life. I expected that the returned veterans, maybe especially the early returned casualties, like the ones we'd transferred by the score from the burning cruiser *Princeton* two years before, would already be making the new case, but maybe it was too early.

In the hall of the old building called "Old Main" I saw the dean. At first he didn't recognize me, but then, with help, he did, and we stood at the newel post by the stairs to the second floor and talked for a few minutes—about enrollment and budget problems, his chosen topics. I stopped by the president's office and asked the secretary if he was in. He was. He asked what I'd been doing in the Navy; I told him and it disturbed him. He told me how difficult it was going to be for veterans like me to return to teaching "youngsters," as he called them—adjusting, and not letting our war experiences affect what we did in the classroom. Still he wanted to hear that I'd killed some "Japs," and so I told him, and even after he got red in the face and started to shake I kept telling him—stories of our boys making sure by keeping the fifty calibers on them until they were ripped to shreds on the parachutes and there wasn't enough weight left to keep the canopy open; and commands like "Mess boys take over; strafe survivors," after the pig boat was hit and going down. "But, President Fairchild," I said as I got sicker inside, "isn't it great to know that we all worked together to win; you here, holding the fort, as it were, and us younger ones out there doing our part?" And all President Fairchild did was shake and finally say he was glad I was back.

But I still wasn't back, and I knew it. I spent that semester in Mexico and taught the following year there in Normal, Illinois. After that it was Ohio State, a Ph.D., and teaching at Wayne State University in Detroit and by that time it was 1950, five years after MacArthur and the Japanese had met on the battleship *Missouri* in Tokyo Bay and the World War II was over. Even with some kinds of new language, words at least, and the ending of one part of my life in a going-away bonfire of momento mori and the unreality of a legal divorce, nothing seemed to have changed much. The veterans who'd come back in droves and went to college under the G.I. Bill opted for reading and a chance to get ahead in the world as it was, to provide statistics in support of a long deceased fiction, and, for a long time, I was one of them. However once time had stretched a veil over the sharp outlines of the maimed and the dead, and over the smallest vignettes of horror—like the puppy playing up front in the PV-2 while we strafed a bus full of people on the island of Truk—once most of that faded into impossibility, it was pretty nice again with the grass freshly mowed, the sky fleece-wisped—and spring come back. Memory is as self-protective as the chameleon's skin, and it covers the body no less. It changes or fades away in the face of overwhelming threat and shows only what will make it unseen. Its billion sensors pick up the clues to survival and cut off those that would cripple and kill. And in the 1950s, even with the after-image and echo of World War II spread across Korea, millions of veteran memories survived in protective coloration and selective hearing.

The sounds of warning bells that were beginning to spread across the country were not heard. Muffled, their tollings lay on the earth like the sound of bells made of meat.

Exercising and Shaving

Several of my friends do exercises—they jog, they do push-ups, they lift weights, they proportion their exercises to give so much for the "lower body," so much for the "upper body." They are much concerned with their exercises, their value, and even their "meaning." They talk about their exercises. They even write about them in their letters. If they had smoked sometime in the past, they no longer do, and if they drink at all it's a little beer or white wine when they're in company—a serious sign that they're really not against a little social drinking.

Now even those of my friends, who do all these exercises, some even investing in elaborate and expensive electric machines, none of them do physical work around the house or on their property. Just about all of them stopped playing sports long ago, if they ever had.

I wouldn't have spent any time or concern with these friends' exercising—that's their business—except they keep talking about it. It's almost as if exercising becomes the meaning of their lives. Well, what the hell, shouldn't we be pleased if our friends have meaning in their lives, maybe any kind of meaning? Or should we?

Imagining what perhaps awful things these people might do if their energies didn't go into the relatively harmless pursuit of exercising, I think we should take comfort in how they are and what they do with themselves.

And then there's shaving—simple shaving—cutting off the hairs on their faces, another activity that keeps a lot of my friends from serious, and perhaps harmful, participation in the real world. They've told me at length about "preparing" their faces with various commercially plugged liquids, colloids, towels, temperatures, and exact timings for all this. And then there's the cutting tool, the razor. None of my friends use the old "straight" razor—it requires too much control on the part of the shaver. It also requires sharpening and maintenance—so that's out. Most of my friends use what's still called a "safety razor." And they keep me informed as to all the "new and improved" safety razors: double and triple blades, some that cut off their hairs *below* the level of the skin—way down at the roots—and razors with swivel cutting surfaces, universal joint handles, and computer control of pressure to the face. As you can see, if you're so inclined, there's a lot to talk about here.

One of my friends, a former salesman of used pianos, can keep telling about his shaving equipment and his experiences with it and his face all through the TV coverage of the days news. And if you ask him a question about anything he's said—well, you're sunk. Comes the deluge!

And then there are those of my friends who use one brand or another of electric shaving machine. You can always tell—even among strangers—who uses one of these machines: They're the guys with the removed hair stubble all over their shirt fronts or exposed underwear. They're the guys who scratch themselves a lot—as those sharp little hairs work themselves under their underwear and into their skin in efforts to transplant themselves. These are the guys who increase their nuisance value by firing-up their cordless, battery-powered shavers during movies or public meetings.

And can you imagine how much these guys have to tell about how their shaving machines work? It's near endless—all about the nylon bearings in the spinning hair-harvesting wheels, the noise repressing insulation, profile-seeking sensors—and the low maintenance requirement.

As with those exercise-friends, these nuts-about-shaving guys find real meaning in their shaving rituals. So more power to these cultural cripples...Shave on, fellas.

Were we to go into matters of "face preparation" and "after-shave" treatments for the face-part of the male ego, we'd be here all night talking about just those two perfumed cauterizes. So we'll dispense with that.

As you might have guessed, there are men who are *both* exercise nuts *and* high priests of shaving rituals. Between these two demanding occupations, exercising and shaving, there is not time left in any day except for keeping their bodies trim (as they say) and the hair off their faces. This is why in the case of these "double-dippers" it is absolutely essential that their wives (male or female, nowadays) must keep employed at very well-paying jobs.

I'll leave it to you to guess just how long this sort of arrangement will successfully continue. For, as you know, these working wives (when female) are exercising and shaving more now than in the past. Sigmund Freud, the frustrated Viennese novelist, would attribute this to their "penis envy." When, as we know, all of it, on all sides, male and female, is only documentation of the grotesque power and success of advertising—and the general lack of meaning it encourages.

How else account for Arnold Schwarzenegger? But remember, he's an exception—he's made exercising and shaving financially, socially, politically, and educationally extremely profitable. This lout has gotten to be a multi-millionaire, married into the Kennedy clan, and appointed by the President of the United States to teach little kids about exercising and the eventual possibility of shaving.

I've Had a Lot of Dogs

During my long life I've had a lot of dogs. I never cared much for cats. I've always gotten along real well with dogs, and to all evidences they've gotten along with me in ways that could be called famous: Dogs and I have gotten along famously.

I like to watch dogs—even dogs who wouldn't be considered "watch dogs." In many ways I enjoy watching dogs more than I enjoy watching people. That may be because when you watch people they get, as some say, "self-conscious," and are often made to feel uneasy. If you watch people they get suspicious of you and suspicious of themselves. Their guess is that there's something odd with people who watch them; most people don't watch other people—so what's wrong with this guy who keeps his eye on you? Also watched people think, because they're being watched, that there's something wrong *with themselves*—something simple, maybe like they're unbuttoned or that the foam from their advanced formula denture adhesive has bubbled out the corners of their mouths as it did, all over Johnny Weismuller's lower lip and chin when they wheeled him in for his very last appearance—to receive an award for his long ago role as "Tarzan of the Apes." But oftentimes watched people may get to think—as the watcher keeps watching—that the watcher is discovering what the watched man or woman has, up until then, managed to keep secret—all the failures that their ignorance or their egos insured; their fundamental insecurity; bad tricks they played on people who trusted them; their sexual limitations; their unsuccessfully masked greed and avarice; their jealousies and hates. You don't have to deal with any of this when you watch dogs. Dogs just *are*. They are never bothered with thoughts of their shortcomings or of suicide—at least I've never heard or known of any dog committing suicide—and lemmings are something else.

Of course dogs can smell better than we can. And unless you perfume your dog or bathe him or her too often, he or she will smell like what they are: just dogs.

But we humans have been taught through the ages to disguise our natural odors—even as our ability to smell has lessened. Still, even with our anti-body perfumes, deodorants, and the like, dogs can smell right through all that, right through to the meat that's us.

Do you know that your dog has its *own* personal smell? Could you smell out your dog in a bunch of dogs—say if you were blind and not allowed to *feel* the dogs? I'll bet you couldn't. I think you might come closer to smelling out your wife of twenty years or your long-serving mistress, but only if you'd really smelled them often and raw, so to speak.

Yes, indeed, I do like dogs. Dogs may be my best friends and, in my experience, they've been—in the long run—more faithful that most people. To me dogs give no evidence of the recently advertised schism of body and mind, no displays of the dog's mind being out of sync with its body. Dogs, lacking anything like our sophisticated language—no matter that some dogs, being harassed by extended demonstrations of Pavlovian Theory are gotten to "say" *hello* or *Jesus Christ*—no matter such conditioned responses, dogs do not speak, read, or write language, as do those of us who claim literacy. No…but what dogs do have is a range of body language far more expressive than most of us have. And this is not so just because dogs run around naked as most of us do not. It's true their entire bodies are there for us to see, all the time. So their body language is there, constantly, for us to "read," so to speak.

In the often mistakenly praised, advanced, industrialized, or post-industrialized cultures, people go around most often with only their faces and hands, maybe their arms, naked. The rest of whatever body language they possess is hidden under their clothes. Hence the maxim: clothes make the man. But clothes do *not* make the dog—whether in advanced industrial cultures or in the backward handcraft cultures. Dogs, in this respect, are more like naked infants.

Yes, in my long life I've had a lot of dogs, but only two children, a girl child and a boy child, who came into the world like dogs—plumb naked—and those were happy days for us. It was only after they learned to talk a little and cover up their bodies with clothes that trouble and misunderstandings developed at one helluva pace.

I'll have to leave this essay now; my dog Rufus is sitting up beside my swivel chair and letting me know from his rich archive of body language—and some deep throated sounds that are neither hello or Jesus Christ—that it's time to move off with him, down the mile long road to pick up the evening mail. Bow wow, I'll be seeing you.

At Diego Rivera's House

I shared a space with Diego Rivera and his wife Frida Kahlo just twice—once in the house of Max Cetto, the architect, in the pedregal, and the second time in Rivera's house in Coyaocan, a suburb of Mexico City. Diego Rivera had already been to Moscow to have his cancer treated—or whatever it was ailing him at the time, and his wife was having a lot of trouble in her rear end and was sitting on an inner tube in a chair by the window. Diego Rivera sat in a huge chair which barely accommodated his enlarging bulk and held forth.

Now even though I've listened to an awful lot of preposterous stories—passed off as true—I never listened to more of that variety of unbridled fiction than what Rivera was putting out that early evening back in, I think, 1948. One of these so-called "factual" reports—given out as if he'd been a live spectator, right there on the scene—detailed how the moon was formed. Another had to do with the Czar of Russia's toilets—another about the actual shape of the Aztec soul, their *alma*, which he described in specific dimensions, shape, color, and density—and so on. Now because this was the celebrated Mexican muralist telling these tales, you listened with more than passing interest. If the tales were being told by some wino in Washington, D.C., you'd just keep going on your way. But, as we said, this wasn't just anyone—not even so special a person as a bonafide wino a few blocks from the President's bedroom. This was Diego Rivera, celebrated painter, more celebrated communist.

All the while Diego Rivera went on entertaining that group of eight people—as I remember—his wife, Frida Kahlo, fidgeted—I must say rather gracefully, if that's possible—fidgeted on her inner tube. I figured, as I saw her doing this—with a perhaps practiced éclat—that she'd long ago heard all of Rivera's verbal inventions and was spending the best part of her consciousness in working up another one of those surreal paintings for which she'd already gained a wide audience.

But I didn't mean to tell you anything about Diego Rivera or about Frida Kahlo. I just wanted to tell you about a Mexican doctor, a Mexican-trained M.D., who came late to this gathering and left early. I remember him most and best for the way he coughed—loud and hardly a rest space between long coughings—each series more and more promising spasms and vomit.

It's wonderful isn't it, what we'll put up with when we're guests in the houses of the famous.

Well, the Mexican medical doctor came in coughing, sat next to a notorious thief of pre-Columbian artifacts—a lean, ferret-faced German who would drive an ambulance onto a new archeological dig where the workers were bringing out pieces of sculpture, ceramics, and so on; turn on the ambulance siren; open the back door; and load up. As soon as the coughing Mexican medical doctor sat down next to this grand-scale thief, the thief got up, excused himself, and left. He hadn't said ten words during the time the doctor was there—maybe three minutes or less.

As soon as the thief was out the door and gone, the Mexican medical doctor said, "Did you hear how that man breathed? I give him no more than a month before he's a dead man."

So it went, there in Diego Rivera's house in Coyaocan, where he sat comfortably in his overstuffed chair and believing, I guess, that he was making assholes out of people—while Frida Kahlo probed about the open center of an innertube for a comfortable place for hers. And while a robber of pre-Columbian artifacts was enjoying his last month on earth—according to that Mexican medical doctor who, I figured, managed to get to the street outside Diego Rivera's house where he went into his last crescendo of coughing, puked, and died.

As I told you near the beginning of this, my intention was not to tell you about either Diego Rivera or his wife—and now I think I've achieved that. As I've been telling you what I've been telling you, my intention has become clear—even to me—it's that I have a very low opinion of Mexican-trained Mexican medical doctors. In some later episode I may tell you how I feel about Mexican-trained Mexican psychiatrists—and how I feel about some of the popular myths of psychotherapy to which the Mexicans—with their Aztec, Olmec, Tarascan, and Mayan roots—have contributed so much.

Nothing Short of Awful

It's nothing short of awful what human beings can get used to, and it's almost as awful that they can get along without.

All your life, it seems, you were being made used to a whole pattern of things like chronological history without space, English syntax, sleeping at night, the syllogism called logic, cleanliness, self-defense, polyphonic music, and something called absolute pitch with the American standard of 440 cycles per second for tone "A" and so on. All your life while you thought you were unique all you were was being made equal—maybe not so politically or socially equal but equal enough not to be legally quarantined for very long periods of time.

After a while—short for some, longer for others—you're in the pattern yourself and hardly knowing it after that "crisis of adolescence" created for the young by the old. It gets to be like knowing where the light switches are in your house, how high and on which side the doorknobs are, and which side of the bread is buttered. It's awful in lots of ways what you can get used to and hardly know, except that you keep expecting what you're used to.

You go to considerable and enjoyable trouble, let's say, making a lot of audio tapes of things you're used to to take with your recorder to Europe. It's an easy way to take a lot of music with you and speeches you took off the television and radio, like Kennedy's ghost-written inaugural masterpiece, and even a whole course in spoken Italian you took off records borrowed from the public library. You play them a lot before you sail and they sound just fine. And then you sail. After you get to Italy and get the children started in school and the rent paid and all that, you find the electrical current is different from that in Texas—160 watts in Florence as against the 110 back home—just like the guide books tell you. So, as you'd planned long before, you buy a transformer for four dollars and put it in the line and turn on your machine. Maybe what you're wanting to hear is your Vivaldi or that rendition of "The Eyes of Texas" that sounds like an annealed brass marching prayer; maybe you want to hear your favorite isorhythmic motet, or just Stanley Czerwinski's "Pickle Barrel Polka." These wants are a matter of taste and time, nothing absolute. So you turn on the machine, the lights light up, the tape reels turn, and the tape feeds past the pick-up heads as usual. You sit back in your 200-year old chair in a 400-year old room and wait for the extravagantly long blank to feed through to the music. But when the sounds come out they are not as expected. They're too slow in speed and too low in tone. So you shift the tape speed from three and three-quarters inches per second to seven and one-half inches per second and everything comes out sounding like a hopped-up hurdy-gurdy. Then there is the usual pulling out and putting in of plugs and fiddling with this and that to see what will happen, but still the music is either too slow or too fast, too low or too high in pitch. And before you go to bed between those invigorating Italian sheets as strong and as rough as square-rigger sails, you mark on the calendar that on the way to the Uffizi in the morning you must see the man who sold you the transformer and get this whole thing straightened out.

No, the transformer man says, he can't do anything about your predicament because Florentine electrical current alternates at 50 cycles per second and your recorder is built to operate at optimum on a 60 cycle alternation. The watts he can take care of, but not the frequency. Can nothing at all be done? you ask, and the transformer mans says it won't make any difference because you can record at 50 cycles and play back at 50 cycles and then everything matches. But you say you have music and plays and speeches recorded at 60 cycles—tapes you brought with you from the United States. Well, says the transformer man, those you can't play here in Florence; you make new ones here at 50 cycles and they'll play perfectly here in Florence. But you say you want to make recordings here and play them back in the States—all on that fine recorder you hauled through Hurricane Carla and clear across the Atlantic to Italy. No, the transformer man says, you play your USA tapes in the USA and you play your Florentine tapes in Florence.

For a spell you stare out the window of the transformer man's shop, out across the narrow street, over the wall and the yellow gray of the Arno to the Piazza Goldoni, and wonder what, in that view, would be most off-tone to Lorenzo if he could see it now. And you think of him and all the Medici with no electric light, and no tape recorders. Nothing you can do? you ask in a final kind of way, and the transformer mans says no—nothing. But you keep the transformer in some kind of odd hope that you can do something about the situation later, on your own. But later when you're back in the 200-year old chair in the 400-year old room you give in to the fact that if you wish to hear the tapes you brought with you, you will have to hear them played either too fast and too high in pitch or too slow and too low in pitch. So, relieved of that, you get engaged with other things like trying to decide why Hugo van der Goes' *Adoration of the Shepherds* looks so much like a perfect painting hanging there in the Uffizi. Certainly the fact that it hangs in that huge matrix of Italian painting has something to do with it—it heightens its Flemish quality. But that alone wouldn't make the blues so perfect as they are, nor create that equipoise of hard rusticity and the miraculous. It must be something about its being both a monumental miniature and a heroic enlargement of life that keeps it singing there in the half-light of the Uffizi.

The days pass and you've driven through Burgundy in snow, stood in the 11th century church of Saint Philibert at Tournus, walked through Cluny in the rain, slept under a huge down puff at the edge of the snow fields at Simplon Pass, and felt Venice alive in the streets of Bergamo, the hometown of Pope John XXIII the 2nd. And when you get back to Florence you turn on the tape recorder with Mozart being played too fast or too slow. But now it doesn't seem so exaggeratedly slow and you let it run that way while you walk on the loggia to see the olive groves with lettuce growing between the trees, and the young men planting with those old sticks we are no longer encouraged to call by their right name. And after a while you are brought into the Mozart and it sounds close to all right.

In a few weeks Vivaldi, Bach, Mozart, Hindemith, the lessons in spoken Italian, and the voices of people on your Stateside tapes actually do sound all right. Then is when you begin to think that it's nothing short of awful what the human being can get used to. But having gotten used to undertoned tonal and atonal music, and even John Kennedy with a base drawl, you realize that it's awful, too, how you could have gotten along for so long without that.

He Almost Bumped Me off My Bar Stool

He almost bumped me off my bar stool. I was just sitting there alone enjoying my own thoughts and some sipping whisky, when this guy—with plenty of room between the line of stools and the tables beyond—rammed into me, sort of at an angle from the back. My reflexes were still damned good in those days—fast—and in this case maybe defensive. When I turned to look at the guy, a fellow about my size and weight, he said. "Wanna make something of it?"

I don't know from where I'd dredged up the guts to respond by saying, "Look, fella, if I did choose to make something of it you'd have a hard time getting home without plenty of assistance." As those words came out of my mouth, I thought they were pretty cute—especially since, all-in-all, I'm a pretty peaceful person.

"What makes you think you could handle me?" the guy asked, looking me over.

"Easy," I said, "very easy."

"How much you weigh?" he asked.

"A hundred and forty this morning," I said.

"Christ," the guy said, "I've got you by twenty pounds."

"Twenty pounds of *what*?" I asked, looking him over as if cartooning the manner in which he'd just looked me over, "twenty pounds before or after you shit," I added, since I suspected this guy was mostly talk, anyway, and since I felt some creative urges floating around my increased heartbeat.

But then this guy stepped a little closer, closed the distance between us that was about equal to the length of his right arm, not counting what now appeared to be a fist at the end. "Take it easy, fella," I said, "I really don't want to be responsible."

"Responsible for what?" the guy said.

"You don't *really* want to know, do you?" I asked, turning to face my drink in a show of unconcern.

"Yes," the guy said, "I really want to know."

At this point I felt the animal taking over in me. The fact of the matter is I felt myself spoiling for combat—even though I was, at the same time, scared. Maybe this condition—wanting to fight—gains its power from being scared. Maybe being scared is what pumps up the adrenaline to go ahead to remove the cause of that scare.

Besides the feeling of wanting to fight this guy, there was also the feeling that none of any of this was really happening nor of any importance. In ways it was like a movie I was watching with me and this guy up there on the screen playing these parts. And in a real way I was inventing lines to speak, gestures to make. It was in that mode, let us say, that I'd spoken the line, "Take it easy, fella, I really don't want to be responsible." And when the guy came back with his line "Responsible for what" and I recited "You don't really want to know, do you?" and the guy said that, yes, he really wanted to know, I had a little trouble with inventing my next lines.

But then, as if written by some anonymous screenwriter, I said, "Well, since you're so unperceptive; am I or am I not wearing a belt?"

"So you're wearing a belt," the guy says, "and what if I take it away from you?"

"In that impossible case," I said, "I have my necktie, see?" and I flipped the wide low end at him.

"So," he said, almost catching the tie as it fell back against my shirt, "I'll rip it off of you before you've got a chance to use it."

"Look," I said, for the moment thinking I'd run out of things with which I could strangle the guy, "have you noticed that I'm wearing high field shoes?"

"You think," he asked, "that you could kick my balls off with those?"

"Oh no," I said, "in my sport that's considered unfair."

"So," the guy says, "you're wearing high field shoes.... "

"With leather lacings," I said, "one in each shoe, just the right length," and I made a gesture at my neck.

At this point the guy got loud, using some foul language and moving around as if he were in the ring, stabbing out sharp lefts and following with a series of right uppercuts. "Take it easy," I said, "U.S. Marines don't have the time or desire to fight fair."

"You're a marine?" he asked, stopping in the middle of one of his boxing demonstrations.

"Yes," I said, snarling a little through clenched teeth, "and we've learned what to do when we've run out of *general issue* piano wire."

Right behind us at a table, a drunken reporter for the local newspaper was telling the waitress bringing him another double brandy, that he was once a serious writer aiming to out do Thomas Wolfe, but that he never got a single one of his stories published. "My trouble was," the drunken reporter was saying, "that I not only liked fresh strawberries I wanted fresh cream with them—so I debauched my calling and became a reporter for this local rag."

"And now you've got both," I called to him past the guy who, I hoped was still thinking of U.S. Marines and their standard issue of rolls of piano wire.

"Both," the drunken reporter said, "and if you'll put away that piano wire, I'll buy both of us some double brandies."

It turned out that the guy who almost bumped me off my bar stool was a cad, a cheapskate, who immediately took up the free offer and moved over to the drunken reporter's table. I made an excuse—something about having to catch a plane. "When you get wherever you're going, send this guy a wire," the drunken reporter said, and laughed like hell—to me that was sure sign that he had the talents of a good writer—of fiction, that is.

Fifty Years Ago in Ajijic

After a few months in the Mexican town of Cuidad del Maiz where my first wife, Barbara, and I had finished writing and illustrating six children's books, we took off for what was to be more of a vacation—less work, that is.

It was in Guadalajara that we got the idea that it would be pleasant to spend some time near a lake. So we drove the forty or so miles to Lake Chapala, the largest lake in Mexico before its water began receding at a terrific rate. Like Mexico City keeps sinking into the marsh below it, Lake Chapala, it appears, keeps sinking, draining away, maybe into a branch of the same marsh. About any of this no one seems to care. After all, as the ads put it, Mexico is *"colorful,"* isn't that enough?

Well, fifty years ago Mexico City was a couple of feet higher than it is today—two feet or more has since descended into the Aztec marsh. And back then, Lake Chapala still had a lot of water in it—even fish. It was real inviting as we looked out at it from the little town of Chapala right on the water. We didn't stay in Chapala, however—the one hotel was too ritzy—that special sort of Mexican ritziness that back then had the ring of one of their tin picture frames. And with the speedboat docks and lobby filled with colonial furniture and Pre-Columbian ceramics, it was too expensive, even if we'd chosen to stay in a place like this, the Hotel Chapala.

We kept on going around the lake to a place called Ajijic, whose claim to fame, let's call it, was a sentimental book written by an American woman who'd lived in Ajijic for a while—the book titled *Dust on My Heart*. She'd left a few years before we drove into the place—and so had a somewhat celebrated pair of homosexuals—one of which, it was said, killed the other in order to avoid the possibility of a love triangle. It happens in the straightest of families.

Besides the natives—the Indians—there was a retired British stationary engineer who'd built a house on the lake, out a ways from the village, and a woman, referred to as a rich, white Russian, who now and then galloped an appropriately white horse along the beach. That was it, except for the Heurers—brother and sister Germans who rented out little adobe and tin houses to tourists. And there were a few tourists in Ajijic—some in the regular houses back from the lake, owned by Mexicans from Guadalajara and Mexico City and rented out from time to time.

Well, I didn't mean to tell you so much about this village, Ajijic—all I want to do is tell you about a series of events that happened around me and my wife while we were there.

We took one of the Heurer's adobe and tin houses, unpacked everything—including all our writing and painting equipment, the latter for making the full-page illustrations for those children's books, paints, brushes, and pre-cut sheets of illustration board.

It didn't take us long to exhaust our interest in the lake—muddy, with evidences of some over-ripe effluvia—and so it was only a few days before we were back at writing and illustrating. We were doing that on the miniature porch of our place when a young man walked up. He was in a regular U.S. Army uniform, ribbons and all, and sporting the oak leaves of a major.

Excusing himself for any interruption, he introduced himself as Major Murphy—Jim Murphy, and he said he'd rented the house of an artist, Ernesto Linares, full of Linares' paintings and that he was having a party for the tourists, like himself, on the following Wednesday. And we were invited.

It turned out to be a pleasant affair—good food laid out on a long table, fresh flowers all over, and plenty of booze.

Among the people there was a professor of Spanish from Berkeley, the widow of the owner of an Illinois coal mine corporation, a retired couple from San Francisco, a real estate developer from Dallas, a couple from Chicago who were collectors of primitive art, a former assistant director for Hollywood-type films including, he said, "Destination Tokyo" of 1943, and a few others.

Major Murphy was anxious to show the house which he'd rented for a month for only a hundred dollars. Every room was hung with paintings—all by Ernesto Linares, the owner, and the major, demonstrating that he knew absolutely nothing about art, praised every one in layman's language mixed a little with some military jargon. For me, in art and painting for most of my life, it was just another well meant but ridiculous performance—like as if I were to lecture about Sanskrit or the anatomy of Cro-magnum Man. But what the hell—if only the major hadn't kept going on and on and on about Linares' big paintings which were, really, pathetic in their obvious and unsuccessful attempts at imitating the often reproduced abstractions of Kandinsky. They were pathetic in the way that much of Mexican painting was then. It seems that Mexicans have their "own thing," which, when they stick with it, comes out okay. But a lot of Mexican painters—especially the younger ones, then lusted to go "big time" international, and the paintings that resulted looked like they were made following instructions the painters got over a very faulty long distance phone line from New York or Paris, or worse, São Paolo.

Well, I was patient enough, I thought, as the major kept on pointing and talking about Linares' paintings until he paused and asked my opinion—"as an artist." I was decent enough, I thought, as I said that I'd be willing to wager a high stack of tortillas that in *one hour* I could teach everyone present how to paint abstract paintings at least as good as any one of those Linares' paintings.

We all laughed. It was good relief to what we'd been listening to. Everybody laughed, everybody but the major who said he'd take up my wager if there was some way to decide whether that was possible or not.

That's when I said, "Look, I have enough paints, brushes, and board to provide any of you who'd like to try your hand.

You could come to my wife's and my place; I'd give the hour of instruction then and you could take your packet of materials, go off for the afternoon—each person by him or herself—and make an abstract painting. Then, maybe the following day, we could reassemble here at the major's place and look at them. I'll bring the booze."

"I'll have plenty of liquor here," the Major said.

And that's what happened: They came by our place the next day, I gave the promised instruction including such time-honored guides as—don't let your colors run off the edges, stay back from the edges a little, avoid leaving large blank areas, in other words, fill up the space, use plenty of color but let *one color* dominate—and pile up the color more in one area than in any of the others. Don't *draw* anything first—just begin putting color on. Remember: You cannot make any mistakes; it's plain impossible and so on.

There was only one question from the group—from the coal mine owner's widow, "If I get any paint on my clothes," she asked, "will it wash out?"

That afternoon, off they went, to be alone to make their paintings.

And the following afternoon we were back at the major's house. Some people had painted two abstracts, and it was the former assistant movie director, named Ed Bernoudy, as I remember, who suggested we stand them around against the wall for everybody to see. Which was done. To no surprise to me, they looked pretty damned good—and everyone was giggling with what I'd call "personal satisfaction."

"The stack of tortillas is yours," the Major said to me, "it's fantastic."

"Not at all," I said.

It was Ed Bernoudy, the movie man, who said, "It looks like a real exhibition—how would we get titles for these?"

"Easy," I said, "let's go down the line, look at each painting—one at a time—and we'll say things, just talk, and you'll see—a perfect title will pop out."

It did, for each painting: titles like "More Is More," "Love Blooms in Narrow Gardens," "As You Were," and "Money Isn't Everything." And Ed Bernoudy was busy writing the titles on the backs, and having done with that he said, "Now for prices—what's each one worth?"

Prices were decided the same way titles were decided. So now here was a group of titled and priced paintings. Time for another round of drinks.

Then Ed Bernoudy said, "We have enough for an exhibition, right here in front of us—first-class stuff. Now all we have to do is find a place to show it—like the ritzy Hotel Chapala! Any objections?"

"Viva!" the Spanish professor said. And so it was agreed.

Back at our place, Barbara and I matted the paintings—wide white cardboard frames, so to speak. It's surprising what neat white mats will do for almost anything. They looked great, real professional. And it was agreed that the whole lot would be exhibited as the work of one man; this would be a one-man show. A name for this non-existent artist was invented: CARLOS BEACLO, and a short biographical statement: Born in Spain, studied with Campendonk and Picabia, moved to Paris and was forced undercover with the Nazi invasion and presently, old and ailing, but still actively painting, lives incognito, someplace in Mexico.

The major had a big, like new, pre-war Cadillac, and that's what was used to take the exhibition, the neatly typed biography, and Ed Bernoudy, wearing a beret and one of the huge diamond rings that once belonged to the dead coal mine owner and now was part of his widow's inheritance.

The major, as chauffeur, drove Bernoudy up to the port cochere of the Hotel Chapala, stopped right there, and Bernoudy—pictures and all—disappeared into the hotel. He was inside for quite a while, and then reappeared, waving us to come in and help.

The scene in the large lobby was something to behold: The owner's wife—a Señora Ochoa—was directing a couple of *mozos* in removing the colonial furniture into other areas—clearing the wall space for the Carlos Beaclo exhibition.

Well, the exhibition was hung, and remained up through *Semana Santa*—Easter week in Mexico. And during that time—by whose efforts I don't know, but I suspected it was the work of Ed Bernoudy—a review of the Carlos Beaclo exhibition was carried in a Guadalajara newspaper—can you imagine? Sure, I don't even have to imagine—I read it.

When we went to take down the exhibition, Señor Ochoa was there—and he apologized for not selling more than two of the paintings, giving the *cash* to Bernoudy.

So, then it's over. Well, almost over. We brought the paintings back to the major's place and had them stacked up there, when Ernesto Linares, the artist and owner of the house the Major was renting—when he hit Ajijic to check on his house, heard there'd been another painter's exhibition, right on his ground in Chapala. He spread out the painting's and looked carefully at them. I was there at the time, and I asked Ernesto Linares if he knew Carlos Beaclo.

After a bit he said, "Yes, I know who he is; I've never met him, but yes, it's plain to see, he studied with Campendonk; sometimes I confuse him with a Spanish musician, though."

So things went, a half-century ago in Mexico. And the story's not over yet. When it came time for Barbara and me to leave Ajijic—get back to the grind back home, and we were saying our goodbyes, all around, we couldn't find Ed Bernoudy at the miniature *cantina* where he spent an awful lot of his time, so we went to his digs. He wasn't there either, and as Barbara and I stood wondering where to look next, I noticed in the wastebasket beside Bernoudy's typewriter table a lot of crumpled carbon paper. It reminded me of the care with which we had to dispose of carbon paper in the Navy during the war. All used carbon paper had to be burned since if you hold it up to the light—sure enough you can read it plain as day, as some say.

So I picked one of the carbons out of the wastebasket, walked over to the window, and held it up.

"Look at this, Barbara," I said. And she read aloud Ed Bernoudy's letter addressed to the Director of the Museum of Modern Art, New York. It praised the art of the newly re-discovered painter Carlos Beaclo and offered his, Bernoudy's, help as agent in putting together a retrospective exhibition of Beaclo's work—right there in New York City.

So far as I know that exhibition was never realized—was it?

I Didn't Go Around the World

Sheboygan, Wisconsin, is only fifty some miles north of Milwaukee, so I drove up there a week or so before I'd be beginning my first teaching job—to look for a place to stay. My contract read for nine months, from September to June of 1935 at a salary of $1026.00. That comes to $114.00 a month—not bad for those times and since I had next to zero in my pocket and nothing in any bank. But I did have my 1928 Model A Ford roadster bought with money I'd made painting wall decoration for club dances, political rallies, and such—total cost of $100.00.

In Sheboygan, after casing the town, I drove out to the north end. Big expensive houses—mansions—floating on manicured lawns, many running east to the tree covered banks high above the lake. I was just looking now, enjoying it. There'd be no place for me out here with the rich, and I knew it, but this was sure a nice place. I rolled along slow, craning my neck. And then across one of those wide lawns I saw, through a big arched window, what looked like a huge Chinese vase standing just inside. I stopped, got out of the car, and took a few steps on to the lawn. Yes, it was Chinese—and right to one side of it, partly shaded, was a woman looking straight out at me...and smiling. When I turned to leave, the front door opened, and there she was.

She looked about forty—later I found out she was fifty—a really good-looking woman.

I told her I wasn't snooping, just trying to get a better look at that Chinese vase there, and she said, "You knew it was Chinese."

"Yes," I said, "I've never been to China, but this kind of thing is my business...art." By then she'd come out on the walkway a little.

"Come in," she said, "and have a good look at it." Which I did.

In the hour of talk that followed she sort of got going when I told her I was the new high school art teacher. She thought that was wonderful, that she loved art—and but for the "great tragedy" of her life, she would have taken up with a career in art, in nature. I wasn't so much interested in this woman's interrupted career plans as I was in this "great tragedy of her life," but I didn't have the guts to ask about that.

She looked rather pretty, for a woman her age, I mean, sitting there on the beautiful settee, crossing and uncrossing her ankles, talking in what I thought of as a refined, exact English, and telling me that she was Mrs. Helen Hainer, born in upstate New York—in or near Saratoga Springs, as I remember—and that her husband was so sick that even the Christian Science practitioners couldn't help. He was upstairs in bed, she said, and when she said that I thought I could hear him tossing wildly and fighting for breath up there—but that was my imagination, I figured.

Mr. Hainer was vice-president of the Volrath Corporation, she told me, known the world over for its pots and pans manufacture—right there in Sheboygan. She didn't appear at all emotional while telling me about Mr. Hainer's illness, which, I gathered, would prove to be terminal, as some people say. So I was wondering if her marrying Henry, as she called Mr. Hainer, was "the great tragedy" of her life—that she had other hopes and plans back then, whenever that was.

Just before I left, Mrs. Hainer said there was a nice big bedroom—unused for years—upstairs, and if I wished I could stay there. "Come," she said, "come take a look at it."

It was a fine bedroom with a big closet, a desk, chairs and, as she pointed out, an antique Jenny Lind bed, named, she told me, for Johanna Jenny Lind, a Swedish operatic soprano of years ago. A large window gave to a view down the bluff and out across the lake—Lake Michigan…really beautiful. The bathroom was directly across the wide hall where a large Regina music player stood. It was of those that played big flat circular brass "records," let's call them—perforated or punched through producing nibs on the back so that when the machine is wound up, the brass records turn, the nibs contact reed-like protrusions that vibrate and give off sounds—real music. I didn't know this when Mrs. Hainer was showing me the bedroom but I found out later when she played it for me.

A week or so later, as Mrs. Hainer and I had agreed, I drove up to the house to take over that upstairs bedroom. She met me at the front door letting me know that Mr. Hainer had died and was buried a couple of days before. She wasn't wearing black, or anything like that. In fact, she was colorfully dressed and smiling a little. I said I was sorry about her husband's death. Mrs. Hainer didn't say anything—she just looked down at the floor and took what some call a "deep breath," and then, very slowly exhaled.

"Come," she said, "I was just having tea," and we walked together into a kind of sun parlor. There was an ornate samovar on a marble-topped table next to another, linen-covered table where the cups and saucers—two of each—were set out, not on opposite sides of the table, but on the same side, and a bottle of Scotch between.

I made some comment about the samovar with its little alcohol flame burning under there, and Mrs. Hainer said it was quite old but still working beautifully. She drew two cups of tea from the spigot and we sat down next to each other at the linen-covered table. She hiked up her dress past her knees as she settled into her chair—perhaps in order to get her legs more easily under the long-overhanging linen table cover. "Sugar?" she asked, and I said, "Yes, a spoonful," and she put it in my cup.

"I'll let you help yourself to this," she said, moving the bottle of Scotch close, "it does wonders for this tea," which she named and which had no meaning for me. So I poured a shot into my tea, and she did the same for hers.

A little later when, to my surprise, our knees, touched under the table and remained in contact with an increasing pressure, I looked straight at Mrs. Hainer. When I felt her hand high on my thigh, I thought of Mr. Hainer, now dead and six feet under, a short chill and a shudder went through me. At that, Mrs. Hainer said, "Oh, my boy, am I hurrying you?" and her hand slid from my thigh. Really, I wish she'd kept it there and gone on up, but I answered "No, Mrs. Hainer, it's all right." I must have sounded unconvincing, because at that she got up saying, "Come, bring your tea, I want to show you something."

We walked through the living room to the library, and motioning to a big leather chair, she said, "You can sit there," which I did. Then, facing away toward a huge table with enormously fat rounded legs, she got down on her knees and "fiddled," as we used to say, with one of the legs, for, maybe, two or three whole minutes. I just watched. It made no sense to me: is this what she wanted to show me—how she could fiddle with a table leg? A sort of "dry run" before getting down to it—whatever it was she wanted to show me?

Well, after a bit I heard a loud click and a door in the table leg opened. Mrs. Hainer reached in and brought out a lot of small cloth bundles. She unrolled them on the table—spread out what was inside—Good God! Jewels, piles of them—diamonds, rubies, and a lot I couldn't identify, spilling over the edge of the table now. "And, they're all mine," Mrs. Hainer said, "all mine, Donald."

I had a feeling that I should say something, but nothing came—not even while she gathered up the jewels, sort of hugging them against herself.

The truth is I was thinking back eight or nine years when I found a broken pocket watch on the loading platform back of the Piggly-Wiggly store. On its caved-in face it said, "Swiss movement, 17 jewels." At home on the kitchen table I got the back off, and sure enough, there were little white and red jewels inside. With an ice pick and a knife I got ten of them out—ten tiny jewels. Come to think of it now, I don't know whatever happened to them. Got lost, I guess.

After Mrs. Hainer's jewels were again secreted in the table leg we had some more tea, and I drank a lot of Scotch without tea. I remember saying goodnight after I'd moved my stuff in from the Ford, and flopped into the Jenny Lind bed.

I stayed in Mrs. Hainer's house for half the school year, close to five months. She told me to call her by her first name, Helen—and she had begun calling me Don. She said that name,

Don, reminded her of Spanish men of high rank. We got along very well, sometimes dancing together in the upstairs hall to the music of that lavish looking Regina music machine sometimes drinking wine between changing those big brass records. We kissed pretty much and "petted," as they used to say—and felt up each other, but, maybe, as Helen Hainer had said earlier, she didn't want to hurry me—which, at the time suited me okay, even though in later years I wondered why it did—or why I said that it did.

Just before the end of that first semester of my teaching art a Sheboygan High School, Helen was sitting in her living room when I came in after having supper at the Ford-Hopkins drug store downtown. She was in a most happy mood, and looking swell. She left her chair, came, and flung her arms around me, saying she'd just received the best of best news. "Yes," she said, "it's come true at last: I'm going around the world with William Beebe—very slowly around, take lots of time."

Now, I knew who William Beebe was—a famous naturalist and explorer who wrote a book I'd recently read, called *Half Mile Down*—all about his going down in the ocean—over three thousand feet down—in what he called a bathysphere.

"And," Helen went on, "it's all fixed, Don—you're coming with me, with us. I'll be your companion, and I'll be yours—Bill understands everything,"

"Bill who?" I asked."

"Why..." she said, "*Bill* Beebe, like I said—we've been friends for a long time—since before Henry and I were married."

Well, I just stood there as Helen Hainer went excitedly on about Bill, and going around the world so slow with him and me. I was wondering why not go around the world—slow or fast—with just Bill, why me too? But I guess I knew the answer to that—and the prospect was not unappealing at first, but not in the seconds that followed with me thinking about Barbara, my girl in Milwaukee, my job—lots of things I had foggily imagined as my future.

And then I had a vision—or a hallucination—very sharp and clear, and insistent. There it was, a picture of the three of us, Bill Beebe, Helen Hainer, and Donald Weismann packed together in that bathysphere, three or four thousand feet below the Pacific or Indian Ocean—yes, and the air hose, the oxygen supply cut off, and then the main cable snapping and the three of us going deeper than even Bill Beebe had planned—down to the very bottom. Yes, and bumping along on the ocean floor in slow motion with the three of us all dead as doornails, as some used to say, in that bathysphere. Sorry Helen, no way.

The next school year, and my last at Sheboygan High, I took a room, by the month, in the old, un-remodeled Foeste Hotel on Main Street. For a while a rumor floated around that Helen Hainer had married William Beebe in some far off place—but nothing detailed or official.

As I sit here now in Texas, and in my ninth decade of life above water, I'm hoping that Helen Hainer, with all her jewels, managed to convince time to run backwards—back before that "greatest tragedy" of her life, as she'd put it, had a chance to happen. Back, way back, before Bill Beebe married some other woman, and Helen went on to marry that now-dead pot and pan man in Sheboygan, Wisconsin.

And, you know—I like to think that maybe I helped assure the undoing of that tragedy by my refusal to enter that crowded and cramped bathysphere.

Why Sam Houston's Wife Left Him

The seven-year drought had just ended in Texas when I was invited by J. Frank Dobie, the Texas writer, along with Walter Prescott Webb the historian and Harry Huntt Ransom, then on his way to becoming president of the University of Texas, out to Dobie's ranch some miles outside Austin.

Dobie drove the old car, and if nothing else happened that day it still would have been a memorable one, for if Dobie had ever learned to drive a car, he had forgotten all of it. Once off the highway, he drove where, it seemed, there'd never been any roads. Sometimes he followed cattle or deer paths, other times the banks of a creek and always too fast with his eyes off to the left and right—rarely straight ahead—and pointing out and yelling out this or that name of some grass or plant that hadn't been seen in the area for the seven years of drought.

At Dobie's ranch house, that very hot day, the Jack Daniels Tennessee Whisky came out pronto—with Dobie saying, "Don't use this elixir as a thirst quencher—that's what water's for; Old Jack is for the soul." So in the hot ranch house without even a fan for a breeze, you find that drinking whisky there is like drinking it in the sun on Pityilu Island, almost smack on the equator. None of us got drunk, still, come to remember it, there was not one present able to make such a judgement.

While Dobie's old Mexican hand went about getting the steaks ready for the fire, the beans, and the rest, we were invited to take a dip in the tank off some hundreds of yards from the house. A tank, as you may know, is a large bulldozed hole made to impound water. This tank was a really big one—maybe one hundred feet across and pretty well filled with those first post-drought rains—muddy, but what the hell; that second fifth of Old Jack had done its soul work.

So then we're in the tank, Dobie and Walter Webb in their underwear, me in my trunks and Harry Ransom walking around the edge in his blue serge suit.

Mainly, Dobie and Webb just floated on their backs and talked looking straight up as if at God. I remember my role as being almost without recitable lines, a kind of walk-on role like that of a butler who helps keep the stage from blankness between the real action and words of the principals of the play. I do remember my calling out to Harry Ransom: "How you doing out there Mr. President?" and Harry answering with, "T.S. Eliot has said yes for a visit this winter," and I said, "Gee, that's great."

The floating talk between Dobie and Webb came and went with the slightest breeze that was just coming up until Dobie asked Webb:

"Any new information about why Sam Houston's wife left him?" I have since learned that this has been a long standing question—in fact that ensuing exchange may have been more apocryphal than anything else.

"Well, yes and no," said Webb. "You'll remember," he went on, "that old Sam Houston was seriously wounded in the Creek Campaign in 1814 at the Battle of Horseshoe Bend."

"Yes, I know," Dobie said, "and that his wound never did heal up."

"And that it stank to high heaven and really sickened Eliza," Webb said, referring the Mrs. Houston—maiden name Allen, Eliza Allen Houston.

"You've heard about that," Dobie said, "it's been known a long time, and it's never been given as the reason she left Sam."

"I've heard about Sam's lieutenant," Webb said, "the one who said that no matter how hard he was pressed he'd never ask Sam why his wife left him."

"Yes," Dobie said, "I've heard that."

"And what Sam said to his lieutenant," Webb said.

"What was that?" Dobie asked.

"Well," said Webb, "he asked the lieutenant if he could keep a secret, and the lieutenant began to drool expecting he was about to get the straight dope. 'Oh yes sir,' the lieutenant promised, 'I sure can keep a secret, sir.' And then Sam Houston said, 'Come closer lieutenant,' and then he whispered in his ear, 'Lieutenant, so can I.'"

"And that's where it stands?" Dobie inquired.

"That's where it stands," Webb said.

"Not much of a story, is it," Dobie said; "about time for those steaks."

And to myself I agreed, it wasn't much of a story—as you've found out by reading this.

Anything Imagined Can Happen

Tom Wolfe in his essay, "Stalking the Billion-footed Beast—A literary manifesto for the new social novel," quotes Malcolm Muggridge as saying, "We live in an age in which it is no longer possible to be funny. There is nothing you can imagine, no matter how ludicrous, that will not promptly be enacted before your very eyes, probably by someone well known."

When I read that in *Harpers* some time ago, I enjoyed what it said, but I didn't believe it. Even though just about all of my friends find it near impossible to be funny—at least in my estimation—there *are* some people who can. And I don't mean people like Bob Hope, Jay Leno, Ronald Reagan, and such. And although I know how our own memory can trick us, I still believe I remember funnier times, funnier people, in the past. Maybe all of us find it easier to be funny when we're young—even though I think I, personally, have become capable of being funnier the older I get. Most of my aging friends, at last respecting the fact of mortality—that they're heading for the hole or the furnace—find it more difficult, if not impossible, to be funny, or, for that matter, entertaining. And my young friends seem to make most of their humor, let's call it, by repeating commercially reproduced jokes, let's call them. They are, of course, funny in themselves, but they don't know that as they go about trying to pile up commercially autographed symbols of material success—for example: Rolex watches; BMW's and Mercedes; five hundred dollar fabric, plastic, and rubber shoes for walking, jogging, playing games, and even for just sitting down while drinking Gatorade, Pepsi-Cola, or Dr. Pepper, etc.

So, even with all this, I still think it's possible to be funny, but I'd agree it's getting more difficult.

About the other part of Muggridge's statement—"There's nothing we can imagine, no matter how ludicrous, that will not promptly be enacted before [our] very eyes, probably by someone well known"—well, about that I had doubts immediately upon reading it.

Convinced partly by myself, and partly by people who have told me so, I believe I have a noticeably above-average imagination. Without a damned good imagination I would never have acted—over a period of sixty years—as if I was a college professor, an artist, a U.S. Naval officer, an administrator, a scholar, a father, and so on. Really, to be truthful, I believe I have one helluva imagination. I've always thought that I could imagine *anything*.

So when I read Muggridge's statement about how we cannot imagine *anything* that won't actually happen sooner or later—and probably sooner. I gave it a lot of thought. I spent some of my valuable time imagining things, events or what you have you, that just will never come to pass in the so-called "real" world.

But you know what? I discovered that anything I could imagine might very well get enacted right here in this real world of gravity, temperature, birth, and death.

Let me give you a very short list of things which, at first, I thought would never be enacted in this life, and which, upon more thought, I came to believe *would* be enacted by live people and before long. This list is not in the order of importance; just a random list:

1) The Pope, whichever one is in the Vatican at the time, will give up the Papacy to marry one of his Cardinals—the Mother Church having previously given its blessing to marriage in which both parties are of the same sex.

2) A large, black, African-American man accuses a small white African-American woman of rape and wins a multi-million law suit in Washington, D.C.

3) The practice of psychiatry is rendered illegal by the United States Supreme Court, the judgement stating that psychiatry is a non-science, and that its pseudo-scientific practices, especially that of so-called psychotherapy, deal only in metaphor and variations of Greek oratory.

4) That due to a dereliction of intellectuals and to their running in purposeless packs after empty abstractions, the climate would be provided for an easy ascendancy of a tele-evangelist to the presidency and a Hitlerian dictatorship in the United States of America.

5) That prime time network television would be legally authorized to have *all* participants—including news anchor personalities, all actors and actresses in soap operas, all masters of ceremonies and participants in talk shows, seminars and incidental programs—all legally authorized to be shown throughout in the nude—naked. The decisive court ruling would have to do with the demonstratable inseparable union of body and mind—and that no expression in language can be complete without attendant exhibition of the unmasked, expressive naked body.

Well, at first I thought I had imagined the impossible. No, not so—and if you don't believe it, do as our imaginary president, George Bush, kept saying, "Stay tuned in."

We Have a Swimming Pool Installed

When it became certain that, yes, that beautiful Madrona tree—called a "Naked Indian" down here because its trunk and branches were as smooth as a baby's butt and the color of a Cheyenne brave—yes, when that Madrona tree was for sure dead, we decided to put in a swimming pool where it had once happily grown.

I shopped around and finally engaged the Austin Swimming Pool Company—with a written contract to construct a pool forty feet long, thirty feet wide, and seven feet deep at the west end and three deep at the east end—a slanted bottom, that is. All the other details—the color and placement of tile, where and how many steps, a ladder, all the details of circulation and filtration—all were set forth in a contract printed on what looked like the highly decorative excursion in bad taste that characterized nineteenth century diplomas awarded for completion of the mail-order course in Spencerian penmanship. This being a while back—1959, as I remember—the cost was firmly established at only $9,000.

Once signed up, the digging crew arrived and began excavating. At the end of their third day at that, the head digger said that their job was complete, and that another crew would be back in the morning—the guys who would put the iron reinforcing rods in place in the walls and floor of the pool prior to loading on and troweling the concrete. This is what's called a ferro-concrete job.

When the diggers left the property, my son and I inspected their work. It looked real good except that what was to be a full seven feet from top to bottom—especially since there'd be at least five inches of concrete laid in the bottom.

Well my son and I got our steel rule and measured. Sure enough, our eyes had not deceived us: it was only five feet, six inches—top to bottom.

Now, since the crew to lay up the steel would be wheeling onto the property at some ungodly early time in the morning—and since I was building a mistrust for guys who can't measure, or were trying to rook us, my son and I decided that we'd deepen the pool ourselves—dig down another foot and a half, at least. So right then we got picks and shovels and went at it. Jesus! That was heavy work. We ran into some rock, luckily the type that's called "rotten limestone" around here. And throwing the dug-up dirt over the side was what some "educators" might call "challenging"; to my son and me it was simply back breaking.

We'd dig and dig and then measure, then dig and dig some more. Around four in the morning, after ten hours of frantic work, we got the measurement we wanted. Seven feet, six inches—that allowed for the five or so inches of concrete to be laid over the iron rods on the bottom.

My son and I, as you'd expect, since we were not well-seasoned diggers—were about as near deathly tired as you ever get just before you die.

Still, having the goal achieved, we lusted for a little more. So we went down another three or four inches and then went to bed.

The crew with the iron rods went to work making the hole in the ground look like a woven iron basket—just great. Once they cleared the property, two days later, the cement trucks rolled in while my son and I watched. The crew went to work as if they were cutting down their time in purgatory.

Now, if you've been following what I've been trying to tell you, then you know that it is quite likely that these guys are going to run out of concrete: They came to cement a pool of a certain size and they were met with a much enlarged one. No one had noticed that, and we didn't tell them—of course not. So...yes, they ran out of concrete while my son and I just watched. The guy in charge, the one in the white shirt, cowboy hat, and clean boots began to raise hell about sons-a-bitches who can't even figure the simple volume of a hole. Another cement truck would have to be dispatched and more concrete brought in from the cement plant sixteen miles away.

After a little bit, the guy in charge came over to me and began to apologize for not only the delay, but for the fact that now there'd have to be joints in the wall—where the new batch of concrete would take up with the old—and he was sorry about that, but he'd see that the joints were perfect.

Now, instead of pretending to eat out the guy for this, I said, "Oh well, Bert, these things happen, forget it." Bert just stood there for a few seconds looking at me and then he said, "You're a Catholic, aren't you? So am I, but I'll get the son of a bitch who's been responsible for this," and I said, "Bert, I'd hate to be that poor Protestant bastard."

Looking for Spies at the Border

It was one of those recurring times when our government—mainly for political reasons—was on a concerted hunt for spies.

I was waiting in line to be cleared by the U.S. customs for re-entry from Mexico. It was very hot and the U.S. officials were taking an awful long time with a very fat Mexican woman. After the usual standard sort of questions, she was escorted into a private area by two female officers and was in there for more than an hour before she emerged and was cleared for coming on into Texas.

After I was cleared I walked up into Laredo to a drugstore. What I wanted after a month in Mexico was a genuine non-amoebic malted milk. There at the counter was this same fat Mexican lady about whom they'd taken all that time in customs.

I took a stool next to her, and after ingratiating myself I said that it was none of my business, but would she mind if I asked her why the customs officials took so much time with her.

She laughed a short laugh and said, "Spies, they're nutty about spies."

"My God," I said, "what would ever cause them to think you're a spy?"

"Well," the fat lady said, "they had trouble reading."

"Trouble reading? Reading what?" I asked.

"Are you a spy?" the fat lady asked.

"Heaven, no," I said.

"Do you work for anybody down there?" she asked, pointing down that hilly street to the border.

"No way," I said, "why?"

"Well," the fat lady said, "they weren't happy how it all turned out, they were embarrassed, sort of lost face, as they say, and might want to get some of it back, if you know what I mean."

"Don't worry about me," I said, "I'm just curious, though its none of my business, none at all."

The fat lady took another spoonful of her banana split, savored it, and then said, "Okay, so it's a funny story, even though while they were doing it I could have killed them."

"I'll bet," I said.

"Are you married?" the fat lady asked.

"Yes I am," I said.

"Children?"

"Yes," I said. "A boy and a girl."

"Well," the fat lady said, "it was like this; you know it's been hot today."

"Over a hundred in Nuevo Laredo," I said.

"It was over there," the fat lady said, "that I had to go to the toilet—and I just don't like to sit on any public toilet seat—so I took a couple sheets of my Monterrey newspaper and put them around—around on the seat, you know?"

"Yes," I said, "more sanitary."

"And I was sweating something awful," the fat lady said.

"Over a hundred," I said.

"When I got to the U.S. Customs," she said, "they must have been looking for some overweight lady spy, so everything I said must have made them think I was her."

"It happens," I said, "and it's not good."

"So," the fat lady said, "they made me undress."

"A strip search," I said, "that's what they call it."

"Uh-huh," she said, "and then they began looking real hard at—you know—at my ass, both of those women officers were down on their hands and knees studying my ass."

"Jesus!" I said, "this is like a bad comedy."

"Not to me, then," the fat lady said. "They even got magnifying glasses, so I asked them what in the hell they were looking for. They didn't tell me right off, but I found out before I left that search room."

"Good," I said, "it wasn't bad, was it?"

"Of course not," she said. "I'm here ain't I?"

"Can you tell me what you found out?" I asked.

"You remember," the fat lady said, "that it's hot and I was sweating. So I sat down on that Monterrey newspaper and the print came off, transferred right on to my ass. And, of course, the newspaper is printed in Spanish and when the print came off on me, it was backwards. It gave them one helluva time reading it with those magnifying glasses—expecting it was some code…or something, especially because it was the *Personals* I sat on—and you know the kind of stuff that gets printed there—enough to make your ass tired."

An Extension
All the Way to Virden, Illinois

When I was teaching at Illinois State University, the university had a program that was called Extension Education. This program was devised to help in-service public school teachers earn some college credit so they could meet state requirements for teacher certification, work toward degree requirements, and by so doing put themselves in line for pay increases.

Classes in this Extension Education program were held in various towns in Illinois and usually taught in an elementary school building or some other public place. All classes were taught at night, since the people attending them were busy teaching, mostly in grade schools, from miles around.

During my first year at Illinois State, I was asked if I'd like to teach an extension class. I didn't find this very alluring until I learned that teachers of extension courses were allowed five cents per mile for driving to and from the particular extension center and two dollars to cover one meal en route. That doesn't sound like much now, but back then high-test gasoline sold for twenty cents a gallon, two dollars could buy a good steak dinner in that part of depressed downstate Illinois.

Well, that year, 1940, I had a brand new Plymouth convertible (cost twelve hundred dollars) and I sure did like to drive around in it—especially at night with the top down and the radio going along with Perry Como, Bing Crosby, the Ink Spots—you name the names from 1940—and don't forget Ben Bernie and all his "lads," as he called them, doing "It's a Lonesome Old Town When You're Not Around," and signing off with "Pleasant Dreams" and "Yowser, Yowser, Yowser" as he always did. Yup, that convertible, my first-ever new car, was a dream on four wheels—rolling.

So when they asked me if I'd like to teach an extension class down in Virden, about one hundred miles south of the campus, I said *yes*—mainly, I think, because I'd be driving that silvery gray dream the 200 miles round trip once a week—with my gasoline paid for—and more: 200 miles at 5 cents a mile meant ten dollars—and with the two dollars for dinner I could have a couple of drinks on the return trip. So I said yes, I'd like to be of service, as I put it.

There was a porch light burning out front as I drove up to the ancient gray school building that first night, and a glow from the room where, it turned out, I'd be doing my thing about the values of art in education.

Well, even though I was only twenty-five years old then, I had one helluva big estimate of my prowess in the world. But when I looked into the buff-colored schoolroom, at that group of about thirty worried-looking late-middle-age and old age people—mostly women staring at me—well, I was sure I'd made the mistake of my life, and I felt a sudden heat under my shirt and a chill in my hands and feet. There they were, cramped into those stationary third grade seats, washed and ironed and their hair set for the occasion. And me, fresh off the open windy road believing, still, that all of the future lay before me—all, or mostly all. So what do you do?

You cover up under a big smile and walk to the little teacher's desk and stand there still smiling—then introducing yourself, spelling out your name, and saying this would be our "introducing session." First I tell them something about myself, my grade school teacher, Ethel Gardner, who opened up the world of art for me—what art has meant to me ever since—most of it true.

Then in order, they introduced themselves, and as their wandering biographies made it clear, there'd be no way to teach a regular campus-type course to these people. It would have to be simplified to the point of disappearance—or made into something quite different—tailored to their measurements, as it were. Which, during the next fifteen weeks, with their help—God bless them—it was.

For fifteen weeks, once a week, I sailed along in my silvery dreamboat, full of music, and myself full of me to arrive and enter each time, into a world of the aging and the old, scrabbling there, on the prairie not so far north of East St. Louis, Illinois. How this worked, I'll never know, but to all the usual criteria it was a roaring success.

When I walked into that buff-colored schoolroom for the last class session, it was all decorated—crepe-paper streamers, paper tassels hanging from the light globes, and a table full of food, and a huge white frosted cake that said in pink rosebuds, "We Love You."

So, the last class session was a party, and when I got into my silvery dreamboat outside, they were all in a bunch in front of that ancient gray building waving goodbye in the dark. And so you wave and pull away in your silvery dreamboat—filled with presents—chicken parts packed in ice, corn, home-baked bread, country sausage, ham, cookies, and all you could name—and an awful lot you couldn't.

I Can Hear the *National Anthem* Playing

I never was in the Army, but before I volunteered for service in the navy in 1943, I was a Civilian Specialist with the Army Air Forces Technical Training Command. I taught radiomen-gunners to send and receive the International Morse Code and procedures for radio, radio-telephone, and visual communication. That experience, which included going to the University of St. Louis for training and then teaching enlisted men in Chicago, gave me my first feelings for the growing military-industrial monster that always seemed to me to be on the verge of going completely out of control, of going off on its own like one of those "things" or diseases in early science fiction.

Early in 1943, while I was teaching at the Illinois State Normal University, I heard a Major Fischer make a speech about how badly the Army Air Force needed teachers of radio communications. I knew a little about radio, mostly from my old brother, Fred, who, years before, had built the first crystal set in our neighborhood. So I got the information from Major Fischer later and went to St. Louis as a member of the seventh class of radio communications trainees. Living in a dark pair of rooms on the edge of Chicago's gold coast, I went to school eight hours a day and three a night, six days a week for seven weeks. In the run-down rooms of the University of St. Louis, I sat through classes in Alternating Current, Vacuum Tubes, Communications Equipment, Radio Nets, Communications Procedures, Radio-Telephone, Visual Signaling, and International Morse Code. With the exception of the course in vacuum tubes, the curriculum was taught by bored men who mumbled material that, when it could be heard beyond the first few rows of the room, sounded like noises from a dying train caller reading from an electronics supply catalogue. Cheating on the examinations was so widespread it appeared total. Some of the class always had the answers almost as soon as the exam was begun and they were passed along the rows as if that was part of the regular procedure.

Teaching and learning the code was something else. For a few hours each day we sat in classrooms wired for sending and receiving audio International Morse Code. The instructors, ex-radio ham and ex-merchant marine radio operators for the most part, sat up front and hand-sent the code to us at our positions at long tables. Working from master copies of five-letter coded groups (KBNOS, QWERT, CDRMP, etc.), the instructor would send five or ten minutes at a given speed and then have our copies checked against his master copy. In the seven weeks I spent in St. Louis that winter, I managed to achieve only twelve words a minute—sixteen were required for graduation.

The night before the last day of classes, class R0–7, that was my class, threw a party at a nearby hotel. Several of the instructors came, including my code teacher, an ex-merchant marine radioman of about fifty. The party was simply a means for everyone to get drunk together inside the protective walls of the hotel. Around ten o'clock I went to the men's room. My code teacher, Gus Welge, really a pretty good guy, was lying stretched out on the floor with his head in the urinal, very drunk and fast asleep. I got down and called his name; I shook him. He was like a corpse, but breathing. I didn't want to leave him lying there, so I muscled him around and over my shoulder in the fireman's lift and began carrying him out when he began to talk, his head hanging down behind my back. He recited some unidentifiable verse and then asked who I was and where we were going. I said I'd get him to a bed in the hotel, or home, if he wished. Then there followed all those air-drawn arabesques and recitations I remembered from the old days with my father and his pals, Johnny Otzelburger, Soapy Wallace, Ed Wink, and dozens more, and after a long time we were out in the street with no taxi wanting to stop for what must have looked like bad news. In the end, I carried Gus Welge all the way to his apartment on the fourth floor of a gray building near the university. We had a last whisky, I put him to bed, and he thanked me, using my full name.

The next afternoon, the last day for class RO–7, Gus Welge, seated behind sunglasses, called for a final code check at sixteen words a minute. I tried so hard on that test that part of me seemed to die. It was obvious, halfway through, that I'd failed: My copy was full of holes—whole coded groups I'd missed. But I went on to the end like a spent bullet that had missed its target. When he called for the papers, I didn't hand mine in. He riffled through the stack and then called out, "Weismann, where's your paper?" and I passed it forward. A little later he called out the names of those who'd done a "solid sixteen," and my name was with them. It was a lie and a thank you bundled in one, and I decided I'd accept it, gratefully. I figured that when I'd start to teach I'd be able enough all the way to twelve words a minute, and that in the time it would take me to get my first group of radiomen-gunners from zero to twelve, I'd have gotten myself to sixteen. So I graduated with the class of RO–7 and reported in for teaching at the Stevens Hotel on Michigan Avenue in Chicago. It turned out that most of that huge hotel had been turned into a barracks; the teaching was being done in the old Coliseum on State Street, the very place where William Jennings Bryan had delivered his famous "Cross of Gold" speech at the Democratic National Convention in 1896, two years before Captain Sigsbee lost the battleship *Maine* in Havana harbor and forty-seven years before I arrived at the front door with class RO–7.

An immaculately uniformed staff sergeant with a huge barrel chest and a sharpshooter's medal pinned on his blouse came out of the room labeled "STAFF" and asked, "All present?" and no one answered. "Right in here and sit down," he said, mostly through his broad nose that appeared to have been broken more than once. "First," he said, "let's get this straight: You're not liked in here for the simple reason that you're civilians. We're using you because we got nobody else right now. And you're going to be teaching soldiers, the men who are fighting this war for you; and you better remember one thing—you better not make any mistakes because the ghosts of those soldiers you kill will be back to bother the hell out of you for the rest of your life. Okay, Code check in the next room—that way. Let's see if you've mastered anything."

We sat down at tables equipped for sending and receiving. "I'll tell you when to put the cans on," the sergeant said, "and keep your hands off those keys. Your code will come off the best punched tapes in the world—no excuse; I'll feed you one minute at four words a minute and at eight; five minutes at twelve, five at sixteen, and five at twenty—and you better have twenty a minute every minute if you expect to do sixteen with those soldiers. Okay, put the cans on, here it comes."

I passed four words a minute as my world blew away and I failed, full of holes at eight. The sergeant looked at me as if I was a dog turd he'd stepped into with his brilliantly shined shoes, "What the hell's with you?" he asked.

"Nervous, I guess," I said.

"Those sons-a-bitches in St. Louis don't know their ass; get in there and for Chrissakes listen to code—we'll check you out tomorrow, and I do me *out*, at sixteen hundred—four o'clock to you," he said.

At four o'clock the next afternoon I flunked eight words a minute on a check run by one of the civilian supervisors, a man named Petkov. I told him I thought it was hopeless, that I'd better just resign and think about what I should do next. "Don't take it so hard," Petkov said, "you think too much. Taking code is just an ear on the end of a pencil, no brain between."

"Maybe," I said, "but I better shove off."

"Hell," Petkov said, "you leave now and you can create all kinds of bookkeeping problems, and this place is all snafued anyway. Stick around; you got thirteen days to pay day. You can sit in here where it's nice and warm and listen to code if you want to, figure out what you're going to do next, and then take the dough and do what you're going to do."

"You know," I said, "I just might do that."

And I did. I figured I couldn't go back to my teaching job, and besides after that farewell party they'd given me when they all said how great I was for leaving a good job with a future and a "C" gasoline sticker, just to serve my country—after all that, I just couldn't go back. So, as the bitter cold days whistled and moaned outside, I sat in the warm little code room, earphones at my temples, deciding what I'd do next. I'd gotten pretty sick of being looked at as if I was a scabby naked man as I went back and forth on crowded streetcars—still in the clothes of a young assistant professor of art—and I figured I'd enlist in the Navy, but first I'd get some money, for what, I've forgotten. So, it finally got settled in me, I'd drive a cab for a while—I knew Chicago pretty well and there are maps—and get four or five hundred dollars ahead and then see about the Navy. Once this was settled, a fine feeling of freedom took over. I came to the code room when I felt like it. I walked around Chicago, saw a lot of movies, watched the ice pile up along the lake shore, sat for hours in front of my old favorites in the Chicago Art Institute and wandered freely about the huge Coliseum with a marvelous sense of detachment.

It was around five o'clock one evening that this detachment, this feeling of freedom, was thrown back into jeopardy. I was walking along a kind of catwalk that ran around the interior of the building, high up three of its walls. From there I could see, almost at once, the entire expanse of the concrete floor below. I thought of Bryan at the convention, the thousands of people and the noise that thundered at the ringing close of his speech that said man would not be crucified on a cross of gold. I thought of the great prizefights that had been fought to the last bell in a ring in the center of that very floor way down below the dust and soot-blackened banks of megaphones, and a string of names I'd first heard from my father—Joe Gans, Pinky Mitchell, Battling Nelson, Harry Greb, Benny Leonard—came singing back to me. But the great hall was all but silent now. Only a very hushed stirring mixed with the distant hum of the glassed-in automatic tape machines held off absolute quiet. Yet down there, spread across the floor, close to a thousand men sat taking code in walled-in unroofed plywood cubicles. It was like looking into a huge egg-crate, each square filled with khaki-colored shapes that moved a little now and then. And for the thousand that sat down there now, there was another thousand back at the Stevens

Hotel that would be coming into the crate at eight that evening, and still another thousand after that. Three thousand men came into and went out of this crate every day, carrying battle gear to get them accustomed to the weight and to the changing shapes of their bodies. What suddenly got to me as I stood there on that catwalk was the fact that whether or not I left this scene of the Army Air Force Technical Training Command, I was already packed into the crate that extended far beyond the walls of the Coliseum outward across the country and into the whole warring world. And then a voice cracked out over a powerful electrical system and hit the still air of the Coliseum with a directive from the commanding officer. The total unified effect of that voice on the thousand men below gave me a deep and lasting chill. It was like nothing I'd witnessed before, nothing: a thousand men sat bolt upright and remained motionless until the words "that is all" came over and then, as a man, they bent back to their work.

My time as a civilian specialist in communications was running out in Chicago. The day before payday Petrov came into the code room and sat down at the far end of the table. "What you going to do?" he asked.

"Drive cab for a while and then join the Navy," I said.

"And see what's left of the world," he said, and I said I supposed so. "Put the cans on," Petkov said, "for old time's sake." So I put them on and as the code began to run I started to letter in the special way we'd been taught—so that the end stroke of every preceding letter left off in the most advantageous position for the starting stroke of the next. My mind was off reading a map of Chicago, the streets and neighborhoods I didn't know about, getting ready to drive cab. My hand kept making letters on the page in front of me, and I watched the neat five-letter coded groups grow in lines across it. It was like absent-mindedly watching a fast moving hand-shaped machine out there on the table all by itself. Then my own hand became very tired. My fingers stiffened up, and I couldn't make them move. "Let's see those sheets," Petkov said, dropping his earphones and coming quickly up to my end of the table. He laid my sheets next to the master, checked the last two, and then, half-smiling he said, "These last two sheets are solid right."

"The hell you say," I said.

"Do you know how fast that last tape was?" he asked.

"I have no idea," I said.

"Weismann, you old malingerer," Petkov said, "you just copied a hundred groups solid at twenty-five a minute—on a typewriter I'll bet you could do fifty."

I went to work the following week, on the midnight to eight shift, seated at a control panel called a BD 157 with my first class of eighteen radiomen-gunners, nine on each side of me down a long table. Within the week the staff sergeant with the big barrel chest appeared at my control panel. "How the hell did you get here?" he asked.

"Sergeant," I said, "I'm just getting to know these soldiers and they got a saying I don't understand."

"What's that?" he asked.

"Fuck you," I said.

With that open invitation, the sergeant came by every night and unloaded tons of invective on me. And although I figure he made captain in the years ahead and was finally fragged in Vietnam, still he provided me relief from the most boring job I've ever done with success.

And then one day I walked into the office of the Navy's officer procurement division in Chicago, answered questions, tried to hide the fact that I'd ever done anything in radio communications, took the physical exam during which a Lieutenant M.D. told me my ears were dirty, and was told to go home and wait to hear from them. I was created an ensign by a phone call from the Chicago office and told to read the *U.S. Navy Regulations*, a copy of which was in the mail to me; buy uniforms; and report to the Navy Training School for Communications at Harvard University. I was much taken by a piece of advice in the Regulations: "Always have plenty of maps with you; you never know where you'll be going." I worked hard at Harvard and was selected for an extra month of super training as an aircraft carrier communications officer and then was shipped to Port Hueneme, California, for training with the marines as an amphibious communications officer. The *Articles of War* were finally read to me and four other officers aboard a merchant ship, the *SS John Shafroth*, as we sailed south of Samoa loaded with gear for amphibious landing. By blinker in the black of night somewhere in the area of the Admiralty Islands, we rendezvoused with the rest of our outfit, destined, according to orders, for a place with the code name "OUCH." (Because it proved so true, I must repeat the following.) The commanding officer of our outfit, a three-striper from St. Louis, came aboard and told us to sit down. "I've got news for you," he said, "I've made the circuit out here, seen all the most recently taken islands, and I want you to know that we'd better hope to God that the enemy is more fucked-up than we are, or we're going to lose this war."

And so the enemy must have been, certainly all the way I went, through New Guinea, the Palaus, and the Philippines. To me the trip amounted to a gigantic stage production of a skewed Brechtian tragedy with all its ceremonially mad, sometimes tragic comedy, interspersed with long soliloquies from fairy tales and *Joe Miller's Joke Book*, butcher shop scenes run on revolving movie screens, unchoreographed Byzantine dances performed in the wings by the brass; a semi-pro travesty, a mock epic, a fiercely poetic mish-mash, a terrible concoction of love and longing, hate, violence, death, and monumental boredom that parodied itself and finally ended in victory.

I can hear the National Anthem playing in the background now—can't you?

How Are Things, Commander?

I though I'd made a mistake in decoding the dispatch that the radio brought that night to the little island off the coast of New Guinea where I was the communications officer. It was addressed to Lieutenant James Rogers on the other side of the island—and I knew that James Rogers was a Lieutenant *Commander*, not just a Lieutenant. But, no, checking the code again, it said Lieutenant, not Lieutenant Commander.

Since the dispatch was classified "Operational Priority"—just one notch below "Urgent," which usually concerns contact with the enemy—I got in my Jeep and ran it over to Roger's tent, where he was sound asleep. I woke him up, put a flashlight on the dispatch for him to read. It said that James Rogers should proceed on the first available transportation to Boston, Massachusetts.

"They got your rank wrong, Commander," I said.

"Maybe," he said, "but they may have already demoted me."

"How come?" I asked.

"It's really pretty silly," he said, "you want to hear how silly?"

"Sure," I said.

"Some months ago," the commander said, "I was on duty out in the China Sea when I saw two of our aircraft carriers sideswipe each other in broad daylight and in an open, empty calm sea. They weren't damaged much, but to have those two ships scrape the paint off each other and the fuss that followed struck me as funny, silly, really. Well, a little later when I wrote to a young friend who I'd been training to be a boxer before I left—the kid's just graduated from high school—I mentioned the incident as an example of the unexpected, maybe humorous things that can happen during a war. The kid thought it was a great story—funny, and from his far-off friend and hero at war in the South Pacific. So he took it to the editor of his high school newspaper who had it printed. Some high school papers get carried home, you know, and this one was.

A father of some other student read the printed letter and hit the ceiling—said it was unpatriotic to make fun of our Navy, and besides, the letter gave away "military secrets."

"Like our ships running into each other, or shooting down our own aircraft? That's hardly secret stuff," I said.

"So—" the commander went on, "this patriotic parent had friends on the local draft board, and one in Washington."

'Ho! Ho!" I said, "Not so good."

"No good for me," the Commander said. "In Washington, as I understand, some kind of committee got to work on my letter—and on me. So here I am, back to the States and already reduced in rank—to stand some kind of hearing, maybe even a court martial. Can you believe it?"

"Easy enough," I said. "I know a sailor who got shipped back to serve time in Portsmouth for running off with one can of peaches that fell off a supply truck."

"So it goes," the Commander said, "well, anyway, I'll get to see my wife and kids, I hope."

Some hours later I drove the commander to the seaplane base where the first available transportation was waiting—a PB2Y, a Catalina Flying Boat—to take him to Hollandia on the first leg of the trip back.

"Good luck, Commander," I said as he got aboard.

"A word of advice," he called back, "If you see any of our ships running into each other, or even sinking each other, just keep your mouth shut—otherwise we might lose this war."

As the Catalina took its long, water-spraying run and then lift into the hot equatorial air, I was thinking back to when I arrived out here. I'd come out as part of a special amphibious outfit. Our skipper had preceded us and visited all of the most recent invasion areas to get the straight poop and make our first landing a good one. We rendezvoused with him in the open sea. He came aboard our ship saying, "We'll meet in the wardroom—all officers." Once all together, he said, "Sit down gentlemen," and we did, with our senior asking, "How is it out there, Commander?"

"We can go into details a little later," he said, "but for now I have only one thing to report." [I know I've reported before what the commander said, but it's stark truth requires I have him say it again.]

So here was our Commanding Officer, fresh from those up front burned beaches, stranded landing craft and all the rest—here he was and about to report one thing, perhaps the most important. "Gentlemen," he said, "I've seen it, and you can keep this to yourselves, but I only hope to God that the enemy is more fucked-up than we are, or we're going to lose this war."

Well, as you know, we won the war—that one, anyway.

Tickets Home from the War

Even among this country's best warriors there's always been talk of getting back home—especially when there's a lapse in the action and time to think in a more consecutive way about other things.

It was simple talking to my war buddy Ben Haffey about going home; he never had any question about it—he had the answer, the solution to getting back home from the day he enlisted in the Navy. He had an ace in the hole—he had colitis—an infection of the mucous membrane of the colon. And he knew all about its behavior: if he avoided greasy foods, all was well, his colon appeared normal, but if he ate greasy foods, or just some grease, his whole asshole area became inflamed—like a five-alarm fire. So Ben, having such personal knowledge of himself as the Greeks had—you'll remember their bumper-sticker slogan: "Know Thyself"—Ben could light up his behind whenever he chose to do so, and the kind of colitis he had was enough to send anyone home, back to the States.

Ben used to say that he had no real worries about the war and his part in it. He used to say that if things got too tough for him he could just eat some grease—a tube of which he always carried with him—get to a doctor or a medic, take down his pants, and exhibit the conflagration. "I carry my ticket home in my asshole," he used to say.

So Ben Haffey had no problem about leaving the war, combat or the Navy—on *his* schedule.

But a lot of others did. And so all kinds of tricks, malingering, and so on were employed by those others. All designed to get back home, the sooner, the better.

One of the means that worked pretty well, especially for medical doctors, was "lower back difficulties." I guess that any doctor worth his fee knows that "lower back ailments"—real, imagined, or pretended—are most difficult to diagnose and treat. So, if a person wanted out, wanted to get back home because of a lower back ailment, he just had to keep up a program of complaint—fall over now and then or yell out in real or pretended pain. It worked for the healthiest person. The trouble was that it took too long. A guy had to go on for months with this charade before the medical authorities would believe the complainer.

A quick way to get a ticket back home—until the trick was discovered and dishonored—was to develop what looked like one or more huge bleeding ulcers down in the stomach. The procedure was simple: first, you had to be near x-ray facilities—on the beach or aboard ship; second, you tore off a little tin foil from your cigarette package, pricked your finger, and drew a little blood; third, you put some blood on the tin foil and swallowed it—tin foil and blood; fourth, you had to dramatically exhibit pain in the midsection with whatever creative possibilities are at your command; fifth, have an x-ray picture made of your stomach—and presto! There it is, clear and convincing, a portrait of an awful bleeding ulcer—and most often your ticket home.

However, as you know, truth and justice will always win out—why, but for that are we fighting this war, after all? So, in time the medical authorities were alerted to this ruse and undid it by requiring x-ray pictures over a period of time—and, alas, the bloodied tinfoil, the fake bleeding ulcer, had only a short life in the stomach. Sorry, no ticket home, then.

It appears that the one sure way to get back home before one's tour of duty or before the war was over took some time and sacrifice but, in the end, it worked every time.

As it has helped so many in so many different ways, it was the *Bible* that could get you a clear ticket back home. And here's how that worked: You must carry a *Bible* with you at *all times* no matter how difficult this can be under a lot of conditions. And you must look like you're reading the *Bible* in all situations where others can observe you. When asked if you'd like to join in in a card game or roll the dice—you say, "Thanks, but no, I'd rather spend my time reading the Lord's words." Especially when there's a beer or booze break, and the boys are thundering off to the fountain of spirits and they say, "Come on along, Ned, they've got real bourbon today," you say again and always, that you're prefer to go at your *Bible*.

After a while, your outfit understands you not as a religious Christian (in this case) but as a NUT—that you're emotionally and otherwise quite unbalanced, you're flatly insane. And unless you're a young Marine in the first wave against an entrenched enemy, *sanity* is a requirement—so off you go nutty, nutty to home. Now, there's truth in the oft-quoted saw that "There are no atheists in foxholes." Of course not. Those guys in those besieged foxholes want to get home! Look! They're reading their *Bibles* between rounds!

Three Scenes from a Long Ago War

He was way, way up there, maybe thirty thousand feet or more, banking and rolling and putting on a show, and we were standing along the rail and craning up at him. "Jesus, what a life," someone said, "up there out of this crap—beautiful."

"And when he gets back, fresh eggs—carrier based, I bet," someone else said, "and a slug or two of whisky. They give those flyboys booze now, did you know that? Right on navy ships, what a deal."

"You mean to tell me you never had booze on a navy ship?" one of the gunners asked.

"I mean, booze served right at you, official booze," the other said.

"Official shit," the gunner said. The fighter way up there was playing with the sky. He looked happy, stunting around with all that power and all that space under him. I'd always wanted to fly, maybe just to do what we thought he was doing up there, feeling free, no assignment, no mission, just flying for the hell of it.

"A Hellcat, isn't it?" the Warrant Officer said.

"Well it sure as hell ain't a Corsair," someone said, and there was a phony snicker because no one ever mistook the gull wing of a Corsair for anything else. Then the little speck that was a plane flashed into a cloud and made that sound that means it's on full rich in a power dive. In another flash it was out, and before it leveled at us someone yelled "Meat Balls!" and we saw the red discs on the wings and fire at the gun ports. The stuff hit the water and then the steel bulkhead behind us and the Zero was gone.

Four of the men I'd eaten breakfast with were bleeding against the bulkhead—just those four and not some other four or two or five, because the shells were spaced that way in the guns of that Zero, or because that hot pilot waggled a little or came a hair to port or starboard as he squeezed, or because the wind, or the air, or the yawing of the ship, or just because.

"It's chicken—the can's open, here, for you," the voice said out of pitch blackness.

"Christ, Wharton," I said, "keep it yourself. If you found chicken around here you deserve it. You not hungry?"

"For Chrissake," Wharton said, his voice spaced between fire. "here, God dammit, take it. If I hold it out much longer it'll be full of shrapnel and we'll both be screwed out of it."

I got out of the hole, but I couldn't straighten up and I stood there on the torn-up beach, bent double, about a yard high. It felt like it was all over. Up ahead I could see the medical pile beyond the dump and I made for it. It took forever. And when I got there there was just a tired-out corpsman. "If you can just vomit," he said, and he gave me a cup of brine, "here, throw it down." But I couldn't vomit and I let myself topple against the crates.

Then the doctor came, "Can't you straighten out?" he asked.

"So far, no," I said.

"Here," he said sliding a sheet of plywood toward me, "I got to go over there," pointing to a black smoking fire across the sand and up into the first stand of trees. "You get down on this, on your back, and try to get yourself straight out." In the time he was gone, I worked against what felt like a powerfully incoming tide filled with knives cutting across my middle. And in the end, exhausted and afraid to move lest I snap back double again, I got myself flat. "Just stay that way," the doctor said when he got back, "how long you been out here?"

"About a year, around here," I said.

"New Guinea before?" he asked.

"Yes," I said. He got down beside me and felt around.

"How'd you like to go back to the States?" he asked.

"No jokes, doc," I said.

"No jokes," he said.

I went double again when I got off the plywood and the doctor walked me that way down to the water; hailed an amphibious jeep driven by a big black man; put a piece of paper, orders, in my hand; and I was taken off the beach. I came to alongside a radar pickett boat, and the marine hoisted me aboard as the jeep banged against it. They put me on a pile of Mae Wests on the cabin deck, and I fell asleep as the pickett boat turned to the open sea. How much later, I don't know; they woke me up and told me I should try to stand up and make it to the patrol craft bobbing alongside. It looked impossible even after I got up: First I'd be way above the deck of the PC, and then way below as the boats bobbed out of time. In the end I stepped off and someone caught me and I was asleep on canvas. Now and then I'd come to, and I could hear the Diesel working hard in a choppy sea, the voices of men aboard and the sound of hand-sent code from a radio, someplace. I kept coming in and going out of the world and it felt like years were passing. Then they put me in a long wire basket and I was hoisted by cable to the high deck of an LST, a Landing Ship Tank. The deck was piled high with crates of blood plasma, all around the 20 millimeter guns, and there was a red and white hand-painted sign on the bridge: THE HELPFUL. They took me down to the tank deck all fitted with triple-deck bunks—bunks for dozens of men and all empty. A doctor came, took me to a lower bunk, told me to lie down, and began asking me questions as I fell asleep.

The doctor was there when I woke up. Everything seemed bright and noisy in a regular way. "How you feel, Lieutenant?" the doctor asked with a big smile on his Irish looking face.

"Okay, I guess," I said.

"How about a bowl of soup?" he asked. The word *soup* sounded real and beautiful—as if I'd just learned the wonderful thing it stood for.

"That'd be fine," I said. While he went to see about the soup, I pulled myself up and discovered that I could move much better. I felt like I'd been on a long and terrible drunk in which I wrestled and fought for days and been beaten over and over. My insides felt like they'd come through my skin and that even though I could stand up straight and walk and bend, I'd have to be very careful not to break or tear anything. "How long you think you slept?" the doctor asked when he brought the steaming soup.

"I don't know, but I feel a lot better," I said.

"We helped you a little," he said, "but you went close to seventy-two hours. Do you know that we weighed you?"

"Weighed me? No, I don't remember that," I said.

"I thought you didn't," he said, "that was something like twenty-four hours ago. What's your normal weight?"

"I used to go around a hundred and thirty-eight," I said.

"How much you think you weigh right now?" he asked.

"I don't know," I said, "I've lost, I know."

"Weismann," he said, "before you put that soup down, you just made a hundred and three."

"Doesn't surprise me," I said, "I've been wearing down, not enough sleep, blackouts, and then, poof!"

"It's an old story," he said, "nothing to worry about, you'll be okay, just take it easy for a while; you can't win the war all by yourself."

That night *The Helpful* suddenly changed course, and you could feel it being pushed at full ahead, high in the water and slapping under the bow. I asked a corpsman where we were headed, and he said the word was that we were going to pick up survivors from the cruiser *Princeton* that was hit and burning. Hour after hour *The Helpful* kept pushing, and twice the guns rattled along her three hundred foot deck—aircraft overhead. And then we slowed and finally stopped dead in the water.

Then they started coming down to the tank deck. Litter after litter bearing men burned black and crusty with their still liquid eyes peeking out, and parts gone from them. The smell of burned flesh, heavy, sickening but with a peculiar affinity for your own sense of smell, like the smell of your own sweat and your own blood and excrement, suddenly pervaded everything and every space. And they kept coming down with ears melted into their heads; noses gone; hands gone; and feet; arms, and legs ending in pointed black sticks like the horseman of the sculptor Marino Marini. Then the saws and amputations, and I suddenly became the healthiest, strongest man in the world, helping hold, lifting, turning them over, lighting cigarettes, and holding them into those holes in those faces of charcoal. I remember: What do you do with these cut-off hands and feet and arms and legs, as I handed another to a corpsman passing. Over the side to the sea, these parts of living men lost forever—and the look of your own, so light in color, so beautiful, so strong and moist and good. And you felt ashamed. And how is it, I still ask and want no answer, that many of these men, crippled and burned, carried tremendous and painful erections. Oh body, we do not know you yet.

"But Doc," I said, "I really wanted to go back to my outfit; there's nothing back home for me now, not until this is all over and done. I've got hundreds of friends all over thousands of square miles out here, but it just didn't work. There I am, Doc, on that peaceful beach the other side of Henderson Field, just waiting for orders; plenty of ice cold beer, nurses even, and a great place to swim. So I come out all tan and feeling great and stretch out in one of those honest-to-God canvas deck chairs to read that last book by Oscar Levant and really everything is just great, fine, couldn't maybe be better. And I'm feeling so lucky and so grateful that I can't wait to get back and do what I can, when, Jesus, I'm doubled up again and I hear rockets that aren't there and see faces I thought I'd forgotten. Doc, what the hell is this?"

Lt. Commander Hollis Summer, M.D. said, "Look, Weismann, it's easy. Let's say you're a woman, the story works better that way, okay? Well, you're a woman about twenty-eight, say, and you have a son age three, okay? And you were told when you had that baby that you couldn't have another. So you got this three-year-old boy, and you know it's the only one of your own you can ever have. So you come out on the porch. It's springtime and everything is just about perfect. Then, as you look out across the porch railing, you see a Mack truck coming fast down the street and in a flash you see your baby boy smashed all over that truck. Now I ask you, Weismann, how do you think you'd feel if you were that woman?"

"Christ, Doc, you know how I'd feel," I said.

"Okay," Dr. Summers said, "now let's repeat this same event, this time smashing to death of your only, never-to-be-had-again son every day for a couple of years, and have you see it as if for the first time, every time. How do you think you'd feel after a couple of years of that?"

"It'd kill me," I said.

"Weismann," Dr. Summers said, "that's about where you're at, only you're not going out on that porch any more; you're going home."

Cuba from the Bridge—September, 1961

The southern coast of western Cuba from four or five miles at sea looks good. It edges a narrow lowland covered in late September with rusty colors and green that look like rushes through the binoculars. As you head east toward the Windward Passage, the mountains climb high against the northern sky and you are reminded of New Guinea—bigger than you'd ever thought, just waiting, and not easy.

Land from well out to sea almost always looks relaxed, and mountains give it a quality of heavy slumber. But the Sierra Maestra with Pico Turquino holding its iron more than a mile above the Caribbean stops out the sky in the silhouette of a partially deserted catafalque, and it gives you the feeling that half of the sleeping or dead are on watch in some other place. Cuba from the bridge of an Italian freighter bound from Galveston to Genoa that September looked good, even noble, but its silhouette—maybe more in your mind than your eyes—seemed to have pieces missing.

Where the Windward Passage points east through both the Caribbean and the Atlantic, Cuba begins to end, and there is Guantánamo—GITMO as you knew it on Navy dispatches when you were less old than you are now. But before your glasses can pick it up there's light smoke on the horizon to the south and soon the low superstructure and stacks of a destroyer—U.S.—the big scanning radar antenna forward and high above the five-inch guns. Then her hull with the squarish numbers and the ship going into a tight circle, looking smart as hell. You feel you've never been a sucker for a brass band, red badges of courage, or the stuff in temples or tents that's half evangelism and half massage. And even though you remember like a broken promise the silliness and measured boredom of almost every part of your own military experience except engagement with the enemy, still the sight of that blue-gray destroyer frothing the Caribbean five miles off Guantánamo warmed you all over, and you smiled and held her steady in the glasses.

The skipper of the Italian freighter turned to you and said a word—blockade—and smiled a lot different from the way he smiled two weeks later when you walked with him down the streets of his own Genoa. Then the destroyer broke her circle and came in on a collision course for the freighter. An unseen signalman aimed his blinker at the skipper and you on the bridge and the light flashed short-long, short-long, over and over—calling to the ship unknown to the destroyer. The Italian skipper had his third officer ready the freighter's light and waited. The destroyer veered off the collision course about six city blocks from the freighter, ran down starboard, and returned on a parallel course about three city blocks off the freighter's starboard beam, still calling with her light. The Italian skipper had Italy's flag raised at the stern and directed his third officer to call the destroyer. So the freighter blinked short-long, short-long over and over at the destroyer—calling an unknown ship; and the destroyer blinked back short-long, short-long over and over, like calling HEY-YOU back and forth. International waters, the Italian skipper said to you, and no war now. And you said yes, wondering how you'd feel if you were skippering a U.S. freighter five miles off Corsica in international waters—that same day—and an Italian destroyer did what the U.S. one was doing now. On watch around Cuba, you thought; the circumstances are special and the bearded one must feel the squeeze. But what about harassment and free passage through the open seas?

The destroyer, trim from stem to stern and without a man showing, steamed parallel, blinking for a long three or four minutes, and the Italian skipper stared straight ahead through the Windward Passage. Then she raced ahead, changed her course to the south, and got under the horizon—all but the top of her foremast and the scanning antenna.

Then two jet fighters, U.S. Navy, came silently out of nowhere, dove, leveled off at about a hundred feet, and blast-roared over the freighter's bridge and out of sight. Dangerous, the Italian skipper said. And he said it again ten minutes later when a bright orange Navy helicopter came in at mast height and circled in a steep bank, two men looking down like into a snake pit at you and taking pictures with a camera that looked like a cannon.

An hour later—fifteen miles by the freighter's speed—the radar antenna of the destroyer dropped below the horizon to the south and a new mast came up fast in the east. Up she came, a small ship, blue-gray, the white numbers—a patrol craft, U.S. Navy. Two miles off she began to blink short-long, short-long over and over and quickly set a collision course, ran it for a minute, and eased as if preparing to come alongside. Then, close, she blinked in plain language—"Where are you from and where are you bound?" Not his business, the Italian skipper said. The patrol craft—and you could picture the junior grade lieutenant commanding—acted sassy in the sea and then sidled close. The Italian skipper looked at you like you were a boy of eight needing help, and he told the third officer to reply with "Galveston-Genoa." And from the clicks of the switch you could read the names as they went to the patrol craft so close you could spit on her deck. She never acknowledged, never receipted for the message, just pulled away and headed south. And as she went you felt sick in a way that was hard even to try to understand. Blockade or no blockade; legal, illegal, or extra-legal, the performance was shabby. It made you think of the catastrophe on the Cuban beaches some months before—a poor show, no matter. And the warm feeling that filled you first at the sight of the destroyer got all mixed up with hot and cold and a kind of sadness reserved for helplessness. "I've got some Marsala below," the Italian skipper said; and you were glad to leave the bridge and talk about something else. "I've bought a house in San

Remo," he said, "two floors—we'll see it in seventeen days if the weather's clear."

The freighter rolled that night. Hurricane Esther had started for Miami a day before and then turned north toward Norfolk, and she'd left a rolling sea far east of Cuba. And before you got rocked to sleep you thought of Cuba and the silhouette of her mountains with pieces missing.

Maybe your kidneys are good, and your bladder big and elastic and you never get up at night. And maybe you left the luxury of nightmares on the threshold of your youth. But this night a roar from your dreams came through to open your eyes, and the cabin got brilliant with greenish light. You sprung from sleep to the porthole and something passed over ablaze. Back in the black you knew it was a multi-engined plane, its powerful landing lights raking the decks of the Italian freighter.

Morning comes like death, inexorably, and the sea was wide open. The course was for Santa Maria in the Azores and Cuba was out of sight if not out of mind. Back of you she lay as surely as she did for Columbus, poor Dewey, Teddy, Walter Reed, and Batista.

The southern coast of Cuba edges a lowland covered in late September with rusty colors and green. The mountains climb high against the northern sky and you are reminded of every one of those South Pacific islands—bigger than you'd ever thought, mysterious, and not easy at all.

Carnival in Florence

Years ago at a carnival in Florence I saw a set-up that if brought to the U.S.A. would make a million dollars for someone with a flair for helping to soak up what's left of the glory instinct in lots of people.

Now just because this carnival was in Florence doesn't mean that it had anything to do with the Medici, the Church, or with art. It didn't. Until you looked close and listened carefully you couldn't tell it from a standard Stateside carnival that works towns in the 100,000 to 200,000 population bracket. There were the usual fried-type eating places and rides—a Ferris wheel; electric scooter cars running on metal floors; a whip; a merry-go-round; and a variety of chair swings, rockets, and airplanes spun around by revolving vertical shafts. Then there were the chance-type booths or concessions—try to toss rings around shiny objects and bottles of wine, or lively rubber balls into narrow-necked bowls, variations of bingo and the like. And then there was the greatest number of shooting-type concessions I've ever seen in a single carnival inside or outside the U.S.A. There must have been twenty of them. The duller ones provided pump rifles that blew out pellets and all you got for your hundred lire was the score you made on the target—no prizes, no awards. In others you used pump pistols with long barrels like the Buntline Special and tried to shoot packages of chewing gum, candy, and heavy-bottomed objects off tiers of shelves.

In the long line of these shooting concessions was the one I said could make a million quick in this country. All it was was an eighteen by eighteen foot canvas booth over the front of which hung a red, white, and green sign (easily changed to red, white, and blue) which gave the name FOTO SHOT. A good enough looking woman, somewhat like a stout *Gunsmoke* Kitty, ran the stand from behind a four-foot counter from which issued four small-bore hard rubber hoses about five feet long. These ran to four good looking steel-barreled, fruitwood-stocked rifles. Back of the counter about fifteen feet there were four metal constructions looking like something Stankiewicz the sculptor might have welded up on an off day. At shoulder height these constructions branched out a foot to the left and foot to the right. On the right side was a target the size of the standard fig leaf for life-size post-Renaissance sculpture. In the center of the target—bull's eye—was a shiny silver button about half the size of the top of the Beta in the standard mass-produced Phi Beta Kappa key. To the left was a camera lens and behind a metal shield, a camera. Above all this there extended a short metal rod topped with a horizontal shelf. After an Italianate version of the big town Texas naturepath of the late 1950s filled this high shelf with silver powder, he gave a signal to the stout *Gunsmoke* Kitty, and you were ready to go—four shots for 100 lire.

She took your money, opened the petcock on the hard rubber hose that ran to your pellet-loaded gun, thus providing your weapon with an unlimited supply of greatly compressed air from the compressor running at the back of the stand, and smiled like Fate.

With a crowd of spectators behind you, you raised the gun, took aim, and fired. And after a while you hit that top part of the Beta, that little dead-center silver button, and POOF! A great blinding flash went off in front of you and your awed and cheering audience. Your pellet had struck home—completed an electric circuit and ignited the silver flash powder in the shelf above your target. You had done it—you yourself—and everyone saw it and knew it to be true.

It seemed real reward enough, the flash as big as an ignited ideal, and homage from the van. But there was still the lingering proof of it all, like tradition; the huge boiling cloud of smoke from the flash powder was blown out over the crowd by a well placed electric fan. And still that is not all. Through the smoke and admiring voices the Italianate naturepath gets to the camera to the left of the demolished target; fishes out the negative you fired into being; and in seconds, it seems, presents you with positive proof of the wonder you'd performed, and the glory of that moment.

There in the damp photograph you stand—in that instant of time, forever. There you are on the firing line, just as your target saw you in the split second when you—by yourself—squeezed off the shot that did it all. And there behind you, your constituents in the van.

I was thinking, as I carried the still damp memento of my glory past the Ferris wheel and home, that FOTO SHOT might not only make a million for some unemployed naturepath—it might also be what some would like to use to render harmless, or declare illegal, any urge to individual glory the rest of us might have in these later constricting corporate times.

Pikeville in Pistoia

It's a long way from Pikeville in Kentucky to Pistoia in Italy, but on that night in Pistoia, now over thirty-five years ago, I sure got to thinking about Pikeville.

It all got started in Florence on a Thursday afternoon in the fourth floor studio of Silvio Loffredo, a young Italian painter. After you've looked at scores of his paintings and prints he asks if you'd like to go to Pistoia for the opening of an exhibition of paintings by five artists of the new generation, himself included, and you say yes, when do we leave. Seven-thirty Saturday, he says, and he'll be waiting at the downstairs door to his building, straight across the street from Andrea Pisano's doors of the Baptistery, fifty meters from Donatello's *Mary Magdalene*.

A little before seven-thirty you drive up and there's Loffredo with another man in a corduroy hat. The pigeons are all asleep and the Saturday night traffic is just beginning to run somewhat wild in those dark streets around the Cathedral, the Baptistery, and Giotto's Tower, which you notice looks dark pink against the blue-black sky. As they climb in, Loffredo introduces his friend, Alberto Ciattini, a poet visiting from Rome, and you're off.

Long before you get the car on the autostrada and headed for Pistoia, a lot of good strong talk full of gesticulations gets going about last year's Venice Biennale, the one coming up this summer with Loffredo invited to represent Italy, and how there isn't abstract or realistic painting—there's just painting. And there's talk about what's getting translated into Italian now; who's getting the play in the U.S., Britain, and France; the "false metaphysic" of Tennessee Williams, as Ciattini put it, the kind of picture of Mexico that D.H. Lawrence gave long ago. F. Scott Fitzgerald, Ezra Pound, T.S. Eliot, and Saul Bellow. The New York painters come into the conversation along with Uccelo, Orcagna, the Congolese, and some fine fish Ciattini had eaten in Rome the week before.

Once on the autostrada, conceived in real Roman scale and efficiency, it passes under the car like a velvet belt and before you're ready for it—the high blue and white sign says the next exit is to Pistoia to the right, and there you turn.

Pistoia is a small town and it's old. Catiline was killed in battle nearby in 62 B.C. and Pistoia was an important community by the 12th century. Camillo Vetelli first manufactured a new kind of handgun here and it took its name—pistol—from Pistoia, just about three hundred years before Sam Colt patented his revolver and set up that first unsuccessful business in Patterson, New Jersey.

Down the dark streets never built for automobiles you go to the Galleria Vannucci near the center of town to find a sign on the door saying the exhibition will open at ten-thirty and that you should come and eat at Mallenotti's. It seems everyone in Pistoia is at Mallenotti's place and dinner is coming with pasta, fish two feet long, meat, vegetables fresh out of the ground, salad, bread as bread ought to be, Chianti as only Chianti is, and cheese and fruit. Around the meal everybody gets going with everybody else in earnest and in fun, in voice, countenance, and gesture, in pantomime and laughter clear across the room. The exhibiting artists, Agostini, Faraoni, Farulli, Grazzini, and your friend Loffredo are introduced to cheers and applause fit for heroes, which they are. They're part of the new generation of Italian painters, and one of them is from Pistoia where Verrocchio worked and Giovanni Pisano and lots of painters centuries before the textile mills and canneries were set up alongside the vineyards. Mallenotti himself comes swinging in from the kitchen, a bread knife in his hand, bread under his arm and sings as he cuts the air to ribbons and everybody coaxes him to the top of his voice.

And then back into the dark street with the cars having to wait or steer around them, all the way to the Galleria Vannucci and the paintings. And in the gallery everybody seems to know the artists and congratulates them in Olympic style. They know art in the way you know your hometown main street—maybe because that's where the Italians have their art, in their streets and all around, all the time. For them art is always present and the artist is always coming.

When the gallery host asks you to say a few words out loud about the exhibition, that's when you think of Pikeville, Kentucky. And all the time you're standing there and trying to talk, Pikeville keeps haunting you. You're remembering years before, when as head of the Art Department of the University in Lexington, carrying the glad tidings of art into Pike County in eastern Kentucky and right into Pikeville on the County Seat on the Levisa Fork. You had some ideas in those days that it would almost be enough just to let people—any people—know of the wonders of art which you'd been lucky enough to be in on since you were a kid. Feeling this way about anything makes a lot possible. Being all fired up about how art can give eloquent or beguiling form to the raw experience of life, and maybe even help cause life to show with some kind of radiance—feeling that way makes a lot possible because your own convictions blind you to the gap between you and those people sitting out there in that bare dead room in the Pikeville Courthouse. And being blind to the gap you seem to pass right over it, which, who knows, maybe you did there in Pikeville with those coal miners whose mines had been shut down for years and whose timber had been cut out of the Cumberlands even before that. But it didn't feel that way.

The man who introduced you was an assistant superintendent of the Pike County School System, one of those who'd gone out of the hills to the State University and then came back. It seemed he felt the gap more than you did and he wanted to help you bridge it by telling those men and women that you'd worked on a ranch for a while in Lightning Flat, Wyoming, and in a lumber camp near Moose factory, Ontario—that even though you were going to talk about art there was nothing odd about you, that you were just a regular guy. And after he sat down and you talked and showed them, you thought how Americans and Mexicans and Frenchman and Italians had made their own experience eloquent in art, they clapped some, and you thanked them and sat down.

After coffee in mugs—it was December and snowing that evening—no one mentioned anything about art or anything you'd said. They talked about the abandoned mines and sawmills and how their sons had gone off to Louisville or St. Louis or clear out to the southwest because there was nothing left in Pike County for them. And they wanted to know how big the ranch was where you worked, and about the tools you used in the Canadian lumber camp, the kinds of trees, and exactly what you did there.

It was pretty clear at the end of that evening when you climbed back into your Jeep for that long ride back to the bluegrass country, that art for them was something way off yonder. It was still for them pretty much what it had been for Daniel Boone and the alligator-horses and for almost everyone before the broadcloth men from Virginia moved in—and those Virginians didn't take so well to eastern Kentucky.

And, you know, it was utterly logical that art should be way off yonder for those people of Pikeville. No man paints pictures while he spends his days scratching the crust of the earth for tomorrow; unless, maybe, he believes in some kind of magic like in the caves at Altimira and Lascaux where the record still shows—or in Pistoia where every tomorrow had to be dug up too, but dug up in view of the victories of a hundred generations before them.

So all the time you're talking there in the Vannucci Gallery in Pistoia in Italy, you're haunted by a memory of Pikeville in Kentucky where your faith in the power of art made you almost a stranger in your own country—and here in Pistoia that same faith was making you almost an intimate in a foreign land.

Evens and Odds in the Odd Year, 1961

I've always said that you never know what *even* things will turn up in *odd* places, and what happened in Mantua that November day is just more clear proof.

After you've taken in the really important Andrea Mantegna exhibition of paintings specially arranged in the Gonzaga Palace and decided that you like the frescoes best because they're closer to Piero della Francesca, you figure there's time to walk though the church of Sant' Andrea and get a feel for the scientific architecture of Leone Battista Alberti. So you drive over and there's a parking place right in front. The huge church rises out of its crowded nest of Fiats and Lambretta motor scooters and makes you feel even smaller and you have a strange urge to run—as if you're late for something. But you don't run, not even with your nice new American passport in the pocket of your West 6th Street Army and Navy Outlet Store trench coat; you know this is a church you're in—no matter what the Pazzi did to Giuliano de Medici in the one in Florence. It's awfully quiet under those great intersecting Roman barrel vaults—hardly anyone in the place and nobody lighting candles. So you stand in the mist gray on that stone floor far below the fake coffers of that rounded ceiling and you feel that you've been here before, many times before. And then you know why, and why you feel like you're late for something: Sant' Andrea is like a railroad station, a very big railroad station. It looks and feels like a railroad station and that you're much too late or much to early for the train. Sure enough there's the information booth under the domed crossing, and the clock and charts of arrivals and departures and lights pointing to this and that all in a kind of altar at the apse end.

So you stand there in the kind of 15th century Italian church that became our 19th and 20th century railroad stations, feeling that you'd missed the train, which—really—you had. And then, not being able to do much of anything about all that you go back outside to your car thinking about smaller things like taking something nice to your wife back home in Florence.

At a vegetable stand in the market you see some good crisp finocchio—that fine vegetable that gives you lettuce, leak, celery, cabbage, and licorice all in one—and pick out two stalks of it. The man at the stand says it costs forty lire and it seems ridiculous to bargain with those sad laughing eyes, so you begin to pay and he begins to wrap up the finocchio in a piece of newspaper. And then you pay him, take the bundle that looks like an oversize corsage that's been fought over, and start across the street still thinking a little about churches turning into railroad stations.

On the other side you realize you're not smoking and that a cigarette might be what you need. So you shift under your bundle and go for the package in your shirt pocket under your slip-on sweater. In the middle of that operation that feels like a news photograph of a sports event, maybe soccer, you notice that your finocchio is wrapped in an English language newspaper. Odd. So you turn your bundle a little and read quite clearly the name GONZALES and the letters DEMO which end at the torn edge of the paper. The slanted tear cuts across the second line of a headline, leaving only the words, IN TEXAS.

And then you read what's left of the article from the left margin to the torn edge: SAN ANTONIO, Nov. 5 (tear); Henry B. Gonzales, a (tear); John Goode, Jr., (tear); lican, in a special Cor (tear); election yesterday (tear); fought on the issue (tear); all of the Twen (tear); sional Districts (tear); gave Mr. Gonz (tear); and Mr. Goode (tear);

zales in the (tear); Mexican ance (tear); to Congress fr (tear):...And so on until there are just a few letters and then none between the left margin and that fateful tear. So you look up at the top and find, *The New York Times* International Edition, Paris, Monday, November 6, 1961. And what you want now is the rest of page two which, you figure, is either hinged to page three, someplace, or just a scrap lying somewhere.

So you go back to the vegetable stand and find the man who sold you the finocchio. No, you didn't want any vegetables, you just want the piece of paper that matches that angled tear down the edge of your finocchio bundle—you want to read about how a friend of yours may have won an election in America.

It's a funny world, the vegetable man says to you, because when he was in Rome selling vegetables for a while before the war the people used to come by his stand, but only to look at some famous sewer nearby; and here you were, he says, not buying vegetables—just looking for a torn piece of paper. And as you hunt through his paper supply you realize that he must have sold vegetables near the Cloaca Maxima in Rome, the huge drain built by Lucius Tarquinius Priscus around 578 B.C. because people like to look at that earliest known example of the true arch in Europe. And for a while you think about how the true arch went from a sewer into Alberti's church of Sant' Andrea and then into U.S. railroad stations. But you keep hunting for the rest of the Gonzales story so you can go into some quiet place and read it and hopefully gloat some.

The vegetable man asks you, please, why did all those people want to look at the sewer in Rome, and even if he was pulling your leg you tell him about the true arch and all that, and how his people perfected the rounded arch, keystone and all. And right in the middle of your own talk you remember that the first known example of the POINTED arch is also in a sewer—in an Assyrian drain dated around 722 B.C. And for a while you wonder to yourself about the pointed arch starting out that way and then going into Gothic cathedrals and liberal arts buildings on campuses around the U.S. But you get into the vegetable man's reserve stack of newspapers and there's the rest of page three of the Paris International Edition of *The New York Times*, and you've got the whole story, headline and all.

GONZALES, DEMOCRAT, IS WINNER
IN TEXAS RACE FOR HOUSE SEAT

On the other side of Mantua where the road goes out toward Reggio there's a little bar, and perhaps no one there could guess who or what you were toasting with those two stalks of finocchio and a torn sheet of newspaper. Viva Gonzales!

Homage to de Stael

In 1958 I stopped to see Lee Malone, then director of the Houston Museum of Fine Arts. He was on the phone and said he'd be with me in a few minutes. I walked out toward one of the galleries where a sign said there was an exhibition of paintings by Nicolas de Stael. I knew a little of his work, mostly through reproductions, and almost nothing of the man. I hadn't come to see the exhibition; I hadn't even known it was showing. I put out my cigarette at the entrance to the gallery and looked up. There ahead of me about twenty feet was a small painting, maybe twenty-four by thirty inches, and with my first look I felt that I'd been stopped in mid-air. Quiet it was, with grayed pinks and velvety black that opened up forward and back and into the whole world. I stood there feeling a great thing happening, and later I *knew* that it had. For three or four years after that, a good part of the world I lived in was the world of that painting, *The Beach at Honfleur*. For years almost every painting I made, and almost every one I tried to make, was another case of trying to repaint or answer that one of de Stael's. The one that came closest, although perhaps no one but I knows or could recognize its lineage, was one I called *War Storage*—grayed pinks and bulky black tarpaulin-covered shapes on a beach—that today reminds me as much of the beach from which I was evacuated from the South Pacific as it does of de Stael's *Beach at Honfleur*. A few years ago I wrote the full title on the back, so I'd be sure never to forget: *War Storage: Homage to de Stael*.

It has been said, untruthfully, that Nicolas de Stael jumped off the Eiffel Tower on St. Patrick's Day, and, truthfully, that Jackson Pollock turned himself over in an Oldsmobile 88, but *The Beach at Honfleur* and Pollock's *Number 1* remain, with all the heritage that gathers as a single voice to call us back to ourselves.

Dear Ted—Two Excerpts

I've just come across some copies of letters I wrote thirty-five years ago to my then-close friend, Ted Rannells, the man I succeeded as chairman of the art department at the University of Kentucky.

We corresponded for over twenty-five years, right up to the time of his death, beyond his eightieth birthday. Both of us being tough idealistic-romantics made it easy to share such thoughts as are in these two excerpts.

And now, with Ted gone to his rewards. I re-say these things to you—whomever you may be as if I were again talking to Ted.

Villa il Portico
Via di Montughi 23
Firenze March 30, 1962

Dear Ted:

It would be a sad mistake to think that for each of us, maybe as far back as very early childhood, there is just one moment, one door, that if failing to open closes away the fullness of life forever. No, the whole long or short life we live is millions and millions of moments, and there are doors aplenty. But sometimes, as with me in Paris, and even more in London, lately, I felt I'd missed whole years of moments and walked an almost endless wall of unopening doors. How else could I explain—were that my interest—the feeling that I was fumbling along that wall again, pitch dark now, back to an unopened door—and that by a magic unknown to chance I found it, opening from the rue de Berri into the Champs-Elysées? And felt my way to some kind of victorious consolation across the Place de la Concorde and into the Tuileries? Must so much wait into middle age, and catch us like this to let us know of the doors we passed and failed to try? Or, more harrowing, were those doors open or ajar with the light showing through—and we failed to see? No matter, you say at last, I have this *now;* and like a man aged backwards into childhood, you step almost innocently through and the Boulevards open to you—and no one you pass need know how you came this way.

In London it happened on the Strand between the Australia House and Trafalgar Square; and on the Victoria Embankment between the Westminster and Waterloo bridges. And then, recapturing the unknown lost, and opened up inside, I poured in the contents of the National Gallery, the Tate and the British Museum, day after day. The sun shone over London and into the galleries, and then, at dinner, I saw a woman who saw me. The mood I thought was only my own luck and extravagance must have carried to her like a familiar song to which she sang the finest words in the sweetest voice. Her name: Cathleen Conway, and two days of my life will always be tied to hers. After breakfast my last day in London, we said goodbye in Victoria Station with all the expansive Weltsmerz of late adolescence—and it turned into a monument as the train pulled away, in vapor, as it should I guess. How strangely human it is that perhaps because of the perfection of those days I shall be reluctant to return to London.

I saw St. Oswald's, the small 12th century stone church at Widford in the meadows where the Windrush runs, and stood in it alone as the birds sang outside against the distant high dronings of our B-50 bombers. In late afternoon I walked around Constable's Salisbury Cathedral, then sat inside as the light went down and heard the balance-release of the 14th century weight-driven clock free the seconds of a March day into eternity. And on another day I was crossing from Dover to Calais on the *Invicta* that saw service at Dieppe and Normandy, and stood aft with a double Scotch in hand as the gulls followed from the White Cliffs. Back in Paris I sat through the Evian-les-Bains noon cease-fire—at a table for one in the Cafe Viel on the Boulevard de la Madeleine...then took the night train south through Switzerland to Milano and on home to Florence.

Yes, I know how the "memories of the Davanzati" can be forever "mingled with memories of that child" you mentioned—the tiny creature with a perfect oval face and splendid eyes. And I am happy that we can write these things to each other.

Yrs.,
Don

405 Buckeye Trial
Austin, Texas
November 27, 1962

Dear Ted:

It has not been easy coming back "home" after a year away, for it was much more than a calendar year, and further than across the sea I went. The "home" to which ones returns, if he is fortunate at all, is in himself—and though to return is part of good fortune, no man accomplishes it without being harrowed, no man re-enters without risk of disintegration, without risk of being consumed.

I have taken many trips. I've been away from home before: as a boy to Yucatan, Guatemala, Mexico, Hudson's Bay, Death Valley, New York; as a young man to Borneo, the China Coast, New Guinea, Guadalcanal, the Philippines, Bermuda, Haiti, the New Hebrides. But in middle age I went where my fathers lived and stayed in their towns and countries for a year that was a lifetime of its own. There, that year, in the presence of greatnesses superseded, outlived, neglected, and denied the lesson of how it runs was taught me. And something of the unbounded optimism, the romantic hopefulness died or was started toward transformation. Whole "settled" areas of my life, the furnished rooms of my house, were disturbed, emptied out. And so I came home. A sense of duty, a responsibility to that myth, a respect for the differences of our private and public worlds made it possible to resume activity back here in Texas. Like the pugilist, all but knocked out keeps his feet and even returns blows while begging the time to recovery of full consciousness or a means to be effective while not fully so, I went about the ring of my responsibilities at home, at the university and in the town. Now, after more than two months, my activity is more than time-begging: a second wind, a new consciousness has come.

As ever,
Don

A Goodwill Trip to Winchester, Kentucky

Thinking of trips I made to enhance goodwill toward the art department of The University of Kentucky during those three years I served as chairman, I'm reminded of a trip I made to the small town of Winchester.

The ladies club of Winchester had written to the art department asking if it might be possible for a faculty member to speak to them about "Modern Art." None of my faculty volunteered, so arrangements were made and I drove to the address in Winchester which happened to be the address of the local fire department. I asked the one fireman in evidence if he knew where the Ladies' Club was, and he said that the ladies met upstairs right over the fire engine.

They were having their business meeting up there, and after the chairlady acknowledged my presence and pointed to a chair near her, I sat down and looked around the low-ceilinged room as she went on and on about things I've long ago forgotten. There were about twenty women sitting in what looked like short sections of church pews. All had their hair done up neatly and some wore hairnets. By my guess, there wasn't one of them under fifty years of age—the women, I mean, not the hairnets, about which I have no way of knowing. As I looked from one to another and thought about the slides I'd be using to illustrate my lecture on "Modern Art," I was thinking that perhaps I'd better not show some of them to this group, now sucking on hard candy passed around by a very old midget-like woman. And now that I'd tuned in on what the chairlady was saying and caught phrases having to do with Christian duty, clean living, and the threat of Communism in the Kentucky public schools, I was certain that I shouldn't show those slides of Dali's nude women with drawers for their breasts; that screaming naked child in a dump heap by Siqueros; Edward Munch's bloody bath tub murder of Jean Marat with the naked Charlotte Corday standing by; that severed gangrenous leg by Hyman Bloom; Ivan Albright's bulging diseased prostitute; and quite a few others.

So, as I sat there without having been offered any hard candy to suck on, I went through my box of slides, taking out those I judged would offend, and which I'd have a hard time defending. I put these in the back of the box, behind a divider—censored out of the lecture.

Now the chairlady was awarding ribbons for a previously held flower arrangement contest. Next were three awards—in this case little boxes of Fanny Farmer chocolates—for what were called "good turns" done by members during the previous month.

As I've often asked myself, "Weismann, what in the Hell are you doing here," I was asking that again inside my head—where whatever I'd planned to say about modern art was dissolving into nothing. All I wanted to do was flee the premises. No way. I was now being introduced as a famous artist who was chairman of the art department of their university, happily married, and the father of a boy child born just a few months ago in Lexington.

I ran the slide projector myself and talked from the back of the room where the old midget-like woman kept offering me some hard candy by holding a piece out to me.

I wound up the talk just short of all those slides I'd deleted. Just before I asked for the overhead light to be turned on the little old midget lady looking into my slide box said, "You still have some slides in here, doctor," and I said, "They're not for this lecture."

"Why not?" she asked. "They're right there in your box, doctor."

"You wouldn't want to see them," I said.

"Are they dirty pictures, or something?" she asked.

"You might say that," I said.

Then the very old midget-like woman leaned close and in a whisper asked, "Naked people?"

"Yes, some," I said.

"What are they doing?" she whispered. I just looked at her; why should I go into that—try to describe some of those images while she sucked more vigorously on her hard candy and nudged against me. "Any of them doing, you know what?" she whispered, and I said, "Doing what?"

"You know," she said, giving me what now amounted to a push..."intercoursing! Do any of those slides show people fucking?"

While I hesitated, the fire house siren went off and you could hear the fire engine starting up below. It didn't startle the ancient midget woman at all, she just kept on talking, now raising her voice above the siren and noise downstairs. When she reached into the box to get at the unused slides, I slapped her, not too hard, on her wrist. "Oh," she said looking up at me with what could be described as a lascivious leer, "you're a bad, bad boy," and then turned and sashayed away as if she was heading down the center aisle to a stage while a pit band played bump and grind music.

Oh yes, I remember Winchester and not because it reminds me of the *Winchester bushel*, a British unit of dry measure equal to 2,150.42 cubic inches, or the volume of a cylinder 18 1/2 inches in internal diameter and 8 inches deep. No, not because of any of that.

Pikeville on the Road to Making Good

I was still in my thirties when I accepted the chairmanship of the art department at the University of Kentucky. I'd come down from Wayne University in Detroit with plenty of energy and a strong will to make good at running things.

Because the art department was suffering some poor public relations, there was an added incentive to make good, not only within the university, but also around the whole state of Kentucky. The retiring chairman had gotten in some scrapes in town and outside mainly because of his heavy drinking and because during the twenty years he'd chaired the department, the general public had gotten the idea that he thought of himself as a superior person. That he drank to excess, there could be no argument. After all, when a professor comes to his classes with his overcoat on backwards and keeps bending up his cars against fire hydrants and telephone poles, all the while smelling like the inside of a whisky barrel and reciting limericks with their punch-lines missing—well, there are solid grounds for the belief that, yes, Chairman Rannells was a drunk. But as for the Kentucky riff-raff's opinion that he thought himself superior—no grounds for that at all: Ted Rannells was a gifted, humble man who, too often, preferred alcoholic visions to a clear-eyed version of Kentucky and its university. I really got to love Ted Rannells, a love that lasted long after I'd left the Bluegrass State, right up to the day Ted, blind at the end and listening to Vivaldi on his phonograph, died peacefully at eighty.

So, with all the good Ted Rannells had done for his students, and for art, his modus operandi created problems for me as chairman.

Much more serious was the case of a young assistant professor, Blake Jones, who took to writing letters and signing himself as chairman of the art department long before Rannells passed it on to me. Whether or not this was condoned by the president of the University, a Doctor Hoolihan who'd earned his Doctor of Education degree from a teacher's college in, I think, Tennessee—whether or not he was in cahoots with Blake Jones remained a question. What was not in question was Blake Jones' sexual orientation, as it's called nowadays; he was a homosexual. And whether or not his personal friend, Doctor Hoolihan was also a homosexual, was never determined.

Just before I took over at the University of Kentucky, Assistant Professor Jones and an unnamed friend were spotted, almost nude, by the state police. They were in plain view, along a not-much-used road, and engaged in what are now called "gay activities," "cornholing and blowing off," as one officer was reported to have called it. All of that not so unusual, not even back then. But what *was* unusual was that that same evening a limousine bearing the number one Kentucky license plate—presumed to be carrying the Governor—drove up to the city jail where Blake Jones was being held and carted him off. He never even cleaned out his apartment; he was out of the state fast, never to return.

Well, along with Ted Rannells' drunken escapades and Blake Jones' run-in with the law, there were some fences to mend—especially in the minds of the public. And I was the new chairman. By the time I left Kentucky for Texas, three years later,

I'd managed to fix up things pretty well. The public, as well as the university, were feeling all right about the art department, with what could be called an attitude of benign neglect.

And how did I manage this? Oh, in lots of ways, but since I want to tell you about a trip I took to Pikeville (in eastern Kentucky), I'll mention only that I traveled all over the state giving talks, dedication speeches, judging art exhibitions, carrying the message that the people's university was on the ball, doing good for youth and for art. I spent a great deal of time on the road and, as I surely remember, I paid for most of the gasoline. But it worked: People stopped talking about drunks, homosexuals, and crooked administrators—pretty much, anyway.

I tell you all this just to remark about my trip to Pikeville, about one hundred fifty miles southeast of Lexington. A trip that in several ways typified most of my Kentucky trips, made in the service of art and public opinion. I was going to Pikeville to judge the artwork—drawings, paintings, soap sculpture, etc. of the sixth, seventh, and eighth grade pupils of the Pikeville public schools and to give talks in the high school and over the local radio station.

It started to snow the day before I'd planned on driving the 150 miles in my 1949, two-wheel drive Jeepster. The roads got so bad that instead of driving I took the Greyhound bus the day before I had to be in Pikeville. It seemed to take forever with the highways banked in snow and stopping in all those towns between—Winchester, Goff's Corners, Stanton, Rogers, Lee City, Ivyton, Prestonberg, Betsy, and into Pikeville. I was the last and only passenger left when the bus pulled up to a drugstore in Pikeville, let me out, and moved away toward Elkhorn City on the Kentucky/West Virginia border. By then it was way after midnight and I had no idea where I'd spend the night. Before the man locked up the drugstore I asked him where I'd find a hotel, and he pointed off in the distance several blocks, then turned off the lights.

It was still snowing, not a soul on the streets, and so I picked up my large suitcase, heavy with a bunch of books I was going to give the Pikeville library, and started walking. Then, sure enough, there was the hotel—a two-story frame building, all dark except for the weakly lighted entry-way and the lobby. The door was stuck, but I got it free and went through. The lobby was larger than I'd expected, wooden-floored with some hard-back chairs against the walls—all empty. No one was at the desk. I put my suitcase down and waited a few seconds before I made a move to ring the rusty bell on the counter.

Before I got to the bell I heard my name called from some place behind me. When I turned, surprised, I didn't recognize the man. "You're Doctor Weismann, aren't you?" he asked, coming forward with his hand outstretched.

"Yes, that I am," I said, "How come you know my name?"

"Well," the man said, "we were watching you when you got off the bus, but I didn't know it was you until you were halfway here."

"Have we ever met?" I asked.

"I'm Ray Kasinski," the man said, "we met once about a year ago—a party given when Ted Rannells retired from the Chairmanship—formally retired, that is."

"I'll be damned," I said, "you remember better than I do."

"Part of my job," Ray Kasinski said, as another man appeared from the back of the lobby, "we're regular old-time Revenuers, Feds. We know there's a big batch of illegal whisky up there in the hills and they're waiting for their contact man—we thought maybe you were the guy."

"And you're sure I'm not the contact?" I asked.

"Not unless you've got the guy in that suitcase of yours," and then they both laughed.

All the time I was judging those kids' art works the following day I was thinking how, if I had known the details—how I might have helped those boys up there in the hills—helped them beat the U.S. Government—and the idea gave me a strangely warm feeling, even though I'd discovered that somehow, someone had searched through my suitcase before I'd gotten it up to my room that had no bath but two Gideon Bibles in plain view on the washstand.

Bill Tabor and the Masons

Bill Tabor has a store and filling station back a way from Farm to Market Road 812 here in south Texas. The store and a few sheds are made out of salvaged wood and stand among scattered junk. The electric sign with half of the bulbs missing says, "Yes, we're open." It's really a place out of an old western movie—something between the remnants of a town and a ghost. Bill Tabor calls it Tabortown and he believes it has a fine future.

Tabertown has the closest gasoline from where we live, so, when I've not been so provident, I buy gas, there—at ten cents more a gallon from a pump that may not measure full gallons. Doesn't matter, does it, when Bill's gas is the difference between an empty tank and the fullness of life.

Bill Tabor, a handsome, deeply weathered, and scarred man of fifty-two was, for years, a movie stuntman. A photograph of him from those days hangs slantwise behind the counter. When you look at the picture it has an especially strong way of tugging you towards thoughts of the sadness of how time passes and us with it.

Even when I'm in a hurry and hanging up the self-service nozzle, Bill is there—usually with a question, like the other day:

"What do you know about the Masons?" he asked, "Freemasonry, like it's called."

"Not much," I said, and I kept myself from asking why he wanted to know. But he went on, anyway.

"I've been having a lot of bad crap happen to me," he said, "an awful lot more than usual, and I'm wondering why."

"Bad crap, like good crap, runs in cycles," I said, using a piece of antiqued economic theory.

"Maybe," Bill Tabor said, "but just look at what's been going on this past month. First the county health board came out here to tell me those five horses I had were underfed and sick and that I had to get rid of them. Then the bank refuses me a loan on my four-by-four. Then somebody from a safety commission drives up to tell me my gasoline storage tank is not deep enough in the ground. Then the promise I had from Budweiser Beer to put on my water-walking act is, all of a sudden, broken, and then to top it off a sheriff's deputy comes out here saying he's had a complaint—that I stole some tools from some guy's shed. All in one month…can you believe it?"

"That's a full month," I said.

"Too damned full," Bill Tabor said, "and I think I know why."

"Why," I asked.

"It's the Masons doing it."

"The Masons?" I said.

"You bet," Bill Tabor said, "the Freemasons and my brother who's a Mason himself."

"They've got some funny customs," I said, "but all those clubs got funny customs—the Eagles, Elks, the Kiwanis, all of them."

"The Masons got lots of *secret* stuff," Bill Tabor said.

"Like secret handshakes," I said, "but what the hell, when I was a kid we had them, and secret codes, and so on."

"Yeah," Bill Tabor said, "but what do the Masons do in those secret temples they have—all those special get-ups they wear and those secret ceremonies. It's not Christian either—anti-Christ."

"How is that?"

"Ask the Catholics," Bill Tabor said, "they don't allow their people to be Masons, they know what Masons are."

"So what does your brother have to do with all this?" I asked.

"Everything," Bill Tabor said. "My brother, who's been against me for the last twenty years, is a Mason."

"So...?"

"It's clear to me, all this bad crap happening to me," Bill Tabor said, "my brother's got those Mason's lined up against me. It's the goddamned Mason's—coming at me with all that secret stuff—making the health people, the bank, the gasoline safety people take my brother's hate out on me."

In what I thought was a transparently kidding, joking way, I said, "Bill, if all this is true why don't you just kill your brother?"

"Five times I've thought of that," Bill Tabor said, "but those goddamned Masons would have him equipped with a bullet-proof vest—goddamned bullets would just bounce off like they were under a secret spell, or something."

"Bill," I said, "have you ever thought of you, yourself, joining up with the Masons?"

"And fight alongside my brother?" Bill Tabor said, "No way, Professor, no way."

Winning the War in Arabia

Somebody stole our Sunday paper out of the slot below our rural mailbox. It's happened before. Sunday papers here sell for a dollar, and anyone running off with them can make a few bucks if they collect a number of them—which is pretty easy since there are ten slots just in the string of mailboxes right here.

At first I thought, the hell with it—what's in the Sunday paper, after all? A little later at breakfast, however, I felt a little lame, lame in my right arm, if lameness is not limited to the legs. There I was at the breakfast table, food and drink taken, and my right arm and hand lying there useless—no pages of a newspaper to turn and say to them, "Same shit, same shit."

So I drove over to Bill Tabor's store, that wild assortment of shacks and lean-tos he calls "Tabortown." I've told you about Bill Tabor in an earlier conversation we've had. He's the one who thinks the Fraternal Order of Masons is out to get him—make his life unbearable, because his younger brother is a Mason and hates him.

I went over to Bill's Tabortown to see if he still had a Sunday paper left. He had more than one, but I bought only one—naturally.

The front page was full of gossip about Saddam Hussein and what looks like an impending war in the Arabian desert. "It's lousy, isn't it?" I said. "If there's a war over there," Bill said, "we'll never win it."

"Well," I said, "we got plenty of practice at that in Vietnam."

"This will be different," Bill said, "they'll just go into those holes and tunnels, I've seen them, been in them."

"For a fact?" I half asked.

"Absolutely," Bill said. "I spent two years over there in the 1950s laying cable for the oil companies. You see," he went on, "there's all that sand on top, but below that there's sandstone, easy to cut sandstone under everything. And I saw those Arabians living and working down in those holes and long, long tunnels; I almost got lost in them a couple of times."

"And you figure the Arabians will go down into them where we can't get at them?"

"We won't even know they're there," Bill said, "we won't be able to find them."

"Maybe," I said, "that would make it easy for our boys—no resistance."

"Arabs are sneaky," Bill said, "and homosexuals, once our boys were past them they'd sneak out up behind them—knock 'em off."

"That's a pretty awful picture," I said.

"Any worse than facing Iraqi gas and germs?" Bill asked.

"I suppose not," I said. "Don't you see any possibility in the event of our getting in a war over there, for us to win?" I asked.

"Only one possibility," Bill Tabor said.

"And what's that," I asked.

"We should have done it years ago," Bill went on, "back in the 50s when we had 100 percent access to that underground world—we could have planted whole nests and communities of them then—they'd have done them in down there."

"What would have done them in?" I asked.

"Oh, they would have done in every last one of those Arabians—you've been around here long enough, Professor, to know that—there's no way, absolutely no way to get rid of them. They'd eat those Arabians down to the bones and not stop there—just keep on going."

"*What* would do this, Bill?" I asked.

"Professor," Bill said, "you know as well as I do, the answer to this war is fire ants—set free to eat up those fucking Arabian Knights of Sadass Hussein."

"Touché," I said.

"No," Bill Tabor said, "fire ants!"

New Patriotic Body Bags for Gulf War Dead

I hear that the contracts are being let to Japan and Taiwan—multi-million dollar contracts for body bags. George Bush is already demonstrating his concern for the casualties he's planned for the land war in the Persian Gulf. But these will not be the regular drab body bags in which the flower of our youth returned from Vietnam. No, not at all: Bush's body bags will be brilliant red, white, and blue with appliquéed American flags. When asked about this, Bush said that "Nothing's too good for our soldiers, sailors, and marines—they deserve the very best, even the enlisted personnel, they all fought and will fight—for freedom which is impossible without oil." Barbara Bush, the First Lady, concurs, as does their son, Neil, a crooked civilian.

Daniel Quayle, the moron who's a heartbeat away from the presidency, is holding out for *two* appliquéed flags on the body bags of those who were sucked up from National Guard units of the type that served him so well to avoid going to Vietnam.

General Colin Powell, Chairman of the Joint Chiefs, has declined responding to any and all questions about body bags and war. He simply says, "Ask the Commander-in-Chief, he runs the plantation." General Powell, by the way, is a four-star general, the highest peace-time rank for generals. Only if Bush takes the country into a protracted land war, will General Powell get a shot at five-star rank like Eisenhower and MacArthur enjoyed.

I'm writing this on the eve of Thanksgiving, 1990. Tomorrow President Bush will visit our poor and ethnic minority soldiers, all volunteers, in the Saudi Arabian desert. This is considered another "photo-op"—an elaborately staged performance to be beamed back to the U.S. to strengthen Bush's chances to be re-elected in 1992. Bush will be using, I wager, that limited vocabulary of hand gestures he was taught by TV experts in 1988. That was when the so-called "image-makers" worked to change Bush from wimp to macho man. It appears that his catastrophic invasion of Panama and the kidnapping of Panama's General Noriega didn't change him enough in the direction of macho man, so I figure he's trying to remedy that by going to war in the Middle East for the oil lobby without real consultation with the representatives of the American people.

Long ago when that retard, Gerald Ford, was president, he tried to beat inflation by manufacturing and distributing millions of plastic covered metal pin-ons that had just three letters on them : W I N, which stood for "Whip Inflation Now." It didn't work. And neither will gaily colored, red, white, and blue body bags. Not even if each one, stuffed with battlefield dead, has an American flag appliqued right on top of where all the cameras can photograph it.

Five and Seven Day Camels

A friend of mine, Roscoe Stark, was a Sergeant in the U.S. Army serving in the transportation corps in Saudi Arabia during the American effort to insure a steady supply of oil for us.

I've known Roscoe Stark for over thirty years, ever since he was a student in my graduate seminar titled "Showing and Telling." He was an excellent student. His seminar paper, "Telling Is Easier than Showing," was a genuine tour-de-force—making the point that telling makes use of language and that with language just about everything seems possible as well as impossible. Showing, however, wrote Roscoe, is more limited. After all, if you hold up the apple or the viper, let's say, well—there they are. All you have to do is place one or the other in the line of vision, and there it is! Simple as that—barring any magic or slight-of-hand indulged in by the shower of the objects. Telling is easier, Roscoe wrote, because you're not limited to the object under scrutiny. With words, the language, you can meander all over the verbal landscape, a fact which makes philosophy, economics, and much more possible even if all you're doing is telling about apples and snakes.

Telling works best, Roscoe wrote, when the person or persons you're talking to are not in the presence of what you're telling about. In this situation you can get away with almost anything, especially misrepresentation.

I thought about Roscoe Stark's seminar paper—"Telling Is Easier than Showing"—when he wrote me about his work the Transportation Corps over there in Saudi Arabia. Maybe the best way to share what he wrote is to quote directly, verbatim of his letter dated August 30, 1990.

"Dear Doc," he wrote,

> "This is a very different sort of life over here—not only the climate and the language, but, more interesting, how things are done. As you know, President Bush is hoping to make Saddam Hussein back down, give Kuwait back and so on. And Bush is figuring that it may take quite a while, maybe as long as it took in Vietnam, almost twelve years, except that Bush says we'll win over here. He figures that in the process we may lose all our regular means of ground travel, except by foot and by camel. So as a Sergeant in the Transportation Corps, they've got me learning about camel transportation. My instructor, the same camel driver [who] was befriended by Lyndon Johnson years ago has told me that there are just two types of camels—the five-day camel and the seven-day camel. The five-day camel can go only five days on its internal supply of water which it is provided with at the outset of a trek; the seven-day camel can take on enough water to last it seven days. The interesting thing I was *told* and *shown* was how it's possible to make a five-day camel into a seven-day camel. What you do is let the five-day camel take on his limit of five days of water. Just before he pulls his head out of the bucket, you stand behind him with a mason brick in your hand and with all your might you bang it into the camel's testicles. This causes the camel to gasp, mightily, and in

the process suck in two more days of water. A five-day camel made into a seven-day camel just like that.

"I asked my instructor if this didn't hurt one helluva lot, and he said—showing me his right hand—"Not at all if you wear a glove, see?"

"I'll bet, [Roscoe's letter goes on,] you're wondering what Arabs do about female camels. My instructor says that's no problem at all. "You see around here a woman is no more than a castrated man—and is treated accordingly. So what do we do with the female camel is bam her in the place where the balls used to be. Works like a charm."

Roscoe added a postscript:

"P.S. I still think it's easier to tell then to show."

I Was on the Roof When the Governor Called

I was up on the roof wondering how I'd go about re-flashing the chimney when my wife appeared below saying that the governor was on the phone.

"The governor?" I asked. "Who is it, really?"

"Says he's the governor," my wife said, "Price Daniel."

"Okay," I said, "I'll bet it's Bill Arrowsmith with one of his Texas pol impersonations; I'll be down."

The ladder was clear at the other end of the 5–12 pitched roof, almost a hundred feet from the chimney, so it took me a few minutes or more to get down and to the phone. I took my time, Bill could wait.

When I picked up the phone, he said, "This is Governor Daniel," and I said, "And this is Buffalo Bill, can I help you?"

"Is Doctor Weismann there?" the voice said, "Doctor Ransom (he was president of the university then) told me that Doctor Weismann could answer our questions here."

About this time I began to feel that this just might be the governor of Texas, so I admitted, without explanation for the shift, that, yes, I was Doctor Weismann.

"Our State Building Committee," the voice said, "is meeting right now—I'm calling while they wait."

Now I settled for it—this was the Governor.

"Yes," I said, "how might I help?"

"We're planning for a mural to be commissioned for a new state office building. The committee is pretty well decided on the design of one of our talented west Texas artists, but the artist wants to do it in ceramic tile."

"Yes," I said, "that's a great medium...been employed for centuries."

"What's a medium?" the Governor asked.

"It's what a thing is made out of," I said. "In the case you're talking about it's the ceramic tile."

"So," the Governor, "it's an all right thing to use in a mural?"

"Oh yes, indeed," I said, "fired and glazed ceramic tile is one of the most permanent in just about all kinds of weather."

"Another question, Dr. Weismann," the governor said, "could it be used on the outside of the building?"

"Oh yes," I said.

"What about inside?" the governor asked.

About this time I got to thinking, again that this just might be Bill Arrowsmith. If the goddamn tile can stand up to being outside in the weather, why ask if it would hold up out of the weather, inside? I thought. But I held on. "Yes, Governor, it ought to do even better inside than out." And then I added, "You know Governor, it's a little like a raincoat—the outside is impermeable, doesn't let the water in, but if you wear the raincoat inside out...well that's another story, the water gets through. But with a ceramic tile you wouldn't have that problem because the mural will never be turned inside out."

"That's right," the governor said, "this mural will never be turned inside out. The artist told us that once it's on that wall with its outside facing out it will stay that way."

"That's the way it should be," I said.

"By the way," the governor said, "what's on the other side—the inside of a ceramic tile mural?" Now I want to remind you that I'm talking to a duly elected Governor of the

State of Texas—once the largest state in the union. I really had a hard time believing what he was asking and saying. I was less cynical in those days, even less disillusioned.

I said, "Governor, all that's on the backside of a ceramic tile mural is the cement that holds the tiles to the wall of the building."

"Yes," the Governor said. "It's pretty obvious now that you say it."

"Like Patrick Henry saying give me liberty or give me death," I said.

"And Remember the Alamo," the governor said.

"How true, Governor," I said.

"While I have you on the phone," the governor said, "President Ransom said you know art from A-Z, and I'm wondering if you would accept an invitation to serve on the State Building Design Commission."

I said I'd be delighted to serve. The governor thanked me and a few days I had a letter from him inviting me to membership on that commission, which I accepted.

I served a while on the State of Texas Building Design Commission. What I remember of all that time was a very long discussion about the color of freshly picked olives. Some ceramic medallions were being designed for the outside of a state building and one of them included a few olives, and the state wanted them the right color, of course. The chairman of the Commission on which I served was a retired admiral who'd been to Spain and evidently looked at some fresh olives. Well, so had I been to Spain—and Greece—but what we saw of olives didn't match, certainly not in color. I held out a long time for my fresh olive color—held out against the admiral's fresh olive color. But after awhile, I thought, "Oh, fuck it" and gave in.

Adjunct Professor

As usual that morning, I was driving to the university for my first class when I saw another professor walking toward the campus. Even though I was not sure I recognized him, I stopped and asked if he'd like a lift. He was carrying two large, heavy-looking books, and he said that, yes, he'd appreciate a lift.

In the time it took us to drive the two miles or so, we talked the usual professor-type of talk—something about the present-day state of education, the economic situation, the politics of organ transplanting, and so on. I wondered what field the professor did his work in—he seemed so broadly educated, it was difficult to determine. No matter that, he appeared entirely at ease and secure in whatever was his academic discipline—even to the extent of coming to the university in bib-type overalls.

Finally, just before I approached the main gate to the university, I asked him what he taught.

"Oh, I don't teach," he said.

"Straight research?" I asked.

"No," he said, "I'm the gas man; I read gas meters. You can leave me out here...thank you."

The State of the Nation and Leon Goertz

Dear Keith; Editor
The Bostonia
Boston, Mass.

It was good talking with you the morning of Shakespeare's birthday. Good to hear your voice, good to get reports from the Boston Front. A nice surprise, too.

Now, since giving your invitation to write an essay on the "State of the Nation" a lot of thought, it's become clear that I cannot write a thousand or so sensible words about "The State of the Nation." Not even our recent presidents have been able to do that. Proof of this should be unarguable in the accompanying pages.

I've chosen to write rather than call you, since I feared you might talk me into and convince me that I could chin myself on my *film-noire*, comic cynicism, and look over the edge into some dream-like vista full of reason and muscular hope.

As Chancellor Ransom used to say to me—and, I guess, lots of others:

Bless you, boy,
My love, Don

Leon Goertz drowned a few weeks ago. Trying to help out a situation that involved someone else's truck and a rising creek, his boot top got caught in the crotch of a submerged oak. Neither would give and Leon died under there. Only fifty, an ex-Marine, and to all evidences in excellent health, he owned and operated Leon's Country Store in Rockne, Texas. Yes, named for the unforgettable Notre Dame football coach.

I hadn't known Leon long, maybe a year since I met him in the Wrangler Bar on Highway 21, about ten miles from Rockne. He had a bronze Marine Corps insignia fixed on his gimme cap which led to my revealing that I was ex-Navy, World War II, South Pacific. He couldn't believe something about my serial number, 289076—too low or too high—and that almost went into an argument. Soon, though, it became clear that Leon Goertz was much more interested in the state of the nation—the United States' state.

Leon Goertz had a surprising lot of information on ready tap. After a while it was clear that what he had was not all that much information, but an awesome memory for almost everything he read in the *Austin American Statesman* and the *Bastrap County Weekly* and heard on television. Down here in south Texas one could argue that there isn't much else, is there? Were I to try to characterize Leon's "positions" on anything from taxation, education, the environment, racism, national defense, the Savings and Loan catastrophe; pornography; the national debt; international relations; and folks like George Bush, Jesse Jackson, and Senator Phil Gramm's wife—well, I'd be met with a fifty-fifty mixture of ambiguity and the impossible. But if I were pressed I'd say that Leon's picture of the State of the Nation was drawn in lines more like those of Jack Schaeffer's *Shane* of 1949 than those of Graham Greene's *The Ministry of Fear* of 1943. Not that the dates matter, though they're both around a half-century ago, and one author is American, the other British.

One night, again at the Wrangler Bar, Leon said he wanted to show me his store in Rockne and to meet his mother. I wondered if it wasn't too late for that—and he said it was never too late to improve the state of the nation, and besides, she'd still be up. Sure enough and she gave us some of her homemade wine out of the refrigerator in the living room. Constantly smiling she said she was against a state income tax and abortion—the Goertz's are Catholic—and that God gave her His blessing with Leon.

Leon's Country Store sits on hard clay just across the dirt road and little down from Mother Goertz's clapboard house. Inside three younger men were sitting on feed bags and good naturedly looking for the right way to bring their three guitars into sync. There was plenty of beer, all from dented cans, maybe the ones Leon wouldn't feel right trying to sell. Leon's younger brother asked me if I knew what *Leon* meant, and I said, yes—Lion. That's right, the brother said, monarch of all he surveys. Leon asked me about the state of the nation—how I felt about how things were going, and I said I thought they were pretty well screwed up, using such as the anti-smoking crusade and threats of cancer for everybody as red herring as the whole world undergoes fundamental changes full of opportunities for the United States while our leaders think only of their upcoming elections. Amen, said Leon.

That's when the older man standing near the beer can crusher introduced himself and said he was a mortician, which was easy to believe. But that's all he said. For awhile it sounded like the three younger men had gotten their guitars going on something like "Waltzing Across Texas," or maybe "Are You Lonesome Tonight?" After all, it was late. And then it got awful quiet with the undertaker standing there just looking at me. So I asked him, seriously, how business was. "People are not passing on as early as they used to," he said.

"Part of the state of the nation," I said.

"To the nation," Leon Goertz said, raising his can of Lone Star, "the National Beer of Texas" as it plainly says right on the can. Then quiet again, and the undertaker staring at me as if he were taking my measurements.

Now, I'm one of those people who, when in a group and that long thick silence descends, tries to relieve it by saying something, sometimes almost anything. Over the years this has gotten me in all kinds of difficulty, just trying to be nice, keep things going instead of waiting and listening and perhaps learning something about the state of the nation. So I asked the undertaker if there were any more or less standard procedures about burying personal jewelry—rings, necklaces, earrings, etc.—on the body. He said wedding rings almost always stay on the deceased, the rest a matter of decision by the surviving "loved ones."

"How about wristwatches?" I asked.

"What about wristwatches?" he asked.

"Do you ever bury the dead wearing their wristwatches?" I asked.

"Never had the problem," the undertaker said, "Pocket watches, yes, sometimes."

"Were those pocket watches running?"

"I don't remember," the undertake said, "besides being in the deceased's pocket where it couldn't be seen it wouldn't matter."

"Pretty much like the state of the nation," Leon Goertz said, "or so they think."

The guitars were going pretty good by this time, and Leon was singing along in German to one of those Elvis Presley numbers that Elvis did in German a long time ago. When they finished, the undertaker applauded while keeping me in focus. "That sounded like pretty good High German," I said to Leon, "I knew German before I learned English right after the First World War."

"The next war," Leon said, "will be like the last big one—Japs and Germans against the rest."

"And what about the state of the nation, our nation, the U.S. of A.?" I asked.

"The state of the nation?" Leon asked, "well, sir, only if we can get cozy with the Japs before they snuggle up to the Germans again we won't be but a little lost ball in that Potomac river."

Then silence and I'm foolishly breaking it again, asking the undertaker, "If you did bury a person with a wristwatch on would you have it running?"

"I don't think so," the undertaker said, "no point."

"So," I said, "if you buried someone with their wristwatch on you'd have it stopped."

"I guess so," the undertaker said.

"Would you give any thought to what time you'd have it stopped at?"

"Never had any reason to think of any of this," the undertaker said, now wanting to skew his gaze.

"Have you ever noticed," I asked, "that in newspapers and jewelry catalogs the watches are often shown as stopped at a certain time?"

"At what time?" the undertaker asked, now getting on a laser track right between my eyes.

"Twenty minutes past eight," I said, "and I bet you know why, don't you?"

That's when Leon Goertz pushed himself away from the roll of barbed wire with the sign, MADE IN THE U.S.A., stapled to it, came over behind the undertaker, put his hand on him, and said, "Don't you know Morgan, that that's the time Abraham Lincoln was shot—in Ford's Theater, Washington, D.C., twenty minutes past eight on April 14, 1865."

"I didn't know that," Morgan the undertaker said.

"That's the state of this whole nation," Leon said, "don't know what or when things happened, don't know what's going on right now, and don't care. A sorry state."

The day after Leon Goertz drowned the sign with the moveable letters outside the Wrangler Bar was spelling out: WE'LL MISS YOU, LEON.

Self-Canceling Laws

Long ago I learned to read, and except for some interruptions—like when the ship went down and I had to spend all my time staying afloat—and when I was a university administrator and doing something that seemed like juggling while playing hide and seek with my paranoiac dean—except for interruptions like that, I've been reading all my life.

I even read reports of what's reported as the activities of our government. I know that I shouldn't feed my growing cynicism by reading reports of new social laws that keep being made—laws about housing, birth control, one parent families, taxation, pornography, and such—I know I shouldn't push myself toward nihilism by reading such stuff. I guess it's how these laws so often prove to be either impossible to enforce, or how in operation they have ways of cancelling out themselves—I guess it's the way so many of these laws—let's say aimed at cleaning up welfare, end up making it worse, that grab and hold my attention.

I've gotten to intellectually accept the macabre charm that these self-cancelling laws have. But one evening I was afforded a first-hand demonstration of just how those self-canceling laws cancel themselves—in the hands of the very people for whom the laws were made.

I was having dinner alone in what to all evidences was a pretty classy restaurant in Trenton, New Jersey—spotless white tablecloths, fresh flowers on every table, waiters in uniforms pretty close to tuxedos, bow ties, and all.

And the waiter was there almost right away, but not too soon with the newspaper-size menu which he handed me by leaning over in a manner pretty close to supplication. It was then I noticed that he had a spoon in his upper coat pocket. I wondered about that. Then, looking around the lavishly appointed dining room, I saw that *all* the waiters had spoons in their upper coat pockets.

I couldn't help myself, so when my waiter returned to see if I was ready to order, I asked him. "How come," I asked "that all you waiters have spoons like yours up there in your pocket?"

"Yes," the waiter said, "it's standard procedure here."

"Some ancient custom I know nothing about?" I asked.

"I don't think so, sir," the waiter said. "It's just part of the policy here."

"Anything you could tell me about?" I asked.

"Well, sir," the waiter said, "I guess so." And then he just stood there while I kept looking from his face to his spoon.

"It's this way," the waiter finally said, "Mr. LaMont, our maitre d', is very fastidious, very efficient. He's worked it out how much time is saved if we drop a spoon—like here at the table—and have to go all the way back to the kitchen for a clean one—no need to do that we have a clean spoon right here in pocket."

It's true that as he went for my entree I was wondering why the bossman didn't require a complete set of cutlery in each waiter's pocket, but I let that remain an unsatisfied wonder.

However, when my waiter returned I noticed that a dark colored string or cord hung out of his fly about two inches. I didn't say anything about this immediately—maybe the waiter just got the end of a draw string on his shorts, or something like that, caught between the buttons of his fly. But then, as I looked around I noticed that *all* the waiters had similar cords hanging out of their flies.

I couldn't resist, so I asked the waiter why, all of his buddies were dangling these strings. "Yes," my waiter said, "we all have them."

"For what?" I asked.

"Since you've asked, sir," my waiter said, "it's the Maitre d' who is fastidious, as I've mentioned."

"Yes..." I said.

"Well, sir," my waiter said, "should we have to go to the restroom—the toilet—while we're on duty, to urinate, sir..."

"Yes..."

"Well, sir, we don't have to handle it, don't have to touch it—we just pull it out with the string."

"A great idea," I said.

"Thank you, sir," my waiter said.

"But," I asked, "how do you put it back in?"

"Well," said my waiter," I don't know what the other guys do, but I use my spoon."

Son Christopher Takes a Blow

The Brewster family, mother, father, and their eight-year-old son, Ben, lived next door to us when our son, Chris, was six years old.

Mr. Brewster worked for an outfit downtown. He did things about stocks, bonds, investments, and such—a non-creative type, making nothing, just moving numbers and abstractions around—but he was already rich. He'd gotten his money-start by buying up old military surplus wooden buildings—dormitories, mess halls, and such. These he moved and painted up a little and sold them—as he said, "to Negroes who could pay cash, who then sold them to Negroes who had to pay on time." In all the time we lived next to the Brewsters I didn't have much to do with them.

His wife Billie, who had a loud raucous laugh that carried right through the walls and closed windows of our house, over a hundred yards away, spent her time pushing her way into "society," which she eventually accomplished—dragging her husband with her—a few years up the road. We had even less to do with her than we had with her husband. Both Mr. and Mrs.

Brewster went to church a lot—had the Baptist preacher to their house and so on. As you'd expect.

Well, on the day I want to tell you about, Ben—you'll remember that was the Brewster's eight-year-old son—laid a lasso rope across the entry road to our place hoping to get our son Chris, age six, as I told you, around the ankles when he came in. Ben hid behind the wall, and when Chris came along he pulled the rope but missed. Then Ben rushed out from behind the wall and swung a punch into Chris's neck. Chris came into the house crying.

I asked him what had happened and he told me that Ben had hit him. "Where?" I asked.

"Here, in my neck."

"Why did he do it?" I asked.

"I don't know."

"Did you hit him before he hit you?" I asked.

"No," Chris said. "Ben just jumped out and hit me."

"From where did he jump?" I asked.

"Behind the wall, he was by the wall."

"Did you hit him back?" I asked.

"No," said Chris, "why should I do that?"

"Well," I said, "he hit you, didn't he?"

After a little, Chris said, "Yes, but I don't have anything against Ben."

Maybe because of my background, especially as a kid, this stopped me: taking a blow and not at least trying to give one, or more, back. That stopped me, and I thought this sounds like our kid is some kind of saint or something.

So, I thought, what if your son is a saint in the making and this thing with Ben Brewster an early evidence of that?

What would be the proper role of parents if they had a saint-in-the-making on their hands? Join the Mother Church to help guarantee the kid's canonization? Pretend that the kid didn't possess these saintly tendencies? Pretend that nothing had happened out there at the hands—or at the fist—of Ben Brewster? Encourage him to watch TV boxing matches with me?

Take Chris over to the Brewster's—talk to Mr. Brewster, the Negro exploiter, and have Ben apologize? No way—I'd not be able to keep my composure—keep from kicking Ben's father in his privates. I really never liked him or his wife—but I guess you've gotten that idea before this.

Maybe what parents should do when they've given birth to a potential saint is just worry and wait.

Well, I didn't share any of these uncertainties with son, Chris.

When Chris asked me if he should have hit back at Ben Brewster, I said that maybe, sometimes, a fella has to.

"When is that?" Chris asked.

Now that's a tough question to answer with all our civilizational and cultural overlay now all but burying our guiding and powerful instincts.

But I went ahead with Chris, anyway—what is a father for but to help guide his son—all matters of saints and sainthood set aside:

I said, "Chris, when somebody punches you as hard as Ben did"—Chris's neck was all red and beginning to swell—"when somebody punches you that hard with no reason, you just have to punch them back."

"But," said Chris, "how will I know when it's a hard enough punch?"

At this point I switched to using his full name: "Christopher," I said, "when the punch is hard enough, you won't have any problem at all—you won't have to think for even a half-second. When that time comes, you'll simply tie into the bastard."

Hiram Block's Counseling Service

For a while I knew a professor of psychology by the name of Hiram Block. For some reason, I feel I don't know him anymore, even though he's still living I guess, and so am I.

Maybe I stopped knowing him because in a quiet, negligible way, he disgusted me—but I won't in any pointed way get into that here.

Hiram Block was never one to miss out on new developments or, shall we say, tendencies or fads in his chosen field of psychology. So when talking to people under certain conditions got the name *counseling*—especially when a person, usually with a degree in psychology, talked to somebody else, that got to be called counseling. That's how Hiram Block and tens of thousands of others across the country got to be *counselors,* they counseled people.

Now when you get to be something with a fashionable name like counseling, you've got to get a special place in which to "do your thing," as they used to say long before Ronald Reagan did his thing—to all of us. So Hiram Block, in those days long before the National Debt was approaching even four trillion dollars, and there was money around the university for those faculty members who had something special to bring to the youth of Texas...Hiram Block got himself a special office and title: Director of Counseling Services. Once so protected and ensconced, Block had the very American desire to grow, "branch out," as others say. I guess that Block just didn't have enough people coming to his counseling office for his services.

So what Hiram Block, professor of psychology and director of counseling services for the university, did was he sat in his office and imagined scores of situations in which people needed counseling. These he listed under what he considered appropriate general headings such as: Matters of Suicide, Matters of Love, Matters of Anxiety, Matters of Family, Matters of Finance, Matters of Sex, Matters of Religion, Matters of Grades, Matters of Lifestyle, and so on. Under these and many more headings he cited hundreds of related situations that he deemed were specific and often causes of disturbed psyches. Then for each of those he outlined what the counselor should say to the sufferer in order to clear up the matter—whatever it happened to be.

Then because, as I've said, there was still a lot of money floating around, he got the university to purchase miles and miles of audio tape, and a system for sending out on the telephone whatever was put on the tapes. What Hiram Block was getting ready was a program like "Dial-a-Prayer" or "Dial Dirty Talk." And he would be the one to talk—or as they say—counsel, on these tapes.

Now, Hiram Block, who looked like someone who'd gone through the dryer but not the washer, was a monumental bore. He relished telling what are still called "Shaggy Dog Stories." Interminably long, drawn out, circuitous, discontinuous, uninteresting accounts of say, a Russian's difficulty in making himself understood to a New York taxi driver, or a dog's difficulty in understanding his master's commands because the master lisped—had a bad lisp. Well, Hiram Block would go on and on and on with such stuff—while whomever he was telling the so-called story to went glassy-eyed and damned near fainted away. This never bothered him—he never even noticed it when whomever he was talking to walked away. He just went on to what he'd settled for as the *end,* the so-called "punch line." Then standing alone, wherever it was, he'd laugh himself sick. On more than one such occasion he doubled up and vomited all over his leisure suit—as if his own "punch line" delivered one helluva blow to his scrotum.

Now, as you've already guessed ahead of me, it was Hiram Block himself—as director of counseling services—who put those hundreds of counselings he'd invented smack on that audio tape—ready for whomever dialed the right number and indicated which particular piece of counseling they needed, or wished, to hear.

Once the system was in operation its fame was assured. The word got around. People from all over, not just in the university area—from all over the U.S.A.—dialed for Dr. Block's counseling. All of them were variants of his Shaggy Dog Stories, often not even completed because Hiram Block had absolutely no consciousness of time or of the length of the tape. It made no difference to him, he just carried on until he got cut off—not matter if it was in the middle of a sentence or even the middle of a word.

Now, I'll understand it if you ask why so many people from so many places—very often paying long distance costs—wanted to hear Professor Block go on like this. Well, I'll tell you: At the beginning of each tape an announcer, not Hiram Block, an announcer who'd had voice training—a real heavy, deep voice, like Tennessee Ernie Ford impersonating a doctor—a voice like that—said, "Relax. This is the University Counseling Service. Your requested counseling will follow. Please remember that should you miss any of what Professor Hiram Block, our director, has to tell you, you may redial this number and the specific tape you requested will be replayed for you. Just relax." Then Block came on like a talking shaggy dog.

It now appears that no one ever got Hiram Block's whole message—his counseling—because he almost never finished a tape, and because this was coming from a great university, the listeners thought they *had been* counseled, but had not paid full attention, or had not relaxed enough. So they kept replaying the tapes—sometimes over and over and over—struggling to be counseled. And as you people who deal with polls and numbers know, this provided statistical proof of the value, need, and success of Professor Hiram Block's Counseling Services.

My Conference with the Chancellor

Harry Ransom was chancellor of the University of Texas then, and I was chairman of the art department. In those years, Chancellor Ransom appeared able to do anything and almost everything—for himself and for the university. Some people thought of him as sort of magician. He had a powerful command of the English language to which he brought a mellifluous and winning flow.

Running the big Art Department in those years was no easy chore—professional jealousies among the faculty, time, space, and budgetary problems, and more important, and making things more difficult, was the fact that I had ideas for the improvement—for the future of the department. And when things had piled up as high as I could take them, I got to see Chancellor Ransom about them—right there in his great offices in the Tower.

I had carefully rehearsed what I had to say, and I was ready. Chancellor Ransom had his girl bring me coffee. It was all very comfortable, and really, at his invitation I began letting him know—not so much about personnel and budget problems as about my vision for the future of the department. When I paused for a sip of coffee, the Chancellor came right in on the beat and intent of what I was saying—wonderfully attuned to what I was saying. And then he went on.

Slowly the space of his offices filled with a honey-colored fog—sweeter and more relaxing than anything I'd ever experienced—on and on, as I felt myself lose my body weight and go under.

I remember, then, shaking hands with him, and just like that I was standing outside his office on a little Oriental rug just standing there, coming to, and wondering what had happened in that office—and what had happened to me, much less what had happened to my vision of the future of the art department.

Doing a Chore for the Chancellor

While I was still enjoying the role of university professor in the arts, I was sometimes called upon to do chores for the chancellor of the university. One of these had me filling in for him at a meeting with William Leer, CEO, owner, and so forth of the Leer Jet Aircraft Corporation and his party.

After doing my duty at that meeting I wrote a report for the chancellor which I've just come across after the intervening thirty years—and here it is, an enjoyable reminder for me, and maybe of some curious interest for whomever might, someday read it.

September 26, 1966
CONFIDENTIAL
Dr. Harry H. Ransom, Chancellor
The University of Texas
Main Building 101
Campus

Dear Harry:
On last Friday, September 23, Professor Helmut

Rehder let me know that since you would be unable to meet with Professor Gunnar Johansen (pianist of California and the University of Wisconsin), Mr. William Leer (executive, aircraft industry of Kansas, California and New York) and his party, you had suggested that I meet with them. This I did on Sunday the 25th. Professors Rehder and Lehmann were also present during the four hours of talk, food and drink.

I cannot be sure that you expect a report of this meeting from me, but since I was treated as if I were some sort of undercover agent with hidden but powerful portfolio, I give you the montage as it rolled out for me.

The Johansen-Leer party flew into Austin from Dallas in Mr. Leer's "Executive Twin Jet" (present retail price c. $700,000) and arrived fresh and rested looking at the Rehder house out beyond Oak Hill, Texas. Since in 1940 I had offered to turn sheet music for Gunnar Johansen at a concert at the Milwaukee Art Institute, and since on that occasion my major graduate professor, Dr. Wolfgang Stechow, was the other half of the piano duo, I met and talked with Johansen at that time. This twenty-six year old meeting proved to be Johansen's way into my tent, so to speak. Even though the rest of the party rapidly became apparently engrossed in Professor Rehder's library (principally in German, and, by my visual guess, comprising approximately 4,000 volumes not including pamphlets), Mr. Johansen asked me to another space in the house. I went there with him, of course. Mr. Johansen was 60 years old on his last birthday, I discovered. He is in terribly good health, it appears; about 5'11" tall and perhaps 170 pounds, stripped. He has those sky blue eyes we find in some blind cowboys. Mr. Johansen neither drinks nor smokes. He is persistent, smooth, and, I figure, with an extraordinary ability to distinguish between the unbuttered and buttered sides of bread. He speaks well, giving some words like accelerator an Italian pronunciation, others a French flavor and still others a trace of German. Being almost completely ignorant of the purpose of this meeting and this quite special talk from Mr. Johansen, I could enjoy something like innocence. This must have engendered an attentive but passive attitude in me, and Mr. Johansen spent some of this time trying to "read" me like an experienced rider goes about "reading" a strange mount. He asked me if I had heard of his "Leonardo da Vinci Academy," and I had to say that I was historically familiar only with the man after whom it was named. Somewhat disappointed Mr. Johansen said, "Good!" He then went into his brief case, a rare looking object of perhaps rhinoceros and gnu hide in sensitive ensemble. From the case he pulled the poorly printed prospectus of the "Leonardo da Vinci Academy" which I enclose for your perusal. Together, then, we went over the prospectus line-by-line or almost so. However, he made an especial emphasis which does not appear in the prospectus; an emphasis on a "jet aircraft pool" for use by a select set of university personnel from a variety of universities. This aircraft pool would consist of a variety of heavier-than-air machines: multiple-engine jets, single-engine jets, propeller craft for short hops and short runways, and helicopters. I did not make excellent sense of this protracted presentation of the needs for a fleet of jet aircraft, but I assume it was related to Mr. Leer's business or even to Mr. Leer's anticipated philanthropy.

Mr. Johansen treated me embarrassingly well—as if I were both rich and powerful as well as handsome, young, and perfectly educated. He worked on me; I made noises without vowels and smoked while looking head-on into those sky blue eyes. Something in the air made me think of a three-dollar bill, well engraved, however. Still, Mr. Johansen was talking in terms of $60,000,000 as you see he has "spelled out" and "broken down" in the prospectus.

Our private conversation ended gracefully with his second glass of plum juice and my third week bourbon. It ended with fine feeling and a perfect neutrality communicated by what I can only describe as a not unpurposively mocked-up mirage. Then we moved into the large room (by this time the game being played in Dallas between the Dallas Cowboys and the Minnesota Vikings must have been concluded and I wondered if I, or my son Chris, had won the two-bits we'd wagered on it) and had open season on conversation. Mr. William (Bill) Leer proved to be quite a guy. About 54 years of age, 5'10" tall, and 195 pounds, he had taken a Thomas A. Edison-type cat-nap earlier because he still had to pilot his jet to Dallas, Madison, Wisconsin (to return Mr. Johansen to his home there), and then back to Wichita all that same evening. He is really interested in flying—as a flyer—and I was happy to be able to recall my own flying experience and so enjoy his very wide and rich experience in the air—even above East Berlin and Moscow! It appeared to me that Mr. Johansen (an *excellent* musician, if I've not made that clear) had a way of playing Mr. Leer. I thought Mr. Johansen laughed too often, too loudly and too long at Mr. Leer's jokes. But, then, I am not an authority on joke-laughter relations.

In "summary," I think and feel Mr. Leer to be a genuine person. So do I think and feel toward Mr. Johansen. However, Mr. Johansen should play the piano more. I think he is looking for a grand complex into which he can retire—the "Leonardo da Vinci Academy." Although not entirely crackpot, his academy is odd in ways that result from an incomplete or uninformed estimate of the state of things today. It appears to aim toward a reverse weltsmerz which fits his own needs to a large degree. I find I have little interest in his Academy—and not only because it is deemed for location in California and not in Texas—but because I think it is poorly conceived and screwy.

Bonsai! Mr. Chancellor,

Yr. Obt. Svt.

Donald L. Weismann

University Professor in the Arts

Mother Teresa Breaks Collarbone

The headline was "Mother Teresa Breaks Collarbone," so I read on to learn that it was Mother Teresa's left collarbone. This meant that she had broken the one opposite from the one I broke in 1930. Mine got broken—sounding like stomping down on a wooden cigar box—when I got tackled and went down sidewise with another guy on top of me—on frozen ground. It was during a football game we sometimes played at the Milwaukee County Home for Dependent Children—always Catholics against Protestants—there weren't enough Jews to make a team.

Reading further about Mother Teresa's accident I found out that she broke her left collarbone by falling from a bed. The news article didn't say how high the bed was from the floor, but I assumed the floor was hard—ungiving. I figured that her bed must have been very high above the floor—high enough for her body weight to have enough time, during the fall, to develop the speed needed to break her collarbone, really a pretty big bone—even in a woman. I thought that, maybe, she was in the upper bunk of a double bunker type bed. This could afford a falling distance of at least three feet, maybe even four. But perhaps she wasn't even in bed as we know it here in the U.S.A. The article said she was at her "Missionaries of Charity" headquarters in India...Calcutta. Maybe she was in a high-hanging hammock, I thought; but the article said, and I quote, "She fell *off a bed*."

Now, as I recall instances of falling from bed—as was often the case with my younger brother, Jack, we never said—as the news article says—that he fell *off* a bed; we always said that Jack fell *out* of bed. And usually he had been sleeping just before he rolled or slid off onto the floor. It's true that, once he was in his fall, he was *off* of the bed, but we never described his falling in that way.

I don't wish to clutter up any further the various stories about Mother Teresa that appear in the world press; all I'd like to do is understand—get a grip on the situation described as breaking her collarbone in a fall *off* a bed. As I read it, it's entirely possible that she was not in that bed she fell *off* of.

She may have been in a pickup truck piled high with mattresses for delivery to her Missionaries of Charity dormitory—and was lying down and resting on the mattress on the top of the pile—sort of like she was in bed, but not really. Then when the pickup hit a bump or a pothole in the road, it tossed her up and *off* she went—not even back into the truck, but out in the Calcutta street. So if the pile of mattresses is construed as a *bed* then certainly it would be correct to report the incident as Mother Teresa's falling *off* a bed. And that would make it entirely natural and believable that as she hit that Calcutta pavement she broke her collarbone—her *left* collarbone, as reported.

Now, as you may know, Mother Teresa is eighty-five years old, and some years ago she was awarded the Nobel Peace Prize. I believe that was before Dr. Henry Kissinger won the same prize for "opening up China," as all the reports had it, and for shutting down Chile as few reports had it—and before Yassar Arafat won it too, for, it seems, just shaking hands with the head of the Israelis—of Israel.

Now I feel pretty certain that being a Nobel Laureate had little or nothing to do with breaking Mother Teresa's collarbone. However, the fact that she is eighty-five years old may have had a lot to do with that. At this time, May of 1996, Mother Teresa is only three and a half years older than I am, and I am well acquainted with how brittle our bones become after, let's say, sixty for those people who've kept in near perfect shape since they were born—and after about forty-five for those who've spent most of their lives as sitting down on lying down spectators—and eating.

Of course there are always exceptions: Look at George Burns, over a hundred, and even the last fall in the bathroom didn't break any of his bones. Maybe comedians retain their suppleness longer than others—look at Bob Hope, Milton Berle, and Ronald Reagan.

Still, Queen Alexandria Victoria, Queen of Great Britain, Ireland, *and* Empress of India, managed to live past eighty-two, and neither she nor Mother Teresa claimed to be comedians, although—if we had all the facts concerning Mother Teresa's falling "*off a bed*" and breaking her left collarbone, we might be led to think she had the makings of one—a very holy comedienne, of course.

End of the Appian Way

It's always good to remember that anticipations can never adequately foreshadow realizations. Realization can far outdo anticipations—as well as do violence to them. There's nothing new in this—and we've learned to cope, no matter how this works.

In a leisurely way we were coming down from Rome through Benevento, Taranto to Brindisi, at the end of that more than two-thousand year old road, the Appian Way, Brindisi is a gateway to Greece, and our minds and hearts were set on Greece across the strait of Otranto, beyond the end of the Appian Way.

The ship we sailed on, a modern Motor Vessel as they're called, had a big swimming pool with tables and drinks around the edge. Almost naked young men and women splashed or lounged about; Italianate gigolos—or so they looked and acted—kept making time with women who looked like they might be school teachers on vacation and full of hope. Nothing wrong with any of this, not even if it brought the *Romans of the Decadence* to mind. After all, the 350 miles of the stone-paved way was built by Romans, not Greeks. Still our minds were on Greece, not Rome.

So the ship plows serenely on, across the Strait of Otranto, southeast among the Ionian Islands—ah! It begins to feel like the anticipated Greece—this blue-blue water, those islands floating and passing.

Then landfall at Patras in the very land of the Greeks. Embarkation, then, and a little clearing, once a park, perhaps, with paper and plastic cups blowing around, falling apart benches near a railroad track.

And a man coming up with badly made plaster copies of Greek sculpture—half a foot high and unsteady on their bases—wanting to sell them—and photographs copied from photographs of dirty French so-called postcards.

So the Appian Way doesn't end in Brindisi. You have to go much further, maybe to Olympia, to Naxos, to the cleared area atop the Acropolis where the Parthenon stands—or all those out-of-the way places still surviving against the ruins created by international, corporate encroachments like that ruined park in Patras.

My Grandmother and Aunt Melba

I heard it said that my maternal grandmother played cards for thirty years, and then one evening she said, "Oh my goodness, they've got the numbers printed in the corners." For over thirty years my grandmother was perhaps counting spots—those little diamonds, hearts, spades, and clubs printed on the cards. At last she was aware of what everyone else knew—what everyone with whom she had played perceived and responded to.

Maybe that's how we learn most of what we learn. In my grandmother's case no one had told her, I presume, and so it took a long trip to revelation. After all she had perfectly good eyes, and if her attention had been directed to those numbers in the corners of the cards all would have been well.

In some cases, however, things are quite different. Take my Aunt Melba, for instance. She'd been flatulent for years—until just the passage of so much wind got to bothering her and she went to see the doctor. She had to wait a while in his outer office on one of those hard varnished chairs but he finally got to her.

She told him of her problem—so much gas—that was all—just too much gas escaping most of the time.

"And that is it?" the doctor inquired.

"Yes," my Aunt Melba said, "there's no smell and no sound at all—just the feel of all that gas escaping."

"Well," the doctor said, "we'll get to that, but first I want to make a complete examination of your sinuses and your ears."

Oh, if only all problems were as simple as my grandmother's.

The Reverend and "Chuck" Heston

It was while the Haight-Ashbury neighborhood in San Francisco was still a phenomenon for the media and a tragedy for its doped-up residents and transients. It was back then when a man who called himself Reverend got a bunch of us members of the National Council on the Arts cornered at lunch. He'd previously been given permission—I don't know by whom—to make a presentation at that afternoon's meeting. What this reverend in a black suit wanted to do was get some of us favorably disposed toward the pitch he'd make right after lunch.

He carried one of those accordion shaped cardboard containers filled with pages of writing and drawings. He said he'd been working with some of the druggies and that he thought their writings and graphics were not only high art, but had been contributing to their rehabilitation into society.

It didn't take long to realize that if this guy *was* a Reverend, the moniker must have been awarded by some fly-by-night storefront operation. He looked a lot like the young Billy Graham and, to a degree, *sounded* like him—especially like the late

Billy Graham who keeps losing his place in the *Bible* and forgetting what his depended clauses *depended from*. You didn't have to listen all that closely to conclude that this guy might be creative, but without any talent—that he was an enthusiastic drifter, a not entirely colorless nut. And the more he talked and the more he showed of himself, the more he revealed that what he was, was a terribly incompetent con man. unlike Billy Graham. He wanted our support in the form of a cash grant for his "charges," as he called them, in the Haight-Ashbury jungle.

One of the things he showed us was what he called a "literary-pictorial" creation. It was a 9" x 12" piece of bright red construction paper on which was lettered—in typewriter size letters, four words: "Fuck the Fire Department."

Charlton Heston, who was in that lunch group, took heavy umbrage at the display and said so in Shakespearean tones—standing up as he decried, much like in some of his movies, especially the one in which he was Moses. However, Chuck's performance (we referred to Heston most of the time as "Chuck," and he liked that)–his stagey performance was not answered by anyone else, and the Reverend produced some typed sheets from his cardboard container—"creative literary works by young addicts in San Francisco." One of these recorded the fantasies of a girl masturbating, another about the joys of gang banging. And then lunch was over and the whole council, staff, and observers convened.

In due course the Reverend got his promised time to present the case for a Federal grant to support the creative work of his charges. When he began to read the essay about gang banging, Helen Hayes, a member of the Council, asked what that meant: What was gang banging?

At this point Chuck Heston, known as a very moral straight-laced Republican and longtime member of the National Rifle Association, took the copy from the reverend and began to read it in that deep-voiced, square-shouldered Shakespearean way that Chuck himself admires so much. As usual, he had removed his suit coat, the better to display the width of his shoulders as being all Chuck and not the padding of any coat. He didn't so much as answer Helen Hayes's question as he boomed out from the script all the bestial, lurid self-evident stuff typed out there—until the

Chairman, Roger Stevens, gave a sign that enough had been done, not only about this literary masterpiece, but also about the Reverend and his group out there across the country in the "City by the Bay." And the sign stuck: After all, Roger L. Stevens, former Chairman of the Kennedy Center, once owned and then sold the Empire State Building—yes, the one in New York City.

I've often thought that if the spaced-out kid who wrote that gang banging essay had ever gotten a tape of Chuck Heston's reading of it, he or she would have made a fortune from it—as comedy, that is, since Chuck has a rare talent for unintentionally making comedians of historical characters like Moses, and all those Romans and so forth which he portrayed, as they say, in the movies. After all, it was a dead cinch, that afternoon, for him to make hilarious comedy of eight guys fucking one girl, gang banging tandem style all in the short time it took a cable car to make one trip up to the Top of the Mark.

Duke Ellington in New Orleans

We'd come through New Orleans with sirens and four motorcycles up ahead, the town blurring past the windows of our big black sedans. The First Lady, Lady Bird Johnson, was up front, the press and members of the National Council for the Arts followed. In the Lincoln sedan with me was Duke Ellington, at that time a member of the Council, as I was. We were on our way to a ghetto grade school where Lady Bird would speak and present the school with a 16-millimeter film projector.

The time was the 1960s, a time of street demonstrations, the Vietnam war, a time that felt for awhile that even with all the empty adolescent idealism, rocky "flower children," body bags from southeast Asia and deceitful politicos—still there was a feeling that things might still be made better, if not in the world, at least in the U.S.A.

Even though I'd know Duke Ellington for a few years, we weren't talking much in that speeding black sedan—just watching the city go by as if compressed or telescoped beyond the spotless tinted window glass. Once, while we were crossing a bridge, I heard the Duke humming. "I think I recognize that," I said.

"I don't think so, Weismann," the Duke said, "I'm just now composing it and wondering where I'll have the winds take over."

We parked in the area barricaded for the cars and began walking the two blocks to the school, Lady Bird and Liz Carpenter, her secretary, in the lead, the Duke and I close behind.

Up ahead a group of young blacks were whooping it up, yelling about killing babies in Vietnam and carrying signs full of mottos in foul language. They looked a big frightening in their tennis shoes, tight jeans, and bare uppers, swinging their arms around as if they were beating off unseen ghosts. And there was a lot of them.

Then one of the blacks recognized Duke Ellington and instantly everything changed.

"Hey!" one of them yelled, "it's the Duke...hi-ya, Duke!" The signs were dropped, they stopped—all smiles.

"Hi-ya," Duke Ellington said, "you being good boys?"

And after shaking hands, giving high-fives, even embracing, they made way for the Duke and the rest of us.

As we were entering the school house I said, "Mr. Ellington, it's really wonderful—here was this bunch of angry guys, you come along, and they sort of collapse smiling into your arms."

"That's the reward," Duke Ellington said, "the reward for walking with you, Weismann."

Can you understand that even though I'd admired this man and his music for a good part of my life, this turn of his mind made me admire, love him even more.

And then, leaving the schoolhouse, a black girl of about fifteen gently caught his arm saying, "Duke, I want to be a singer, how can I ever get an audition?"

He stopped right there at the busy, noisy intersection and leaning toward the girl said, "Here, sing in my ear." Which the girl did as Duke Ellington appeared to listen with care and concentration. And when she'd finished he had her write her name and address on a piece of paper he gave her.

There have been times I've wondered if that fifteen-year-old black girl ever heard from the Duke.

I'll put my money down that, yes, one way or the other she did.

Well before Duke Ellington died in the summertime but sent out his Christmas cards ahead of time, there was just a three-word message to all of us: "I love you."

A New Violin Glue

For that first year of the National Endowment for the Arts, 1966, the budget was small—six or eight million dollars. Nothing like twenty years later, at which time the budget was about a hundred and eighty million. I started my six-year tenure on the National Council the same year the Endowment became a reality. From my prejudiced point of view I think that the twenty-six original members of the Council were the best—they were mostly artists, writers, actors, and musicians, not just rich people who gave money to support the arts.

On that first Council were Isaac Stern, the great violinist, and Leonard Bernstein, the celebrated composer, pianist, and conductor. We had a great chairman, Roger Stevens, a multi-millionaire real estate king and a phenomenally successful discoverer and backer of some of the best plays to make the New York stage. He was not from a wealthy family. He made it himself, even to buying and selling the Empire State Building. Roger Stevens was, and still is now, a genuinely secure man. In his own gifted way he took no shit from anybody. He was, and still is, a fine example of the highly informed, courageous, intelligent, free man. And because of this, the council, under his chairmanship, operated in a wonderfully open and free way—as it awarded that six or eight million dollar budget in wise and valuable ways.

And this is where we come back to Isaac Stern and Leonard Bernstein. On one of Isaac Stern's concert tours he met a Greek, appropriately in Greece. This Greek had his reasons to believe that a most crucial element in making excellent violins was the glue used to hold the instrument together and contribute to its tone quality. And Isaac Stern gave this possibility serious concern. The Greek took him to his workshop where he was—according to him—on the verge of arriving at the perfect glue—of discovering, at last, one of the secrets of the greatest violin craftsmen. He told Issac Stern that what he needed for this realization were certain chemicals and equipment that would cost, in U.S. currency, nine hundred dollars.

Well, when a great violinist like Issac Stern is given to believe that it's only the lack of nine hundred bucks that stands in the way of creating violins that could challenge those of Andrea Amati and Antonio Stradivari—well he's going to see that this man gets those nine hundred bucks. And, besides, what an excellent project for a National Endowment for the Arts to support, he thought.

Well, it came to pass, as old-fashioned story tellers say, that a meeting of the National Council in Washington, D.C., Issac Stern presented the case for supporting the Greek's—really Stern's—request for a grant of nine hundred dollars.

Now, as you may know, Isaac Stern is a Russian born Jew, and Leonard Bernstein is a Massachusetts born Jew. There are only two years between their birth dates. They are both virtuosos, full of energy, articulate, superb entertainers—and to watch and hear them together is well worth any admission—makes even an untalented person wish their secret was in their Jewishness and that they—those other untalented, or even talented persons, were themselves Jews. And if this is racism, let's make the best of it.

After Isaac Stern's introduction of the matter of a new glue for violins, Leonard Bernstein spoke up in support. Now here they were together, dead serious, but lubricated with the best talents of the best early 20th century comedy teams, and going at it: a real show.

There were a couple of members of the council who must have thought that this case of a Greek and his glue wasn't worth their time, or that it was transparently silly, and they said so. There ensued some of the rarest exhibitions of logic, illogic, irony, and repartee that I've ever been privileged to experience.

If you've ever watched Bernstein conduct—if you've ever watched Stern, standing or sitting, go to the top of his virtuosity, then you've got some feeling for what these two soul-mates can do in defense of something they both strongly believe in. In this case, a Greek and his dream of the perfect violin glue. All the while they exhibit a joy of life that winks at its own ridiculousness. I'll tell you I value that one hour of the Sterns-Bernstein performance more than any other during the remaining six years I served on the Council.

Just before Chairman Stevens asked for a hand vote on this perfect glue case, one of the Council members asked Isaac Stern if the man over there in Greece was really a Greek.

"Well, yes," Stern said, "a Jewish Greek," and he brought the house down.

The recommendation to award that man nine hundred dollars went through without a dissenting vote and with a standing ovation for the Sterns-Bernstein team.

Now, if you ask, "Did the Jewish Greek perfect the glue?" all I can say is nothing further was heard of the man or the glue, not in the following six years I was on the Council, anyway.

But should that matter? Not to me.

Visit to New York

Coming back from someplace—oh yes, now I remember—I was returning from Montreal after a three-day meeting of the National Council for the Arts—where the level of abstract talk full of untested generalizations had gotten to me in a way that not even all the booze at noon and dinner and in the evening could obliterate. I don't mean to sound superior to the people or the talk that made up these meetings—It was just that I'd had enough of people exhibiting their personally held images, their little homunculi, and the talk that had a powerful way of denying the very nature of art and its one-on-one relation to human experience. I don't mean to belabor this, nor, by implication, suggest that, were I in charge, I could run this sort of meeting any better. It's simply the way government-sponsored meetings go, I guess.

In a way it's a little sad that after five years on this particular Council, I couldn't feel any better about how things had been going—and how, I'll bet, they're still going.

Well, I'd planned this Montreal trip—all at government expense—to give me three or four days in New York on the return. I thought it would be good to get to a couple of museums, the Met, the Whitney, and some galleries that were showing the current work—the hot stuff, along 57th Street. After all, art is my business and has been, in painting at least, since I was twelve years old.

So the airplane takes off for New York. You've surrendered part of your life—and you trust it's not your last—to this pressurized, cramped existence in an aluminum tube where well made-up young women tell you about face masks and oxygen, but nothing about parachutes. And then, through the windows which keep getting smaller each year—the clouds come down, hauling the heart-rending blue with them. And so you go, suspended.

Even before the descent is begun, a cheery captain is talking over the static loaded intercom. He's telling us that there'll be a little delay—traffic over LaGuardia is heavy, a few planes ahead of us—and so on.

After a while we descend into a wide holding pattern over New York. We are, as they say, "in the stack," and keep flying in a circle. The cheery captain—even more cheery now—comes on to let us know that it's a beautiful day in New York, temperature seventy-two degrees, and that our turn to approach and land will come soon.

But it doesn't. The bar is re-opened and those well made-up young women, more and more smiley and cheerful, come on with the cart loads of booze. After my second bourbon, we're still circling well above and often well beyond New York City.

So, each time around, I'm looking at that phenomenon down below, all that stuff piled up and spread around, distant and remote as it is for most of us—not clusters like Rockefeller Center, which the Japanese bought—we've walked around there, and up and down the so-called "Avenue of the Americas"—not those postcard places—rather the South Bronx, the darker parts of Harlem, and all the unevenly distributed skidrows.

So I'm up there and getting funny ideas about forgetting going to museums and art galleries, and instead spending my time down there in those other castaway places. But what if a close-up view, as I walked around, got me to thinking that I could spend my life better trying to help those awful situations? Maybe then I'd feel better than in these meetings of the National Council for the Arts—and even my teaching of the history of art made me feel—get my actual hands at work down there where I might help make a real difference.

So the plane keeps going around and around high in the air, insulated, while the captain talks cheery down home talk, and those pretty women, all smiles and perfect teeth bring more booze—helping my fantasy go its way.

I see myself down there—calling home from a torn-up public telephone booth—telling the wife that I've got to stay, that there's stuff down here that I know about from boyhood in the slums of Milwaukee, and that since I feel I can help, then it's my responsibility to do just that.

And then I see myself in those downward streets—a do-gooder from far off—being understood or misunderstood, it wouldn't matter which, and night coming on and me, knifed and dead, for a few lousy bucks in that South Bronx street now passing under the plane, at last cleared for an approach to land.

A hard landing, that series of bumps—reality—and finally taxing in. On the ground in New York I hear myself say...Fuck New York, and I walk as fast as I can, then run, to the Braniff ticket counter—and get the first plane back to Texas.

Fascination and Self-Fascination

The other evening, I was reading again—after all these years—*Every Man a King*, the autobiography of Huey P. Long. He was shot, as some of you may remember, in 1935, the same year I graduated from college—so I'd read a lot about him while he was still alive. A farm boy who did the whole legal education thing in seven months, he became Governor of Louisiana at thirty-five, U.S. Senator a few years later, and was headed for the presidency when he was assassinated, the same year, 1935, that his book, *My First Years in the White House* appeared.

Well, reading Huey Long's autobiography again, my fascination with the man and his career was revived. What a character! A man with an insatiable lust for power, a clever demagogue who bludgeoned or bought the members of a lazy or sleepy legislature and managed to achieve a virtual suspension of democratic procedures. And there are those who believe that, yes, he would have been elected president had he not been killed. Huey Pierce Long was a fascinating man, but more significant, he was fascinated by himself.

You know, fascination is the name we have for a state of being that is in *no way* simple. When we are truly fascinated it's as if we are under a spell—we are enthralled, held by some charm which is, or seems to be, irresistible. I remember talking to a downed Marine fighter pilot—during the war, in a hospital—where he was being, as they say, "rehabilitated." We had a couple of long conversations that covered lots of subjects, but the leitmotif back of everything he said was simple and strong: It was his fascination with, and desire for, combat. Not a bad state of being for a fighter pilot in a hot war—no matter which side he happens to be fighting for. And this fighter pilot was no raw kid. He was about thirty years old, a major, lots of experience, and he knew what he'd been doing in the air with that machine and what it had been doing to him. "Sure," I remember his saying, "sure, it's pretty terrible, but it breeds its own awful fascination that keeps a guy going—and you feel you can't put it down, even if you'd want to."

And, less dramatically perhaps, was a conversation I had sometime back in the 1970s with a genius-type who said he was in what's called public relations—and when he came right down to it, he said he was in behavior modification. One of the things he said, at a side table during a political meeting in Austin, Texas, was that conditions at the time were such that he felt—or actually believed—the time was ripe for recognizing that with the proper "know how" a guy could cause people to believe *anything* they were "directed" to believe. He didn't say *almost* anything, he said *anything*. And it was clear to me that he believed just that. This man talked like someone bewitched, someone under a spell. He was *fascinated* by the techniques, the measured procedures for getting people to believe in certain directed ways. Another case of fascination. He even wept when he told how he, operating alone, could convince intelligent people to do his most ridiculous biddings.

Of all the cases of fascination I've heard about, including even the fascination that Richard Burton had for Liz Taylor and that she had for him, the cases that interest me most are those that have to do with an individual's fascination for himself or herself. By this I don't mean a fascination for a person's body parts, or how they breathe or defecate. That sort of fascination may be quite normal—a recognition of the mysterious qualities of the living organism. No, what I'm interested in is those people who are so enthralled by what they *think,* that they act as if they are under an almost constant but always powerful spell like heavenly revelation. This spell works to cause them to believe that what they think is always right, that they have the correct answer to just about every question, that they know what's good for everyone—and that *only* they have this power to know. They are held by the charm of this which, for them, is irresistible. In a sense, once they are in the throes of self-fascination, they are helpless except to fuel this fascination with actual physical acts that support it. And these throes of self-fascination may chain together and last for the person's whole lifetime. This, I figure, is how in varying degrees, it was for Adolph Hitler, Martin Luther, Napoleon, Richard Nixon, and others I'm sure you could cite.

Sometimes, even though the deeply self-fascinated person may, by his or her public actions, cause them to appear insane, that is not always the case. Especially, if by some seemingly accidental congruence of their pronouncements and the climate of the times, they come to be respected as reformists, leaders. Certainly that was the case with Adolph Hitler—unlike the cases of all sorts of persons who underwent only intermittent self-fascination or who were limited to what could be called a "half-assed" self-fascination. And, incidentally, there is nothing more sadly comical than the performances of a person who has only a half-assed fascination with himself. In this respect, people like Ross Perot and Aimee Semple McPherson come to mind.

Now I've known some half-assed self-fascinated people, but only one completely self-fascinated person. And should you be looking for one, my personal experience would direct you to the three best places where you might find what you're looking for: Number 1, where politicians gather; Number 2, the military, especially among the higher rated enlisted personnel and the commissioned brass; and Number 3, academia, the professors, the administrators. The one full-blooded self-fascinated person I got to know is from the academic group. So far as I know, this man has lived almost all his life in a state of being under a spell, a charm, a complete fascination for himself—his weird conviction that *truth* is his and his alone. In a way, he always seemed to me to be self-hypnotized even when he talked and acted like anyone else, but only to gain a tactical advantage over the other "ignorant" people. At first Newt Gingrich struck me as this kind of self-fascinated academic: he had the Union Card, the Ph.D. degree, and the manic drive to see to the details required to enhance the spell under which he operated and to acquire the power necessary to reproduce his concept of truth in the minds of others. But Newt turned out to be a wind bag; he just talked like he was genuinely fascinated by himself; he couldn't convince himself about what he said—the charm was not on him. He turned out to be a fake as soon as he met even mildly strong resistance.

The academic, full-fledged self-fascinated person comes through, usually in ways comparable to those suffering from the disease known as epilepsy. Not in its extreme form, known as the *grand mal* in which there's all that falling down, foaming at the mouth, and so on. No, not that form of epilepsy—the milder form called the *petit mal* which lasts for only a short period, from one to thirty seconds but which does involve a disorder of cerebral function and a clouding of consciousness.

It has occurred to me that these short cloudings of consciousness and their outward effects in the face and manner of the deeply self-fascinated academic can be, and often are read as deep philosophical pauses in whatever he may be saying at the time. And should this *petit mal* progress a little toward a *grand mal* with some limited thrashings about of the body, this can be construed as oratorical visual aids, so to speak, to what the possessed person may be saying or trying to say. But never forget, no matter these disorders of cerebral function—and perhaps partly because of them, the deeply self-fascinated person is a spellbinder—able to pass his spell to his listeners.

Although some writers on the subject attribute the oratorical and gestural force of the self-fascinated academic to the dance named for the 4th century Sicilian martyr, St. Vitus, I have not given much credence to that explanation—even though St. Vitus is recognized as the patron saint of dancers and actors, and is called one of the "Fourteen Holy Helpers." Rather, I give more credence to the similarity that may exist between the conduct of the deeply self-fascinated academic person—especially when he or she experiences temporary defeat—and what I often witnessed as a little kid in the downtown areas of Milwaukee.

Back then public drunkenness was much more common that it is today. It seems that then there was almost always someone, man or woman, staggering along the street, babbling or shouting out. For me it was only when these drunks stopped and began to spin around before falling down on the pavement that my interest got fired up. People quickly surrounded the writhing drunk, and almost always someone in the crowd yelled out, "Get an ambulance, *he's got the snakes*!" During those incidents, and way back then, I never got the classical idea that the possessed drunk was fighting off serpents, fighting off evil, as in the celebrated 2nd century B.C. *Laocoön* sculptural group. To me it seemed that he was enjoying his great power in making all those almost impossible bodily contortions, sort of like a circus clown or freak—sort of like how I think of the completely self-fascinated professor about to get *his* way, *his* truth in a performance before a supine faculty senate.

However, in either of these cases—the through and through self-fascinated academic as an epileptic or as a drunk with the snakes, generally manages to hide the extreme evidences of his or her malady by limiting its public display. Usually these abnormalities are reserved for the isolation and protection of a locked bathroom or a room in some distant motel where he or she can masturbate away some of the pressures they're undergoing. But sometimes these pressures surface uncontrolled in the person's home where he or she often beats his wife or husband and abuses the children.

You see, these select personages think of life in or out of the home as a debating society in which no matter what the judges decide, they always win because, simply, they're entirely convinced that they're right.

Now, out of deference for the whole unwashed population, the non-elites that exist outside the self-possessed self-fascinated person, out of deference for them, my candidate for first prize often flatters them into an unknowing submission. This submitted group then becomes his willing constituents—somewhat like those thousands of so-called volunteers enlisted in the cause of Ross Perot's reform political party. As we know, however, this didn't work for the simple reason that Perot is not a genuine self-fascinated person. He's just a phony, an obscenely rich nut with no corresponding bolt.

It's tempting to go on wit this, to tell more about this perfectly self-fascinated academic man I've known. Tempting, too, to reveal his name, but, after all, who knows, he may still be living. So I shan't go on—believing that with the few tips I've given you, you'll recognize him when and if he turns up either as President of the United States, or as a corpse—shot to death at breakfast—perhaps by his wife.

Weismann, What Are You Doing Here?

It was the first European trip on which we'd taken both our children, Christopher and Anne, ages nine and ten. It was 1961. I had what's called a "research leave of absence" from the University of Texas, to go to Italy, to make contact with the young upcoming Italian artists, talk with them, see what they're doing, and make what sense I could of that in comparison with what American artists were doing over here. At least that's what I wrote in my application for the leave.

In Florence we found a pleasant run-down villa on the via Montughi, we got the kids started in an Italian school run by two Irish nuns—the *Instituto Santa Reparata,* and I went to work with a list of artists that, in time, I'd be interviewing. Both Anne and Christopher picked up the language at a surprising rate, partly because we'd made the trip from Galveston to Genoa on an Italian freighter—two weeks in transit with an Italian crew who took to the kids right off. It was like two weeks in a speeded-up course in Italian, and their mother remembered it from years before when she studied for a year in Tuscany. Christopher made friends with his classmates and Anne, besides that, convinced us she should continue her riding lessons begun in Texas at a riding academy there in Florence where an Italian Army Cavalry captain did the instructing. He held forth in the center of a huge sawdust and earth ring in an eighteenth century building that must have started out as an opera house. There were loggias high up the sides of the ring where my wife and I often sat alone watching the riders below. Except for the gently expressed commands from the captain and the muffled sounds of the horses' hooves as they made that big circle, it was quiet in a way that encouraged something like meditation—thoughts of the ambiance that's one's self.

On more than one afternoon, sitting up there in a worn overstuffed chair with its remnants of gold leaf still showing, that old question I'd had so often and in so many places came back, "Weismann, what are you *really* doing here?" Oh, I knew I was there with my wife to watch our Anne, in full riding get-up from polished boots to crop and cap, perform so earnestly and so well. But the question asks more that just "what are you doing in this decaying Florentine opera house with its subtly rich aroma of horses?" It seems to be asking "what are you doing here *on earth,* Weismann, in this life?"

Then there was that rainy day in Florence when I found myself part of a small audience in the large conference room of the Leonardo da Vinci Society in the Corsini Palace at Number 10, Lungarno. The program, a lecture by an American woman, a gifted photographer, who'd taken to scholarship and was doing research about the nineteenth century daguerreotype camera. After being introduced she went to the lectern, adjusted her large feathered hat and started talking in a sleep-inducing monotone, first about the *camera obscura* and then the "pin-hole camera." After slowly working her way into the fifteenth century, decade by decade, she wisely gave credit to Leonardo da Vinci, a reproduction of whose self-portrait hung on the wall behind her as a centerpiece in the line of portraits of the past presidents of the Leonardo da Vinci Society. As time passed and I began to doze off, I noticed a large dark insect that looked like a cross between an orb-weaver and a wolf spider making its way from the portrait of the first president of the Society—named on a big brass plate, Francisco Gioli—to the seventh president, named Dario Lupi. In the long time it took the spider to make the entire trip, the woman photographer talked her way to Jacques Mandé Dagurere, the French scene painter who invented the daguerreotype camera. Then reams of statistics—that only 187 true daguerreotype cameras were built, and all of those between June 15 and August 15, 1839, that only fourteen of these are now in existence, and so on. And as she droned on I was asking that old question—or it was asking me, "Weismann, what are you really doing here?"

I've found that if you live long enough you're bound to find yourself in places and situations that don't give easily to explanation, and some actually defy explanation. Like that time on a little island in the South Pacific while a few of us officers were sharing a quart of bourbon, a Japanese infantryman in immaculate uniform emerges from the brush, his empty hands held forward to me, surrendering. What in Hell was *he* doing here? And I? Oh, I know the obvious answer: Weismann, you're in the Navy and there's a big war on; we'll take the Jap back to the ship with us and those who do such things will interrogate him, and with luck discover exactly what he was doing, all alone, on that island. Just part of your job, Weismann. But all that leaves a lot unanswered. Like that time in Cody, Wyoming—just coming into that bar and dance hall, the "Bronze Boot," and everything stopping; the music, the talk, everything and a spotlight drenching me in light. And I stand there as the band strikes up with "Empty Saddles." Over the years I've become somewhat accustomed to this sort of thing, but I'm still facing the question, "What are you doing here, Weismann?" Later, it helps when I'm told that I was mistaken for one of their own—a spitting image of a rodeo performer who'd broken his back a few weeks before and would never ride again. But the question never stops being asked.

And how about all those times I've been hauled in as a robbery suspect, and for murder in Blue Earth, Minnesota—just because, like myself, those other people don't know what Weismann's doing here. As I've said, if you live long enough and remain rather more plain that fancy, you're bound to find yourself in places and situations, neither of your own making, that pose the old question—maybe especially for guys like me who were never convinced that they knew for sure where they belong. Not that

I ever took the words to that hymn seriously, "I'm a stranger here, heaven is my home."

So here I am now, sitting in that vaulted conference room of the Leonardo da Vinci Society as that woman goes on in infinite detail about all the varieties of cabinet work housing those 187 daguerreotype cameras, cabinet by cabinet. And although, unmercifully, I'm hearing every word she says, I'm off some place else and being hounded by that old question. It's true that if I grapple with it I can *explain* some of it pretty well even while *understanding* it eludes me.

The fact of the matter is that I was there in that conference room because my son Christopher did not need a haircut. If he had needed one, I'd have taken him over to the barber shop on the Vittore Emmanuele II where his hair would have been cut and I would've been looking through Italian magazines while that woman photographer went on without my knowing a thing about it. But my son did not need a haircut, and that meant that the time was open for my daughter to go riding in that slowly decaying opera house I've already mentioned. It's near the main Florence railroad station so there's hardly ever any parking space in the area. So I drop her off at the riding academy telling her that I'll be outside waiting for her when she finishes.

Now the opera house was too far from our house to make it seem reasonable for me to return home and then drive back to pick her up. That's when I remembered the invitation our landlady had given me to hear the woman photographer and so I drove over to the Corsini Palace where the Leonardo da Vinci Society was meeting and where there was plenty of parking space. And after a while I am in that conference room, caught like a piece of fully clothed flotsam between the facts that my son's hair didn't need cutting and that the Corsini Palace is not far from where my daughter takes riding lessons.

When I realized that I'd been caught in this circumstantial net I sensed a vague danger in the situation; what might happen next that would have me asking "Who's in control here—and what in Hell am I doing here?"

As I walked the long aisle out of the Leonardo da Vinci Society's conference room and into the street where I began to run as if being chased to the opera house-stable, I was thinking of all those things in history that may have been precipitated in situations like this one, just ending for me. At the point where I began to fear that my daughter might have been kidnapped because someone, some place, had dropped a basket of eggs—or something even more ridiculous than that—I felt a cold sweat all over and ran even faster.

And then I saw her, a little up ahead and all smiles, running toward me. No question now. I knew *why* I was there and exactly *what* I was doing there: I'd come to pick up my beautiful ten-year-old daughter who was asking, "How was the lecture, Daddy, or wouldn't I understand?" And I was saying yes, she wouldn't understand it, even if I could explain it, which I thought I could, but just barely.

About George Rickey and Olga Schubkegel

Back in the early 1950s while I was running the art department of the University of Kentucky, I did a lot of things I haven't done since, like attending meetings of State and National Associations of art educators—groups dedicated to broadening, if not deepening, the teaching of classroom teachers who, along with all the other subject areas covered in the primary and secondary school would do something about art in their regular classes. Also these associations developed standards or guides for those who would be supervisors of art in the public schools— sort of "art specialists."

For a few years this kind of responsibility—attending those meetings—was acceptable to me, but once out of Kentucky I never did that again. For one thing, the people in these organizations like the National Art Education Association, the Kentucky Art Education Association, and others, registered as pretty dull with me.

So, while still in Kentucky, which was described for me by an old Blue Grass hand as an eddy in the stream of life—where genealogy was history and where art was family portraiture—while still there I went to one of those art educationist's meetings at the state college in Murray. It was an annual meeting of the Kentucky State Art Education Association, so there'd been a lot of time—a whole year—to plan for it. Art educationists from all over Kentucky and adjoining states attended, as well as some artist-type speakers from far off.

After all this time I've forgotten almost all of what happened at that meeting. However, two people out of the couple of hundred or so who attended have survived in my memory for the forty-five years or so since then and now.

One was a somewhat celebrated sculptor by the name of George Rickey, who'd now be over ninety years old if still alive. I'd known him for some years before this meeting in Murray and because his sculpture was what's called "mobiles" and were designed to be activated by the movement of the air, and also because he farted a lot, we called him "wind art." He was a nice enough guy, overweight, never hearing anything you said to him, but still a pleasant enough character. His father had been some kind of engineer or repair man for a company like the Singer Sewing Machine Company or some company that manufactured metal door and window frames so there was always quite a supply of metal strips and the like in the Rickey family's basement. This is what the young George got interested in—this metal supply in the basement. In the few extended conversations I'd had, over the years, with George Rickey, I don't remember his ever having mentioned his parents, his education, what he'd read or seen—none of that; he'd just tell about all those stacks of metal strips in the basement.

It's not surprising then that George Rickey got to putting these surplus metal parts together to create mobiles. Even by the time of the Murray meeting he'd already won some recognition and acclaim. In fact, the art historian-critic, George Heard Hamilton, had recognized Rickey as worthy of mention in his big book titled *19th and 20th Century Art* in which he said that, and I quote, "George Rickey had positively affirmed the virtues of mechanics in his exquisitely balanced stainless steel constructions which embody a knowledge and control of motion different from Alexander Calder's mobiles, which are at the mercy of every wayward breeze."

So you see, mothers and fathers, just because your son goes off by himself into the basement and spends hours down there does not mean he may be doing something anti-social or dirty down there.

The other person at the Murray meeting whom I remember—in fact will never be able to forget—was the art supervisor, if I'm remembering correctly, for the Gary, Indiana public schools. Her name—and I am not making this up, as Dave Barry of the *Miami Herald* keeps reminding his readers—was, and is, if she's still alive, Olga Schubkegel. She came with a national reputation for what she was able to have her primary and secondary pupils produce—rather professional appearing paintings, reminiscent, a little, of the then current and popular art style called "abstract expressionism" mixed with echoes of Grandma Moses' primitivism—but still with a unifying character, almost as if created by the same person. At least that's the way they appeared to me in the large exhibition that Olga Schubkegel had shipped ahead for display at the meeting.

Of these two remembered people, George Rickey and Olga Schubkegal, it was not Rickey, the artist, who was, shall we say, was "lionized" at the meeting. It was Olga Schubkegel. She was a physically attractive woman of about forty-eight or fifty. She spoke well, communicating her educational interests with a quality of sincerity and command. She moved gracefully but often with a suddenness and quickness that surprised me, as if she'd come apart at the seams. You, whoever you are, will be correct if you assume I'd taken more than a passing interest, but rather one that wondered about how this woman got those kids in Gary, Indiana, or wherever, to make paintings that could compete with some making the best galleries of the time. I figured she'd all but done them completely with the kids, whose names appeared on them, just watching.

Compared to Olga Schubkegel, George Rickey looked and moved around like a slob. But he kept very busy. You see he'd just invented a package called a Moby-Kit—a neat box with a supply of parts, metal strips (echoes of his basement beginnings), wires, little pulleys, and swivel joints intended for sale to kids. I saw him sell several of these kits to some primary school teachers who looked a lot like him, but dressed better, and cleaner. He really kept at it, this selling, I mean.

So, even though the meeting progressed through all sorts of discussions, in groups with leaders, note-takers, and summaries, I remained a kind of umpire skirting the edge of the outfield.

Now both Rickey and Olga Schubkegel had come to Murray in my car from Lexington, Rickey had left his car back at my house and Olga Schubkegel had come there by train from Chicago. The plan was that after the meeting the three of us would drive back to my place, and Rickey would pick up his car and drive to another doings, and hopefully more sales, further down south. I'd take Olga Shubkegel to the train station in Lexington for her trip back to Chicago. The drive from Murray to Lexington, over a hundred miles, was filled with Olga Schubkegel talking, continuously, about how she got her kids to make such adult paintings. "I never touch a brush or anything else to their paintings," she said, which to me verified that she'd all but done them from beginning to end. Mile after mile, she made me sicker to my stomach. And "Wind Art" Rickey farted a lot. An awful trip, really.

Okay, so we get to Lexington; George Rickey says his goodbyes and takes off. I never saw him again. There's still two hours before the late train to Chicago, so my wife and I are stuck with Olga Schubkegel. And she kept on talking until it was all but impossible to stand it any longer. But thank God, she'd soon be on that train. Truly a light at the end of the tunnel.

Olga Schubkegel took a terribly long time to put on her "train make-up," as she called it, but we were finally on our way along the night streets to the railroad station. As we approached it the train was already pulling out and I stood there watching that lighted logo on the back of the last car disappear down the track.

Now don't ask me what happened after that; it was just more of the same. More interesting to me even after all this time is how I was struck by that disappearing train, down and away in the night—with that lighted logo slowly darkening to nothing. Right there on the platform with Olga Schubkegel I became all alone, a solitary memory bank recalling every good possibility, I'd missed every fulfillment of promise that I'd missed just by a hair, by a mere second or two.

So—alone—you stand there savoring all the might-have-beens and feeling just a little sorry for yourself: If only you'd done this or that—and not missed, how might it be now?

But then coming back from reverie there's Olga Schubkegel with her little suitcase, standing right where you'd left her on the station platform and still talking. And you think, ah yes, and how about all those other things that had missed *you*—Weismann? Like that car careening out of its lane and coming straight at you on that iron bridge in Scranton, Pennsylvania, and like all those bullets, shells, that found home in the guy right next to you.

So, who knows, maybe Olga Schubkegel, that talking machine dressed as a woman who took too long putting on her train make-up, caused something awful to miss me.

So thanks, Olga...sure we'll put you up for the night.

No Question: Smoking Is Bad for You

I, for one, have been surprised by the success of the forces aligned against smoking cigarettes. The strongest and most violent of these forces is the body of *former* cigarette smokers. The assumption appears to be that a *former* smoker—a person who may have chain-smoked for twenty or thirty years and who reformed, as they say, is better and more healthy than a person who never smoked at all. This situation is like in the old Senator Joe McCarthy years when the belief was that a *former*, card-carrying Communist was far superior to just an ordinary citizen, a regular lifetime red, white, and blue American. Remember Whittaker Chambers?

Former cigarette smokers and all those people convinced of the basic evil and rottenness of the human body—old-time religionist fundamentalists—seem to have gotten together in what are now called in political circles "Summit Meetings." In these meetings these dirty-minded people are sort of like Holy Rollers wallowing in the dirt of all others except themselves. This wallowing has eventuated in all sorts of pronouncements among which was an elaborate one describing and damning the vile habit of smoking—especially of cigarettes.

When a former children's specialist named Doctor Koop was appointed Surgeon General of the United States, he produced statistics showing that cigarette smoking causes heart failure and cancer, mostly, but not limited to, cancer of the lungs. Now I have no argument with what this ex-children's specialist was saying. After all it's very likely a fact that human lungs were not intended to breathe much more than just oxygen—not carbon monoxide and whatever it is we are forced to breathe that comes out of all those automobile exhaust pipes which are year-in-year-out just ahead of us and blowing it at us—or the equally noxious stuff that's blown at us from our air conditioners when we shut our car windows in efforts to hold out those automobile exhaust fumes. I have no argument, really, with Dr. Koop. In fact he was right on target when he said that war—with poison gasses, nuclear radiation, and microbes, not to mention bullets, shells, missiles, grenades, and all the conventional stuff—that war is also bad for the lungs, the heart, and every other part of our bodies, as well as for the mind, if that's different, separate from the body. No, no argument with Dr. Koop: Smoking is not the best thing to do to our bodies. I believe this just as surely as I was once led to believe that I'd go blind, insane, and die—the whole body, not just the lungs and heart—if I masturbated. Of course, as we know, it's not the most popular belief to hold, nowadays—especially since it was admitted how widespread masturbation has been through the ages even if a lot of that pleasure was gained not by going at it directly, but by riding horses, bicycles, motorcycles, lumps in the upholstery, or just rubbing against table legs or door frames.

No, no argument on the health score: It's the self-appointed "I'm better, holier than thou" folks who liken cigarette smoking to ingesting offal or rotten pig intestines dug out from the environment-choking garbage dumps which they ignore. To these people, cigarette smokers are dirty organisms that should be sealed off from clean sane people who believe that blacks—niggers to them—give off offensive and unhealthful odors and therefore cannot be lived with—certainly not close-up. These are the same people who believe they, themselves, do not pass urine or feces, and never fart. They work at clogging up their pores with anti-odor pastes and sealing waxes, thereby holding in their sweat.

As I said earlier, I've been surprised by the success of these reformists, how they've pretty well managed, so far, to create a tremendous body of second-rate citizens: all those people who smoke cigarettes, herding them off to back rooms and basements, out of airplanes, trains, taxicabs, and meeting halls.

But maybe I shouldn't be surprised at all: rounding up and herding the cigarette smokers with the zest of on-marching Christian soldiers gives them a feeling of doing good in a world gone bad—something that's do-able for them in the face of all the other, more important things they ignore or feel they'd fail at. In this sense, hunting down and reviling cigarette smokers constitutes a red herring dragged across the trail of earth-shaking issues they can thus deny the existence of. It gives them something they can do, and maybe we are fortunate that they don't put that effort behind banning Shakespeare in the schools, joining the anti-family planning crusade, the anti-pornography-in-art bunch, the so-called "pro-life" enthusiasts, the anti-Semitics, anti-Asians, anti-blacks, and all such.

Maybe we—all of us—not just cigarette smokers, should be thankful that one helluva lot of people stay put and use up their energies against smoking. It's a relatively harmless occupation for people who might be doing a lot worse.

As the old Wyoming sheep herder said, "To hell with the one; I'm seeing about the ninety-nine."

The Powerful Mystique of Graduate Seminars

He had been president of an eastern college for ten years when he retired and returned to Texas, the place of his birth and where he had taught once upon a time.

The university was pleased to have him join the faculty of a department called the Department of Government, which he did as, of course, a full professor with everlasting tenure. He taught two courses: one an upper division one, the other a graduate seminar—both in subjects having to do with "Government."

Now in academia—as I've observed it during the four decades I've served in that club—the aim of most members who have attained at least the class of Associate Professor with tenure is to get their salaries increased and their teaching load decreased—less work, let's call it, for more money. And more than that, these academics lust to teach any *graduate* students—and these not in a regular classroom situation, but in what's most often mis-named "seminars"—groups of graduate students, seldom more than ten or twelve (often only five or six), seated informally in arrangements resembling circles or ovals, often in over-stuffed furniture in carpeted, air-conditioned rooms with dimmers on the lights. The boondoggle, which has become the pervasive form of much of college and university teaching during the past many decades achieves its most pristine form in *Graduate Seminars* listed under the catalogue descriptions of the so-called Social Sciences and the Humanities—and most often taught by full professors, who, because they have convinced the administrator that they are doing valuable research teach only *one Graduate Seminar*—two or three hours in, sometimes, a weekly meeting. It's great, I want to tell you—I've done it, but only until my out-dated Protestant ethic scared me into going back to big lecture sessions where I had to come prepared every time—and put it out to three or four hundred at a crack. The thing about running a *Graduate Seminar* is that the professor can get away with almost anything—come unprepared, then just ask the students question. Isn't it the old saw that it's not answers that count, just the questions? And don't many professors claim that they "learn more from their students than the students learn from them?" In this regard, if this is true, I've wondered why the professor was paid a salary instead of the students.

Well...I didn't intend to say so much about the boondoggle character of many graduate seminars in the Social Sciences and Humanities areas, but you'd be safe considering what I've already said, for I've been a student in graduate seminars in three big universities, and I've run them in a few. And more than that, I've listened to half-drunk colleagues confess their seminal sins on late Friday nights and their denials on the following Sundays. I guess what gets me is not so much what goes on in so many graduate seminars, but rather the mystique that's been built up around the very words: *Graduate Seminar*—like the "Holy Land," and the full, lifetime tenured professor-in-charge, a kind of priest, a shaman.

So...to remind you how this part of my not-so-abusive diatribe got started—remember, we were talking about the President Emeritus of that Eastern college returned to Texas for his last transfiguration as shaman of a Graduate Seminar in the Government Department at a university in Texas. He presided over his Graduate Seminar on Wednesday evenings from 7:30 to 9:30—the same time during which I taught a class of sixty—subject, *Classism and Romanticism in 19th Century American and European Art*. I taught this class in a room built like those in old medical schools—lots of bolted-down seats in rising tiers from where the doctor lectured over the cut-up cadaver.

Well, high up there in the row close to the ceiling sat one of my students who happened to be the wife of that President Emeritus. Her name—Phoebe. So with the lights on dim and me showing and talking about a slide of an Ingres drawing, I heard a thump and excited sounds from Phoebe's seat, way up there. Always ready for almost anything to intrude from the outside world of reality, I switched the lights on bright and shot up the aisle to that top row. There lay Phoebe out cold on the floor. We went to work on her—an ambulance was called—and we worked some more.

Then, as if from a world beyond, she opened her eyes and her breathing returned to what may have been normal for her.

"I'll call your husband," I said. "What's the number?"

"Oh," she half-moaned, "please don't do that, for God's sake don't, please don't interrupt him—he's doing his *Graduate Seminar*."

So you see what I mean about the awful mystique that's been woven about the concept: Phoebe would choose to die rather than interrupt her husband's Graduate Seminar. May Jesus or some fallen angel help us!

Leaving the Town and Gown Club

Partly because of situations way beyond my control, such as beginning first grade when I was only four years old, graduating from grade school at eleven, because "they" skipped me a grade, and out of college at nineteen—partly because of such happenings, a lot of my friends are older than I am. In some cases, quite a bit older. This helps account for the fact that as I move closer and closer to ninety, a lot of my friends and acquaintances are dying off.

Never one to go energetically about trying to make friends, I never had an abundance of them. So from a starting supply of friends that never was a lot, there are logically not so many left now. It seems that almost everyday I read that another one has gone down the tube, so to speak. Naturally some of those leaving have dropped out of being "close" friends—drifted apart, as some say. Yet in their time, and mine, they certainly were my conversing friends.

Now not all that attends the reduction in the number of one's friends is bad. There are positive dividends. For instance, there are less birthdays and other holiday postcards to send out, less letters to write, less phone calls to make, and less to receive. The steady dwindling of friends means less gifts to hand out or mail away and, of course, to receive. More subtle is that having less old friends relieves one's memory of lots of responsibilities. By that I mean what you already know from your own life's experiences with friends: It may be a fact that a serious and compassionate person—in efforts to further and keep friendship relations—presents himself or herself in ways conducive to the understanding of the friend in question. This means we represent ourselves differently to different people. And we have to remember who we pretend to be to each of these people. One friend, let us say, got the idea early on that you were jovial, another that you were a charming wet blanket. And if you have lots and lots of friends—to them you are lots and lots of different people. This is not hypocrisy; it is closer to respect and love and what journalists and preachers often refer to as "caring"—being a "caring person." You care enough for your friends to be whatever they care for.

Well, as more and more of the old friends cash in their chips with public notice, or just disappear silently from life's landscape, you're relieved of more and more of your caring impersonation. I'd guess that no one would argue that this shrinking of the masquerade is not welcome. It certainly is—being less and less of what others expect you to be—jovial, devil-may-care, always "friend-in-need," good drinking companion, great listener, good scout, relaxed, and uncomplaining. Yes, being less of all that and more yourself more of the time—no matter how harrowing that may be!

So old friends keep dropping off like flies, as my Uncle Feodore used to say. And he ought to know: He died almost friendless and penniless. But then he had the time; he was ninety-four when he or someone, perhaps a lone surviving friend, threw in the towel.

And as old friends just "pass away," as most Protestants allude to death, you get the idea more and more brilliantly that your own turn is coming—not suddenly, but slower, like seepage. As the essayist would say: The fact of mortality gets pretty roundly exemplified.

I think that all I've been saying here contributed to the reason I finally resigned from the all-male Town and Gown Club which was founded here in Austin, Texas, close to a hundred years ago.

I'd been a member of the Town and Gown Club for almost thirty years. Because I taught at the University, I was in the quota of members called "Gown," the name deriving from the tradition that once had academics wear gowns. The "Town" quota included men from town selected because they'd made successes as lawyers, doctors, automobile, and beer franchise holders, clerics, chain store owners, that mis-named group called "developers," and so on. From year to year, some members left the University or the town and were replaced. This didn't happen so often and as a result this group of men, as a group, kept aging, "running in place," as my sixth grade calisthenics teacher, Mr. Zinsmeister, might have called it. And they kept dying off—and will, of course.

Well, the exact times of these deaths—the evening it gets announced that, sure enough, old Barney Craftsman had gotten the sponge treatment—these *exact* times were nothing extraordinary. What got to be extraordinary to me was how long and how painful it took some to die—meeting after meeting fading away, "feeling the blow of the cold," as the Germans have it. After the summer recess there were always a few who'd had it happen: shuffling along now, not walking; bent over where they were once pretty perpendicular to the floor; eyeglasses thick enough to be aquaria and bumping into things; palsied hands that made it hard to hold the forks and harder still to spear the chicken-fried steak though the creamed gravy; spilling their ginger-ale, mumbling like maybe the clots had at last gotten within striking distance of the brain, hearing aids falling out onto their vests and hanging there without them even noticing it, and all those canes, walkers, and some wheelchairs.

Now I'm a pretty optimistic guy—not that I ever fall on the floor in fits of optimism or joy. I've been in situations that most people would agree were pretty bad, like standing there while they bulldozed all those Japs into pits at the end of the Momote airstrip in the Admirality Islands—when not all of them seemed to be dead, and watching that old man carry his testicles in a kind of homemade wheelbarrow as he made his way in the New Guinea bush, and, worse in some way, being an almost innocent bystander to political horrors worked in the back alleys of a few of our nicest cities. Still, as I said, I'm a pretty optimistic guy. And, almost contradictorily, I'm what at least *I* call myself a *realist*: We live, and after a while, short for some longer for others, we die—or as my father used to say, while he could still say, "we croak." Incidentally my father who, himself, was kept actively living by virtue of heroic performances of medical science, still referred to medical doctors as "croakers." No matter that. As I said, I believe myself to be a realist and that the life we have is always, at every instant, held precariously. And we shouldn't be nervous about this. There's no need to—that's just the way it is.

So, to refocus, as some say, on the Town and Gown Club and why after almost thirty years as a member I've resigned. It's simple: It got to bother me to the point of melancholic boredom to present myself every so often to watch those who were on that monthly calendar being overtaken by the sadly ordinary facts of diminution and disappearance.

For those of you liking some comic relief from this, let me say that a Welsh friend of mine, not yet dead, has told me about a Welsh friend of his who died at home in Wales. By his last testament his wishes were carried out. What he wanted was that his remains be boxed and all that, and that as his friends and enemies came to look at the box a recording of Kate Smith singing *I'll Be Seeing You* be played over and over while a greatly enlarged photograph of himself, hanging right over the box, smiled, almost laughed in derision to those below. His wishes were carried out. And then what was left of him was carried out as Kate Smith, long dead, continued singing until the lights went out and with it the electric current that fed the phonograph. With my Welsh friend's friend still smiling and waving in the dark.

But to come back to the Town and Gown Club: You see, it got to be like seeing the same movie over and over. Sure, I've watched some movies more than once, some, maybe five or six or more times—but, brother, from my point of view they had to be great movies, the kind that keeps revealing new dimensions in itself—and in me. The Town and Gown movie, so to speak, was not a great movie to begin with—and seemed to get worse the more times it was run. The same size on the same screen.

So, to preserve the metaphor, I walked out. Besides, I'd eaten all my popcorn.

My Last Day of Teaching

No different from the preceding twenty years—there they were coming in through the triple doors at the back of the auditorium, and me watching from a wing off stage. Four hundred and fifty of them signed up for my class, *The Visual Arts As Experience*, taking their seats and this being the first session of the new semester, and not knowing what the course or the teacher would be like, they're quiet and looking toward the lectern on stage.

In the wing, I know that I cannot do this again. I just cannot pump myself up one more time. I cannot lecture to another class. After all those years, I know it's over—no question now. There had been other times that felt something like this: that I was at last run down, tired of hearing my own voice, tired of believing that, yes, I was getting to them out there and that I was doing it all for them, instead of feeding my own ego—that heady feeling of my own power over those college kids.

But this time it was a sure thing: This was the end.

But how to tell them that this class they'd signed up for wouldn't be offered, that they'd have to go through all the bureaucratic mess to find a substitute course that they could fit into their schedule of classes? How would they take this? Why didn't I quit during the summer, before this fall rush? No matter any of that—it was over and gone for me, and they'd just have to do what they'd have to do. Simple as that.

So you walk out, center stage, and just look at them.

Then you say, "This is course U.C. 320, titled *The Visual Arts As Experience*," and that it "*was* scheduled to meet at 3 P.M. on Mondays, Wednesdays, and Fridays." And you say it that way, in the past tense—that it *was* scheduled. Still you can't quite say it outright, not yet, that the course had been canceled.

So you go to the huge blackboard, saying that it might help to know *who was* scheduled to teach this class—who you are.

With your back to the silent class, you begin to letter our your name in large letters that will carry clear to back of the hall.

"My first name is Donald," you say to the blackboard, slowly lettering it out:

D O N A L D

After that you put a big letter L and a period, standing for the middle name. And as you look at that abbreviation for the name LeRoy, you think of how you must have gotten it—who thought it up? Your pa? No, he was someplace else when your mother had you there with Doctor Ingham in that house on Island Avenue in far away Milwaukee. A neighbor? A friend? Hardly. And no uncles or others in the family, living or dead, ever had the name LeRoy. It must have been, for whatever reasons or non-reasons, your mother who gave you that name.

So, as you keep pressing down and rubbing the chalk around on that period after the letter L, you say, still to the blackboard, "and in case anyone should ask what the L stands for, you can tell them it stands for LeRoy, the name given me by my sainted mother—dead these last forty-seven years."

And you stand there, staring at that period big and clear on the blackboard—for what seems like a good part of forever—while nothing but what feels like eternal silence stands like a solid block behind you.

Then someone back there, snickers—then laughter, coming up strong, invades the hall.

Then you turn from the blackboard and there they are now, coming to their feet and applauding like mad.

So what did I do? I raised my hands above my head like boxers do when their victory is announced, bowed, returned to the blackboard to letter out slowly the last name as the 450 college kids responded by repeating every letter after me—every letter louder than the one before

W E I S M A N N

with a final roaring cheer at the end.

And with that I commenced my next ten years of teaching.

Shortest Valedictory

While I was deciding—after twenty-seven years on the faculty of the University of Texas, to call it quits, to retire—I figured in all the variables and the unknowns I could recognize or imagine. I didn't go about my decision in any manner that could be called light. After all 1981 was forty-six years after I'd done my first day of teaching as head of the Art Department in Sheboygan High School. In a sort of real way, teaching had been my life. And I'd run things in academia, too—and especially at the University of Texas where my role was often heavily political up to and involving the Board of Regents, the Governor, and even the President of the United States. So this decision of 1981—after serious and prolonged thought—including if I'd be able to live the rest of my life, and that of my wife, on the retirement allotment, Social Security, and some small investments.

Well, having decided to retire, I walked over to let my Dean know that I was declaring to call it quits.

That's when my Dean delivered perhaps the shortest valedictory ever delivered—smack out loud. He leaned back in his swivel chair and said, "Oh shit, Don." That was it. Period.

There Are Ways and Ways

I had often talked with him and served on committees with him, a very nice guy, Director (or whatever he was called) of the University of Texas main library. As time went on and ideas about improving the library—open-shelf availability of its resources, enhancing the rare books collection, and a generally more "aggressive" attitude toward seeking out and securing new acquisitions, Alex Moffet was thought of as an obstacle to development. Committees were appointed by the University of Texas administration ostensibly to help Moffet improve or change his ways, but clearly these "helps" were aimed at getting Moffet to resign or retire. He wasn't an old man, a little older than I was back in the 1960s, but after a while he got the message: retire or get fired—with a pension, of course.

It was right after he got this message that Alex Moffet changed in quite noticeable ways. A tall man, he'd always walked with a light stoop—his back bent forward a little and the shoulders a little rounded. But once he'd decided to quit trying to defend his long perfected mode of operation, I noticed how his back straightened giving him another inch to his height, and how his shoulders got thrown back, making a veritable straight horizontal across the back of his neck. And although he was never a sour-puss, he began to smile a lot. He appeared on campus in a brand new lavender colored Lincoln Continental automobile which he drove with a new abandon resembling a bit the driving habits of the highest paid professors of physics and business and the richer freshmen students. It was obvious that Alex Moffet had now retired.

That part of the Moffet story gave me increased positive warm feelings toward him. For a short time I'd see him driving on the campus in that lavender car and smiling. We'd wave to each other. It appeared that Alex Moffet was now a happy man. But then, suddenly, he just died. The amputation, though a relief, proved to be fatal.

Quite different is the story of my high school English teacher, a short, bouncy, fast-talking man of about thirty-five when I first met him in 1928. To me at fourteen years of age, this man, Bertram Shoemaker, seemed a hero—not of the first grade, perhaps, but still a hero. He'd been a sailor in submarines during the First World War, he knew a great deal about American literature, had a Masters degree from the University of Minnesota and, he said, was writing a book about his experiences in the Navy—titled *Sunless Seas*.

By the time I was a junior in high school, two years after first meeting him, it had become clear that Bertram Shoemaker was a drunk—not at school, but every place else. The hero feeling faded, and I began to feel sorry for him. Not just because he was a drunk—after all, my father was one too, and I had learned to live with that. No, not just because Bertram Shoemaker was a drunk, but because of other of his habits like repeating over and over stories he'd told me many times before, and never getting back to finishing his *Sunless Seas*, often reading me the same first two pages of it—out loud and with lots of dramatic gestures.

Maybe because I thought I was doing him some good listening as one member of a very small and continually shrinking audience, I kept in touch. Twenty-five years after I'd first met Bertram Shoemaker he chose to retire early, at age sixty, from the Milwaukee Public School System. Unlike Alex Moffet he didn't change into a happier man. He never got beyond those first two pages of his *Sunless Seas*. It was as if his life had ended back there with the Armistice of 1918, but he continued to live. And so, as I figured it, he launched a conscious effort to remedy that: he drank enormous amounts of whisky almost continually. A slow suicide, a certain death.

The last time I saw Bertram Shoemaker he was sitting up in bed, naked, with his skeleton showing clearly through his translucent skin and drinking from a quart bottle of whisky. His wife, who managed to keep things together by selling Spencer corsets right there in their little apartment, was standing across the room, and when I looked at her she was turning her head slowly from side to side with no expression showing in her small pale face.

I didn't go to Bertram Shoemaker's funeral, but I heard that his mother, an eighty-five-year-old warhorse Theosophist, had his body shipped to Oyster Bay on Long Island near the sea.

Now, when I retired at sixty-five, well into two decades ago, I didn't suddenly turn into a happy man as Alex Moffet did, nor did I hurry death along as Bertram Shoemaker did.

No, I've been what must be considered a happy man for most of my life. I don't mean that I've danced and giggled my way through. There's been bad times—some at home when I was a kid, the war, divorces, losses of brothers, a mother, a father, and more than a few deeply loved ones. But the stretches of times between such unpleasant and trying times have been happy ones. Indeed, besides considering myself one of the luckiest men alive, I consider myself one of the happier. Of course there have been those people, men and women along the way, who thought I was playing the fool, pretending to be happy, joking as I went along. Among some of my friends I was thought to be, and often they said so—"the funniest man alive."

I retired for the simple reason that I'd had fully enough of the academic brand of life—sixty years of it on one side of the desk or the other. In that time I enjoyed some "celebrity status," as some say, as an educator, as an artist and writer, but I didn't retire in order to give full time to my art, my research, or to my family. If I retired for any "reason" other than merely being tired of the academic drills, it may have been to more freely enjoy what was left of my life, and maybe by this and that, but informally and without design, make some sense of the life I'd lived up to then.

I didn't feel any "load" on me to do this. Simply it seemed no more than another page in the same book which, as yet, hadn't reached the blank end-pages and the hardcover back. And never being one to make specific plans far in advance, I didn't make but very few—only those of the practical sort: money, some protection for the future.

A friend of mine, a woman who'd labored for a few decades as an administrative assistant, announced early what her main plans for retirement were: number one, she was going to learn to play the piano; number two, she was going to learn a new language, perhaps French. For a little while after she'd retired she tried to do that, but what happened was that she took to drinking wine—first by the quart and then by the gallon. Advised by her former boss that all that wine would do her no good, she shifted to eating ice cream, first by the pint, then by the quart. The rented piano waited, the French books stayed on the shelf, and she quickly became enormously fat, a cripple, fell down on the floor of her kitchen, couldn't get up, and died there in the empty house.

I'd known this woman for decades, since before her divorce when her hair was still an oak color and she moved in an almost sylph-like way. She'd always had plans, *specific* plans, for the future. Now, don't get me wrong, I don't think there's anything wrong about planning. I've done plenty of it, but *specific* plans—especially long range ones—I've found out, have their own traps, their own built-in denials.

I know a man who said that since he was eight years old he has had the specific plan of being chosen President of the United States of America. And it's true that he's worked hard and long at that. But in the scores of years that have passed since that early decision, he has never managed to get elected to anything. He hasn't taken to booze or ice cream, nor—in my considered opinion—has he become a happy man like old librarian Alex Moffet. What his retirement will make possible for him is beyond the range of my guessing. In the past he has said that one of his heroes, "Stonewall" Jackson, the celebrated Confederate General who was killed by fire from his own men, was expressing his own specific plan when he, "Stonewall" Jackson, said, "I'll camp at the crossroads and the enemy will never know from which direction I'll attack." If that is the retirement plan of my friend...well, I think it's much too specific—too specific to succeed anywhere intact. Still, I'll visit that "crossroads" every now and then to see how he's doing. He's really a great guy and very successful, but it's damned sad that he got so early obsessed, with such rigid plans.

And when I visit him I just might play the part of "the funniest man in the world" as I go about the long term effort of making sense of my life.

I Tell My Dog about George Burns

This was the day, March 9, 1996, that the death of George Burns, the comedian, was announced. He was one hundred years old and, according to his old friend who was at his bedside, George Burns died peacefully as his life ebbed away. The television announcement was accompanied with film clips of George Burns and his wife and partner, Gracie Allen, doing their special kind of comedy—reminders, for me, not only of George and Gracie, but of that part of my life that ran along parallel to theirs.

I was alone, sitting in my TV chair, when I got the news. Only my dog was there—lying right near and staring up at me. Her name is Buttons. She's about seven years old. We didn't give her that name; her former owner did and wanted that name to go with her; to whomever would claim her there at the Humane Society pound, which because when I was a boy I was, for a few years, in a sort of orphanage named the Milwaukee County Home for Dependent Children, I call the pound the Travis County Texas Home for Dependent Dogs. I think Buttons appreciates this linking of our lives.

Buttons is what appears to be a successful mixing of German Shepherd and Daschund. She weighs a little over thirty pounds, has a beautiful brown and black coat, and is extremely intelligent.

People I meet on morning and late afternoon walks with Buttons often stop to admire her. "What kind of dog is that?" they often ask. Now since no records exist for this dog, there is no way, for sure, to know what breed of dog she may be, so I just tell these inquisitive people that she's a "New Zealand Tracer"—first as a joke and then, because they think I'm serious, I become serious: "Yes," I repeat, "she's a pure bred New Zealand Tracer." One lady walking a honey-colored Labrador said she'd never seen such a breed and I assured her that now, at last, she had. Funny how deep-in one can get, isn't it; especially if you're just enjoying life.

Well I'm sitting there watching and listening to the television celebration of George Burns's life and death while Buttons stares up at me. She's a great watcher and a terrific listener, so I begin to give her some clues to how my life intersected with his and Gracie Allen's—at various times and places.

I tell her how, on the radio, they entertained me, made me laugh when I was cooking in a lumberman's camp near the James Bay in Ontario, when I was in the Navy and hearing a re-broadcast in Borneo and in a lot of bus stations airports and saloons across this country, as well as at home. And the *voices* of George Burns and Gracie Allen coming through on the television report, brought back especially clear pictures of one of my favorite roads of this country. On a roadmap it's numbered Highway 93 and it enters northern Nevada at a place called Jackpot. From Jackpot it runs south through a place called Thousand Springs then through Wells and with the exception of the town of Ely, on down through a great emptiness—mile after mile of virtually uninhabited semi-desert country—the kind of country in which corporate America would now like to dump its tons of nuclear waste.

I drove this road first in 1937, over sixty years ago. Long stretches of it were like some of the pictures we've seen of the up-close surface of the moon—a land still devoid of people and their usual baggage. Back then I had the road virtually for my own every time I drove it right up to the last time just before the war.

I never had a "mission" or "reason" for what I was doing out there, no clear target at the end. I was just *going*. Excited and happy as if I was the first man in God's still unplanted garden.

And when night came with nothing but the road in that fan-shaped light ahead, more than once the voices of George Burns and Gracie Allen came to me over the radio.

Yes, I was telling my dog Buttons all about that, and later about these same voices and their moving images right there in front of me on the television screen. Yes, I told Buttons, we had a lot in common—Burns and Allen and me—how the time of our lives ran together, overlapped, no matter that we never actually met, and no matter how near or far we were from each other.

After a little while Buttons got up from the floor, took the two or three steps that lay between us, put her head in my lap—and, I'll swear to this: she raised her head…and smiled—yes, in a manner so wonderfully characteristic of a genuine New Zealand Tracer.

Rick and Thoughts of Failure

Even though it's been fifteen or twenty years ago, I can still vividly remember that evening. It was in early March, and that means that here in central Texas spring is well begun—some trees are showing that delicate yellow-green, the Spanish oaks are shedding last year's leaves, and little shoots poking up all over the place. Renewal, as some call it, is in evidence almost wherever you look. Sometimes it makes a guy feel pretty weak, of no account, with all that happening in the nature outside himself.

I'd had a good day; the family was in good shape and the school year had only about sixty days to go to what's still called Commencement. Of course I was already savoring the end of another term, and maybe a summer of "creative" work, as we like to call it.

In many ways I'm either what's called "a good soldier" or just plain stupid, if there's a difference in the academic infantry: I just barge ahead, often on backwaters of liquid offal—doing my job and lots more—keeping up and, most of the time, glad to be alive. I give positive, often eloquent advice to students—advice I regularly couldn't follow myself, but true, good advice just the same.

Well, to come back to that day in early March, and to the evening when I was sitting on the terrace looking across the valley way off to San Antonio and having a tall bourbon. It got to be near midnight when the phone rang. It was my old friend, Rick, professor of anthropology and world class authority on Latin America. I was surprised that it was he who was calling at this late hour—must be serious, Rick is an early-to-bed, early-to-rise type.

"Are you busy?" he asked, and I heard an uncharacteristic undertone in his otherwise flat-out voice.

"No," I said, "I'm not busy."

"Can I come over…now?" he asked.

"Never a better time," I said—this being a small evidence of how I live my life.

Now Rick lives in the same high class, expensive, booster-type suburb of Austin that I live in—not that we join in with the residents, not very often anyway. But that's neither here nor there, as the TV weatherman so often implies. The important thing is that since Rick and I live pretty close, he was over at my place in record time, and looking a little sad.

I still had half of my bourbon and asked Rick if he'd like a drink. Like most of my friends from liberated backgrounds he enjoys good whisky and now cigars after giving up cigarettes.

"No, no thanks, no drink, thanks," Rick said. Now I knew something heavier than dust was in the wind—especially since after refusing the offer of a drink, he just stood there, as if it was still my turn to talk—so, as if we'd both missed the same train and were standing on the platform with our suitcases, I said, "Well, what's up now, Rick?" and after a small while he said, "I'm a failure, a flat out failure, Don."

Now, even though I try to disguise it, I'm a deep thinker, really a kind of radical philosopher which I hide in jokes I invent—the jokes arising out of, but not betraying, the deep moral, philosophical well from which on occasion I hoist them. So, from that well came this pronouncement, "Rick, there's no need to feel bad if you've discovered you're a failure—everybody fails."

"How's that?" Rick asked.

"I mean," I said, "that anybody who sets goals as difficult to achieve as you have, they have to expect that some may miss the mark...fail."

"But look at you," Rick said, "you're not a failure, you succeed over and over...all the time."

"It just looks that way, maybe," I said, "but only to others, not to me. Everybody worth their life fails. Look at Jesus—nailed up, and lucky maybe not upside down—a real true failure."

"Jesus, a failure?" Rick asked.

"Indeed he was. How would you like to wait all that time before people thought you were not a failure? Rick, whatever gave you the idea that we do not fail in this life? What makes you think you should succeed with everybody else failing? Success in any big way in this life is a plain home style myth."

"I think that's horseshit," Rick said.

"Success or failure," I said, "is not the issue—whether a person fails or succeeds is not the important thing."

"So what is important?" Rick asked.

"The important thing—since failure is guaranteed, like death, the important thing is to fail in your own style," I said, "and Rick, you've got style."

"Fail in my own style," Rick said reflectively. And then after a long pause, "Yes, by God, in my own style. I'll have that drink now."

The next afternoon Rick called me at my office, saying, "I went from your place last night feeling pretty good. But for the life of me I can't remember why."

"Don't worry about it," I said, "at times every one of us fails to remember and that's not important—just so we fail to remember in our own style."

Rick, a good long-standing friend, did not hang up.

Inside the Austin City Limits

I had planned on going to England that summer of 1936—and I would have if I hadn't had a real smash-up in my 1928 Model A Ford roadster outside Manitowoc, Wisconsin, in October. So come late June with the depleted savings of my first year's teaching at Sheboygan high School, I headed out instead for where it was cheap to live—Mexico, with the peso at twelve and a half to the dollar.

I was still twenty-one that June, and maybe already thinking that Milwaukee, where I was born, was not where I was intended to die.

In the summertime of the preceding years I'd hitchhiked a lot. Just looking around at Wyoming, the Dakotas, the still-lynching southeast—the northeast all the way to Halifax and points between. I'd learned to travel light, never more than ten pounds including a sketch pad and some drawing materials. Even back then I knew I was an artist, and the stuff I made convinced a lot of people, even a couple of hot-shot critics in Chicago and Philadelphia, one of whom said that my paintings "made the ordinary seem extraordinary in a mysterious way." I've never forgotten that.

Through the middle of the country from Milwaukee south, the summer of 1936 felt like a model for Hell—really hot!

The sun went down as the pickup driver said that this was where he turned off—almost a mile north of the Austin, Texas, city limits, on old U.S. 81. A breeze had come up, and I began walking in...cool against my wet shirt, and a sky of unlimited blue, at once above and all around me.

On my right, a big used car lot looking like some artifact from a long forgotten time. No one around, no salesman, no customers. Just lying there, as if for some unannounced appearance.

Brightly colored pennants, strung along wires over the huge lot flapping in the breeze and besting the gold of the west.

I stood there as if commanded to do so and felt a mysterious peace reserved for those who die without pain—as if I were in a place ahead of my time, ahead of schedule or, way *behind* schedule, back in early boyhood watching a kite my father flew for me, and then let me hold the string as it danced against the same unmarked blue. A first time back there, and now *another* first time inside the city limits of Austin.

You know, it doesn't take the Grand Canyon, the Pyramids of Egypt, or the flickering lights of Tangiers at the Gates of Hercules to stop a guy, make him feel for an instant the magnificent wonder that resides in himself as well as what's "out there." And this, with all his vulnerabilities submerged, lost, in that special, protected moment saved out of the long paragraph of time.

I didn't know it, back then over sixty years ago, that something like the mood created in me by that extended moment, hovering over and around that Texas used-car lot, would carry me back to Texas eighteen years later—where, with time out for a foreign war, trips abroad, and all the rest, I have remained, and happier, I guess, than most other people.

Glad to Be There...and Here

A rainy March day and I'm sitting here in the studio-workshop I made out of the two-car garage not so long ago. I look out to the southeast from where the warm air from the Gulf of Mexico is coming, gently but with a little gust now and then. Once the sun comes out there's going to be flowers all across these fields. It's really spring again, another beginning—the ancient pattern.

They say—some people who report such things—that it's the burgeonings of spring, the feel of life coming back in everything, that makes some other people feel inadequate—that they keep dying while the nature around them gets infused with new life. And that's why some of these people commit suicide, those statisticians say. In these latitudes, anyway, and they have the figures to prove it.

I've never felt inadequate with spring, and I've seen a lot of them. What happens in me, if I take a good pause and look around me at this annual miracle, is an easy slipping into a reflective attitude. With another future happening in front of me, I sense its beginnings in last winter's rains and in-foldings. And I sense my own beginnings.

Here, this St. Patrick's Day in Cedar Creek, Texas, spring has me thinking, and wondering too, how it is that for most of my life—almost from the beginning—it's been the appearance of the stuff of this world that has fascinated and held me. And without demeaning them by considering them in this word, "stuff," I mean to include people, animals, bugs, the wind, rain and snow, and all the rest. What I mean to make point of is the *appearances* of these: how they appear to me, how I am given to *see* them; how they reveal themselves to me in their particular silences.

Long before the man or woman or child comes up to me, long before I meet them in the hall, the field, on the stairs or the landing, I sense I am in communication with them. Their very *appearance* is telling me, and I am listening. And then, when they speak out in words, I feel I am listening to them, but in a different way—all the while the silence of their appearance keeps telling me, and my silent appearance keeps telling them.

The academic would say that what I'm saying here is simply something about visual perception—how we see, and with all the cultural modifiers, interpret what we see. And that's acceptable to me. But what I'm getting at is the virginal quality of vision—the powerful first impact that goes with sight, how the very presence of light, color, and shape in space gets to us and affects us in much more than superficial ways.

It's the miracle of vision, how our eyes bring the world into us, that's played into my hands ever since I began to remember. And played into my hands by causing me to use those hands to draw and paint in a natural celebration of whatever is seen.

The very first drawings I made and can remember were of things I saw around me—and that was early…when I was six or seven years old. And I kept at doing that for the next ten or fifteen years—making drawings and paintings of the city stuff around me: the streets and houses, the railroad sidings, the piles of coal along the river, the circus when it came to town, the long lines of men and women lined up at the soup kitchens during the Great Depression, and all the little details of Victorian buildings, water hydrants, sewer covers, tire tracks, and telephone poles. In the 1930s I was what was then called an "American Regionalist," celebrating the ordinary visual facts of my close-up world.

Then, along the way, and no doubt partly from the pressures of what the "famous" artists were doing, I tried my hand at giving shape to my *feelings* about what I was seeing. So, naturally, this led to what's called *abstract* or *non-objective* paintings. I had a lot of what's called *success* with those paintings—even sold quite a few. But the satisfaction of celebrating the actual, optical world—and its mysteries—was for me missing in these private, introverted, self-referring works. And after a time I stopped making them. In fact I stopped making any drawings or paintings. That is until I made my first extended trip to Europe. There the impact of all that new stuff of foreign worlds had me, once again, wide-eyed, engrossed, marveling at the specifics of the objective world—and, again, marveling at the mystery of the utterly real. So I went back to the world in years of drawing and painting it.

With all the valuable happenings of that first year in Europe, it's clear now that the most significant for me was re-discovering the richness and specificity of the surrounding objective world, and how it continues to stand out there in space and color as a fundamental clue to where I stand and what I'm about.

Not that any of this will make me appear different to those of you who have seen me through the years. I'm still the same guy—the same guy who, after all that's happened in the intervening seventy-five years since he was six or seven years old is back where he started—and glad to be there—and here.

Ode to Retirement

Of the eighty-four years of my life up to this very time, I've spent seventy-five years in school—either as a student or a teacher—save for about three years spent as a communications officer in the Navy here and overseas. Even the time I spent with the Army Air Corps Technical Command—prior to my enlistment in the Navy—I was teaching. Teaching radiomen-gunners the Morse Code, military radio procedures, and routine maintenance. I am both a retired Naval officer and a retired university professor.

With exception of the World War II military years, my education and experience has focused on art—the performance, history, theory, and criticism of the visual arts. I've enjoyed some national recognition as a painter, and I've published in the history and theory of art. I've served on state and national boards and committees that have to do with the arts. Long ago I was President of the Illinois Art Education Association; Committee Chairman for the arts with UNESCO; a special arts consultant with the United States Information Service in Florence, Italy; a member of the Arts Council for the National

Endowment for the Arts by appointment of the president—and so on.

I recite all this only to evidence the fact that almost all of my life has been spent with art and peripheral matters. During that time, at times, I worked to clarify, understand, and illuminate a lot of what Susanne Langer called "Problems of Art." I dealt head-on with the so-called "problem of *form* in art," history and historicity in the art literature, classical and contemporary aesthetics, the creative process in art, objectivism and non-objectivism in painting and sculpture, the role of art in society, the artist and society, the interrelations of the arts, art and human experience. I even jousted with *meaning* in the arts. I guess I did passably with all this and more, and I received awards and honors enough—certainly more that I ever had reason or gall enough to expect.

Along with the academically certified performances I kept making through the years, there was a constantly haunting suspicion that those performances were just that: performances, and performances that had been choreographed by others than myself—choreographed by other historians, other critics, other forces. This may have been the case, since I was almost always aware of both my irregular academic training and my mistrust of those considered to be excellently educated in the history and theory of art. Also a certain skew was introduced into my teaching by virtue of the fact that I'd been a practicing exhibiting painter from the time I was sixteen years old. Art history reads different for an artist than for a person who is exclusively an art historian. Still, seemingly without thought, I did try to imitate the "pure bred" art historian as a kind of "cover" for what I couldn't keep doing, anyway. And it was this "imitation" that lent a certain feeling of falseness in my style if not in the substance of my teaching. Maybe most other people didn't notice this, but I certainly did. Still it didn't drive me to visit psychiatrists or counselors; things would have to get terribly, terribly bad for me before I'd submit to those sorts of exercises in true or made-up confessions. I just went on and on, year after year, balancing the academic part of my life with marriages, children, travel, and lots of physical undertakings—single-handedly rebuilding a two-story house, building garages, sheds, and even a gazebo which overhung (and still does) a cliff. And there was the building of those hundreds of feet of dry stone walls, some twelve feet high, that filled-in chunks of otherwise "unusable" time.

Long before I retired, now nineteen years ago, I had, in subtle and difficult ways to describe, abdicated my imperfectly adopted role as an academician. Little by little I was using the history and theory of art as helps in describing and understanding my own personal experience—helpmates in efforts to make sense of my own life. In retrospect I think it was this selfish appropriation that may have made my large lecture classes, sometimes as many as five hundred in them, as successful as they were. I know that I'd stopped admiring the "objectivism" of my colleagues, and not especially because my students scored better in the long run than students turned out by those who taught in ways similar to the once-popular time-filler called "painting by the numbers." No, I stopped respecting the cool objectivism of my colleagues in the humanities just as I had Marxist determination when I was an undergraduate over seventy years ago and attending meetings of the John Reed Club. Somehow I just could not ignore those living young warm bodies—those students—set in front of me each and every class period, anymore, it appears, than I could deny my living self.

Well, I got out of teaching before they "found me out"—if any of those "*they*" people ever cared who I was or where I was at. And it should go without saying that I, myself, often wondered who I was, what I was about. This didn't bother me much, since it's one of my non-academic assumptions that everyone has the same wonderments about themselves. If you seriously ask any person who he or she is, and where they're at, you're going to get some pretty ambiguous, often ridiculous, responses. And you're going to be suddenly cut-off in your questioning if you ask the "why" question. So no sweat about wondering who I am and where I'm going—that's just natural, part of the adventure.

What was interesting was that once out of teaching the history and theory of art—and I'd been slowly wiggling out of that for several years—once out of the university, most of the stuff of the history and theory of art got evaporated, steamed off my gray matter. It got so that if I was asked by some passerby how to spell Grünewald, I'd have to think hard, and, as often as not, get it wrong. And as for the formal relationships that characterized Mannerism, Nazca pottery, or the Saite period, forget it—ask somebody else. It required no effort on my part to relegate such to some dead area of my brain—it just blew away like leaves into an ocean or into a deep wide tank-trap on the other side of the horizon.

In all this, I didn't experience any sense of loss. Maybe because all that categorized information had never really been mine; it never got *inside* me. It was worn like a coat, not a consciousness. The only art-type book I wrote after my retirement was on contract to a university press run by friends who wanted, terribly, to have it done—a book about a relatively unknown painter of Longhorn cattle and their western ranges. I got paid a lot for my work and the book was a best seller for the press. Once I saw the finished product—pages and pages of full-color reproductions, all on heavy, expensive glazed paper and all the words spelled correctly, I recognized it for what it was—a fifty-dollar-a-copy travesty—a sort of parody of what I'd left back in those university halls. It seemed to help when I gave my outsize writer's fee to the Salvation Army. I have my own way of tithing.

Years before my retirement from teaching and in connection with a lecture concerned with the late 20th century American art, I made a point about the power of the art brokerage to determine which artists got the big plays and, along with everything else, made lots of money as their artificially boosted stock sold high on the market. This high powered commercialism serves to sharpen the difference between money value and aesthetic value, between commerce and art—and, for me, an opportunity to talk about the equation of money and success, and how the American system is structured to encourage the making of millionaires. From limited but no less supportive personal experience, I told that class that if that's what they most wanted to be, the road to even obscene riches is clearly marked and open to anyone—save the bottom level of retards—anyone who will dedicate his or her life to just that. While the boos and cat-calls died out I outlined a sample case, made up on the spot.

It concerned the progress of a near destitute man from hand cutting bird-call whistles out of aluminum salvaged from used beer cans all the way to his millionaire status as the owner-operator of a huge multinational toy manufactory. The story made point of sacrifice of just about every regular feature of what's called a "normal life"'; work twenty hours a day, sleep no more than four; forget sex except what can be taken on the fly or advance the project; limit friendships to those who can help; employ ethnic minorities at the lowest pay; avoid unionization of labor; use the media for whatever help it can provide; stay clear of the law, remembering that what's called "extra-legal" is not illegal; keep tabs on how the big successes in the oil, chemical, pharmaceutical, and other industries achieved their successes. And above all, don't give up; believe and continue to believe that any set-backs are only temporary and that the last laugh—all the way to the bank—will be yours.

And then you're in a position to consult the art brokerage, the dealerships which know all about tax breaks and how to "guarantee" that what you'll purchase will rise in cash value…etc. So back to talking about monetary value and aesthetic quality of art.

Some time later, in somewhat the same context, I made up another story of the artificial inflating money values in art. This one had to do with a disgruntled American artist who cynically sets up an exhibition of human corpses—found objects, *objects trouves*—and trucks the cadavers across the country to a gallery in New York City. And once having voiced this invention, it stuck with me—not as a story about art and its commercialization, but rather a story about the credulousness of human beings, the surreal character of American life, and a partial victory over meaninglessness. This became the core of my book, *The Twelve Cadavers of Joe Mariner*, which I mention in *Mysteries of Photography*, the piece that ends this book, *The Stuff of Stories*.

As I approached the date I'd set for my retirement from the university, the cloak of academic propriety I'd worn all those years just slipped from my shoulders and I felt a great relief.

So then there's retirement to a house and land far from the town where, I imagine, the university with its fifty thousand students and thousands of faculty still stands. Retirement to south Texas with a wonderful woman who would never purport to know all about me and the world in which we live—but who perhaps comes pretty close to that.

And what do I do with my time now—the kind of time I used to use performing as a high-level impostor of an academic man? Well, along with tending this south Texas acreage, I write—write short things and whole books, some of which even get published. But they're not about art or its history or theory—not about any of that in a head-on way as I used to deal with it, but sort of slant-wise in narratives that, on the surface, may seem to be about something quite different. I guess that's the way my convictions always ran—as threads, as stories sometimes difficult to find, in the fabric of personal experience. There is something self-defeating, I think, in attempting to get at history, art, or love in a direct, head-on way. A person has to sidle up, be asked in, so to speak, and with no fears of vulnerability, let his own experience have good play. This is how history, art, love or what have you gets *into* us, becomes part of us.

So now the stories that used only to haunt me as ghosts come forward, and with encouragement flesh themselves out and into the kind of active life we were always meant to share.

And now as I put down this pen and read it back, it's not all clear to me why I've written like this. That may be the trouble with putting words down on paper—there they are, pretty much, just as you thought them—but, once written, they come through in a time different from the time in which they were written. And not only is the time different from the time in which they were written, you, the writer are a different person—maybe because you thought as you did when you were making those words.

Long ago when my mother called out to us kids standing more or less in a line and looking out the front window into the street, "Get out of that window, you make this place look like a butcher shop," I believe I knew, then, what she meant. But I don't know now.

Or when she said also long ago, "Stop running around that table, Donald, people would think you're possessed," I knew what she meant then: I just stopped running around that table. But now I wonder, not so clear now.

But the day Tony Balistreri brought his father's horse up onto our front porch—and I was talking a long time into one of the horse's ears—my mother came to the front door. She wasn't angry about the horse being on the porch. She just looked long at me and asked, "Do you think for one minute that that horse knows what you're talking about?"

And I said, right off, "Yes, he does."

Mysteries of Photography

I'm one of those people who enjoys—no, more than enjoys, I love to look at photographs—old ones and ones made just last week, or yesterday. Best of all, I favor photographs of people, known or unknown to me—or at least photographs that include people.

As you hold that photograph in good light, and maybe scan it slowly under a magnifying glass, there that person or group of people stand, sit, or recline exactly as they did in that split second—maybe twenty, maybe fifty years ago. There they are, holding forever what that camera saw as it clicked and made them, in a sense, eternally in that other present.

If you spend time doing this—looking at photographs, images of people and their once-upon-a-time physical ambiance—something like mystery takes over. This may be the truest if those you're looking at are of people you know, or once knew—friends, lovers, family. Long ago, let's say, you knew them well in life, and now they're beyond that. But there they are in that single movement of that single, lost day years ago. The sun was just so high, the light across their faces, the breeze evident in the trees behind, and blowing wisps of hair across your father's or your mother's forehead—all of it, and more, under your magnifying glass. The mystery of it is almost scary. I don't mean that the process of photography is mysterious or scary; it's what these images in black and white or color can *do* to us. If you're not careful, staring through that magnifying glass, you're apt to move right through it—back to that time and place with those people—enough so you hear yourself talking to them, and them answering. It's spooky.

And if what you're looking at are not old *still* photographs, but *movies* of those people moving and talking—you'd better watch out or you'll disappear from your chair in front of the VCR, join them, wherever they seem to be, right in front of you, and maybe never return—not even to stop and rewind the VCR after the credits roll over.

For some of us who identify, perhaps too easily and too completely, with other people, this can happen even with the talking, moving images of Humphrey Bogart, Orson Welles, Ingrid Bergman, even Lyndon Johnson. But it can happen more forcefully with movies in which the actors or actresses are, or were, your personal favorites.

I met Lee Marvin way over thirty years ago. I was standing out on the apron of the stage introducing the next film at a film festival in San Antonio when I looked down into the fourth row and recognized the white-haired man as Lee Marvin. He was looking straight at me. Pointing at him, I made like my right hand was a gun, my index finger the barrel and worked my thumb, and "fired." Then Lee Marvin brought up his right hand, squinted, and "fired" back. That's how Lee Marvin and I met. And so we went on until he died some years ago at the hands of a rare virus, as Lee's wife, Pam, put it. We had been great friends.

I had a book, *The 12 Cadavers of Joe Mariner*, come out in 1977, and Lee liked it one helluva lot. He wanted it to be made into a movie, and he actually lusted to play the lead, that of an artist en route across the country with his exhibition of twelve embalmed corpses. He and Pam even decided who should play the feminine lead, Gena Rowlands. With Lee's close collaboration—often accomplished over the phone or out at his place in Tucson or mine here in Austin, I wrote a screenplay for the book. Happy times those—lots of laughs and just enough booze.

And there were those times when Lee would call much too early on a Sunday morning. Usually at those times Pam was visiting her folks in New York and Lee had gone on a bender. Incidentally I never saw Lee drunk, never even more than plain mellow. One Sunday morning we talked for three hours. He said he was sobering up and stopped every so often to get another cup of coffee, saying, "Hold on, I'll be right back."

I could go on, but we were talking about photographs and movies and the way they give a rare quality of permanence to the most evanescent—the way they deny all time except that one instant when the camera clicked, or that series of moments in a movie when the wind was blowing the high grass just exactly as it was a week or decades ago, or a person—let's say your friend, now dead—walks again in only the way he could walk and speaks only as he could.

Lee Marvin made lots of movies, some poor, some very rich. I own a video of his titled *Monte Walsh*, one of his best, I think.

The other evening I was looking at it again after some time, and there he was: Lee walking along the wooden walk of that deserted street in that perfect mock-up of a Western town of the 1880s. For sure there he was—a real presence, so much so, that I found myself getting out of my chair, going toward the telephone—just to call that number, (602) 299-2818, and ask "How are things, Lee," and have him come on saying, "You know, I was on the phone with Robert Mitchum the other day and when I asked him how things were going, he said, 'Worse.'"

But, of course, I didn't get all the way to the phone—I can usually sense the difference between the possible and the impossible—most of the time, anyway.

What is possible is stuff like making the words in this essay—a one-way observance of our ridiculous will to deny the running of time and the finality of death.